Praise for *Covering the Curriculum with Stories*

'Creativity is high on the national agenda, the curriculum is changing significantly and those who work in schools are being encouraged to personalise the experience of their pupils so that the learning is memorable and real. *Covering the Curriculum with Stories* is a delightful resource for all those who want to ensure that children learn effectively through dramatic play and that they have fun too.'

Steve Munby, Chief Executive, National College for School Leadership

'*Covering the Curriculum with Stories* is a marvelous resource which underpins the magic of story telling at its most engaging with a detailed and thorough explanation of why learning through story should be part of very young child's inheritance. I thoroughly recommend you do more than buy it – buy it and cover your curriculum with it as well!'

Alistair Smith, Chair of Alite and best-selling author

'In *Covering the Curriculum with Stories* Sharon and Paul Ginnis have produced a genuinely integrated learning resource. They have combined their expertise and experience in a rich and stimulating portfolio of activities centred on storytelling. Stories are fundamental to learning: across the ages, every culture, faith and philosophy has found its most powerful expression through stories. Sharon and Paul have captured the power of storytelling but have added the impact of drama, the disciplines of literacy and, crucially, underpinned everything with strategies for effective learning. These stories develop a range of skills but they also introduce moral issues, problem solving and decision making strategies and everything is underpinned by a focus on personal relationships.

'*Covering the Curriculum with Stories* is a powerful resource in its own right, but it is also a model of highly effective professional practice which will influence the organisation and teaching of the curriculum in schools.'

Professor John West-Burnham, Honorary Professor of Educational Leadership, University of Hull

'We are all capable of creating great stories and we can all learn while we play. These are the two beliefs at the centre of a truly inspirational but deeply practical resource from Sharon and Paul Ginnis, *Covering the Curriculum with Stories*. This must surely be the most comprehensive approach to using stories to explore almost every nook and cranny of the school curriculum. It also just happens to be full of wonderful ways of helping pupils to become more effective learners. The stories are engaging and varied. There are suggestions for activities to suit every type of teacher. It is, in short, a gem of a resource; one that every primary school should rush out and buy right now.'

Bill Lucas, best-selling author and Chairman of The Talent Foundation

'If only the entire school curriculum were built around such imaginative and engaging resources and activities as these ...'

Professor Guy Claxton, Visiting Professor of Education, University of Bristol and creator of Building Learning Power

'I heartily recommend *Covering the Curriculum with Stories*. Sharon and Paul Ginnis have developed an excellent resource combining story telling, drama, creativity and play. As the authors recognise, young children do not learn to be more creative simply by being given more freedom to play. The resources that they require in their play are crucial, and the resources that are of most importance are cultural.

'Throughout *Covering the Curriculum with Stories* an emphasis is placed upon children developing their communication and collaboration skills and their creativity as they learn to learn through play. These are the same curriculum priorities that I have identified in my own research. These attitudes, skills and understandings are increasingly prioritised by developmental psychologists and early childhood educators, and are now also being identified as being of special importance by politicians and economists in developing the knowledge society of the future.'

Professor Iram Siraj-Blatchford, Professor of Early Childhood Education, Institute of Education, University of London

'Sharon and Paul Ginnis are very rare as educators in that they have a deep belief in student-centred methods, combined with unbounded creativity and down-to-earth practical ideas. Any teacher would be lucky to have this book as a resource, as the rich opportunities it provides for learners to be involved in problem solving, questioning, playing and drama are enough to last a school year, and more, ensuring they become part of their daily thinking habits.'

Dr Donna Brandes, International Consultant in Student-Centred Learning, Australia

'This is an exciting book. Exciting in many ways. Firstly, it is hugely heartening to find 'learning through drama' being presented in such an accessible and lively way that teachers cannot fail to want to try out the ideas. For too long now the arts have failed to take their rightful place – at the centre of the curriculum. At last the energy has come full circle; and here are the experts, Sharon and Paul, offering a fabulous resource to enable all Foundation and KS1 teachers to re-energise their teaching. Yet thankfully this is no 'quick fix' recipe of ideas – it is an extremely thoughtful, erudite, well worked-out, cross-curricular resource. The authors have thought through every angle that any teacher, whatever their experience and background, would possible want explored. The authors are obviously excellent practitioners, which means the ideas are tried, tested and incredibly workable.

'I cannot recommend the book highly enough. It is exactly what creative, concerned teachers are looking for.'

Jenny Mosley, Education Consultant and Trainer

'The Ginnises have created a breathtakingly comprehensive, creative and effective series of resources that will give teachers nowhere to hide. With this resource every teacher in the land will be able to lead wonderfully creative lessons that bring the best thinking, acting, playing and learning out of every child.

'This series is a huge undertaking and a huge achievement and deserves a place in every school.'

Ian Gilbert, Trainer, best-selling author and founder of Independent Thinking Ltd

'This inspiring publication is about the education of young children, offering clear, vivid, thoroughly tested guidelines on how to harness their creative instincts in order to meet the requirements of the curriculum.

'Sharon and Paul Ginnis have developed the use of dramatic play linked with the building of stories, which not only opens up pathways to all the basic subjects and skills, but also creates an atmosphere in the classroom of group discipline, responsibility and fun. Above all it challenges children to think – and to enjoy thinking.

'Experienced teachers will be able to free-wheel with the book's rich ideas and beginners will find the step-by-step instructions both exciting and safe.'

Dr Gavin Bolton, Reader Emeritus, Durham University

'Using drama for learning, being a sort of 'universal joint' to engage children with the curriculum currently required by law, has become of interest again recently. Teachers are weary of the requirement to concentrate upon content-based study and are seeking respectable academic contexts which can challenge their students to think, study and engage with the real circumstances of their existence.

'Throughout our lives we all spend a great deal of time telling and listening to stories and we easily forget how these engagements inform and influence us. Technology has added tremendously to the availability and usage of story. Newsprint, television, the internet and radio have added to the literary and oral forms we all experience. This book makes sensible, detailed and informed contributions that help teachers to understand why it is important to harness stories to serve curriculum learning, by explaining the transition from the literary form to the dramatic form.

'Roger Barnes a psychologist at Newcastle University said to me, "Schools may not be safe, but drama can be a safe place to learn in and from." This book endorses this opinion.'

Dr Dorothy Heathcote, Hon DLit (Newcastle), Hon DEd (Derby)

'Sharon and Paul know how young children learn. Combining methods from the long-established tradition of drama-in-education with their own original ideas, they have created worldly-wise, lively and rich scenarios that are guaranteed to produce profound learning. It's a long time since teaching was this good.'

Peter Batty, Head of the Education Development Unit, St Martin's College, Lancaster

'When weighing up the potential impact of any educational resource, I first and foremost think as a parent. The sixty four thousand dollar question is always this: would I want the teachers who teach my own children to discover and use this resource? With *Covering the Curriculum with Stories* the answer is an immediate, unequivocal and enthusiastic yes!'

Mike Hughes, best-selling author and Independent Trainer and Consultant

'*Covering the Curriculum with Stories* is an excellent resource which will be welcomed by teachers, student teachers and, of course, pupils!'

Professor Christine Skelton, Professor of Education and Director of the Centre for Research on Education Policy and Professionalism, Roehampton University

'*Covering the Curriculum with Stories* offers a clear, step-by-step guide to creating exciting and meaningful literacy based projects. The level of detail and range of resources provide teachers with the tools they need to develop tailor-made, cross-curricular activities that really do capture the imagination of our young learners. This book is an excellent, well planned and easy to follow guide, perfect for the newly qualified teacher and for those wishing to add excitement, fun and creativity to their lessons.'

Simon Cooper-Hind, Headteacher and Consultant Leader for the National College for School Leadership

'Human beings of all ages love stories, and story telling, whether written, oral or visual is an important aspect of most cultures internationally. Stories involve characters, plots and meanings so we not only enjoy stories, but learn from them as well. This is why this book is such a fresh approach to education for younger children – it combines enjoyment with learning. The six hugely entertaining and engaging stories can be used to promote thinking and to develop other important skills right across the curriculum. Moreover, the first part of the book provides an extremely useful and practical guide for teachers as to how they might want to use the book with pupils. The book is an invaluable resource and, like Paul's earlier book *The Teacher's Toolkit*, should be part of any teacher's or school's collection of classroom materials.'

Professor Clive Harber, Professor of International Education, University of Birmingham and previously Head of the Schools of Education at the University of Natal, South Africa and the University of Birmingham

'*Kim, four, spends a busy November morning digging up earth in the garden and filling little cardboard boxes with it. When her mother asks her why, Kim explains that these are to be her Christmas presents for her brother and the other boys she knows. "What boys like best is to get dirty and play in the mud" Kim tells her mother. "When the snow covers the ground, they can't find any mud. So I am going to give them some for Christmas."*

Joan Beck (in *How to Raise a Brighter Child*, Fontana-Collins, 1967) recognised that almost all small children possess a considerable amount of creativity and adventurous thinking, and that this can be cultivated by deliberate encouragement and opportunity. Sharon and Paul Ginnis share this conviction, which underpins the approaches they provide in *Covering the Curriculum with Stories*.

'This excellent resource allows children to engage with scientific discovery, experimentation, exploration, imagination, curiosity and enquiry, and provides them with opportunities to generate ideas, recognise relationships and find answers to questions. It also helps busy teachers to work together with their pupils on play-based projects that develop their creative thinking and learning skills. The stories are interesting, engaging and fun, as are the activities. Pupils will enjoy them enormously and the process of learning they promote.'

Andrew Herdman, Principal Development Officer, Neath Port Talbot Education Authority

'Everett Reimer observed that some true educational experiences are bound to occur in schools, but that they occur despite school, with all its compulsion, regimentation and coercion. This happens because there are some teachers like Sharon and Paul Ginnis who set out to make the experiences in classrooms as lively, interesting and enjoyable as possible. This book is to be recommended to all teachers who want to join them using the techniques of dramatic play so intelligently articulated in this handbook.'

Dr Roland Meighan, formerly Special Professor of Education at the University of Nottingham

'Stories are magical. They provide the most effective routes by which children make sense of the world. If we believe that education is a moral enterprise, and we aspire for our children to become personally successful but also to use their gifts to build community and enhance the common good, then we must educate them to think critically, value differences and embrace pluralism.

'Sharon and Paul show us the way! Practitioners in early years will welcome this book as a scaffold, supporting their desire to engage children, make learning joyful and plan for cross-curricular outcomes with clarity and vision.'

Yasmine Thebault, Early Years Adviser,
Department for Education, Sport and Culture, Jersey

'A wonderful aid to the teaching of drama from writers who have a wealth of experience at the "chalkface". *Covering the Curriculum with Stories* ensures that teachers can "tick the necessary boxes" while retaining the story and play elements of education which are essential to the real intellectual, social and emotional development of children. I can see this book becoming a bible for busy teachers.'

June Maidens, LGSM, MBE, founder and co-ordinator
of Atherstone Children's Theatre Workshop

'This is a user friendly and informative book that will support teachers to understand and practise successful story-drama. Sharon's and Paul's own imaginative and successful practice shines through!'

Patrice Baldwin, Norfolk's Adviser for the Promotion of
the Arts in Schools and Chair of National Drama

'These story-based projects are brilliantly effective and great creative fun. It is wonderful to hear staff, pupils and parents talking so enthusiastically about them. Pupils play hard, work hard and think hard. The result: more enjoyment; better behaviour and very efficient coverage of the curriculum.'

Jayne Loft, formerly Headteacher, Coedffranc Infant School, Neath Port Talbot

'*Covering the Curriculum with Stories* … and covering our young people with creativity, joy, fun and co-operation! This beautiful book presents a wide open door to, and a guided tour of, an arena that offers wonderful opportunities to everyone who wants to work with young people in ways that empower, enliven and enthuse. We learn why we should, and how we could, use stories, drama and play to unwrap and enrich the curriculum. The book's sound rationale and crafted, detailed guidance is a gift to all classroom teachers. We will all want to take part in these magical adventures and see our youngsters grow and develop through this collaborative approach to learning.'

Pam Walker, Education Development Officer, East of England Co-operative Society Ltd

'Sharon's ability to engage pupils in the learning process, especially through drama is amazing. Through these creative projects she is able to deliver curriculum content and improve thinking skills in a way that is unique and incredibly effective.'

Cliff Chipperfield, Head of Quality and Standards,
Department for Education, Sport and Culture, Jersey

'I will definitely recommend *Covering the Curriculum with Stories* to our student teachers. The authors present a well-informed and rigorous challenge to educators – both current and future – and demonstrate how the curriculum could (and should!) be transformed to re-inject the fun and excitement that ought be at the heart of children's learning.'

Jane Davies, Senior Lecturer, School of Education and Lifelong Learning, University of Sunderland

'*Covering the Curriculum with Stories* takes your pupils to places you can hardly imagine.'

Tony Witte, Headteacher, Norbridge Primary School, Worksop

'The theoretical justification for the teaching processes used, and for the attitudes and skills which will result from this approach, is presented in a way that is both attractive and compelling. Sharon and Paul stimulate and support teachers by providing a comprehensive portfolio that would enable even those new to this way of working to gain clear insights into what is possible. A great read and a wonderful resource.'

Janet Meighan, Trustee and Secretary of the Centre for Personalised Education Trust and Co-director of Educational Heretics Press

Covering the Curriculum with Stories

six cross-curricular projects that teach literacy and thinking through dramatic play

Sharon Ginnis and Paul Ginnis

Crown House Publishing Limited
www.crownhouse.co.uk

First published by

Crown House Publishing Ltd

Crown Buildings, Bancyfelin, Carmarthen, Wales, SA33 5ND, UK

www.crownhouse.co.uk

and

Crown House Publishing Company LLC

6 Trowbridge Drive, Suite 5, Bethel, CT 06801-2858 USA

www.CHPUS.com

Published 2006. Reprinted 2007.

British Library of Cataloguing-in-Publication Data

A catalogue entry for this book is available
from the British Library.

10-digit ISBN 190442497-X
13-digit ISBN 978-190442497-0

LCCN 2006926988

Illustration: Sue Hagerty
Design: Paul Barrett Book Production, Cambridge
Printed and bound in the UK by
The Cromwell Press, Trowbridge, Wiltshire

This book is dedicated to Clare Downey who died on December 25th 2005. An enthusiast for learning who cared deeply about education and was a loyal, caring friend and colleague.

Acknowledgements

Many people have helped to bring these ideas into being and supported us as we've tested them, refined them and finally written them down. We thank everyone who has had a part to play in getting this book completed, in particular:

David Bowman for his faith in the ideas, for his patience and for maintaining a good spirit at all times.

All the team at Crown House, especially Tom Fitton who toiled endlessly.

Special thanks to Mike and Pam Cousins, our exceptionally talented friends and writing partners whose contribution to this book was invaluable.

Clare Ginnis, Steven Ginnis and Helen Ginnis because they are a source of endless joy and share in our lives with such enthusiasm and grace.

The rest of our family for understanding what it takes to write a book, for constantly taking an interest in what we do and for all the words of support and kindness. Thanks to our mum's, Monica Robinson and Jean Barber, to Cliff Barber, to John and Mary Robinson, to Trish and Andrew Pitcher, to Debbie and Jon Ward, to our nieces and nephews, Nicola Robinson, Amy, Daniel and Megan Ward, to Uncle Stanley and Aunty Barbara Bentham.

Gemma Tatt who is charming and thoughtful and becoming a talented and creative teacher.

Jane Ryan Caine and John Caine, Peter, Sally and Sarah Batty, Steve and Jacqui Munby, Janet and Roland Meighan, Pete Duncan and Donna Brandes, who are close, trusted friends and colleagues who share ideas and fun in equal measure.

Cyd and Jon Cray, GGD Emily and Jemima Cray, David and Kathryn Bell, for being wonderful, caring and loyal friends with ready words of encouragement whenever they are needed.

June Maidens for being an inspirational drama teacher, playwright, talented director and faithful friend.

All the wonderful people Sharon worked with in Atherstone Theatre Workshop over the years, especially Maggie Williams and Beth Lester.

Geoff Rayson because his English lessons were always interesting and he shared his love of stories, drama and poetry so eloquently.

Andrew McCallum and the Birmingham Arts Faculty Team of the 1980s and early 1990s; they were the best of times …

Susan Birtwhistle for sharing a passion for the arts and being such an encouragement. Primary school teachers and headteachers in Jersey for keeping creativity high on the agenda, promoting the teaching of drama, pursuing high quality teaching and learning and being exciting and talented people to work with.

Sarah Johnson, Yasmine Thebault and Cliff Chipperfield, States of Jersey Department for Education, Sport & Culture, for making creative things happen.

Jayne Loft and all the staff at Coedffranc Infant School and Margaret Thomas and all the staff at Neath Abbey Infant School, for their creativity, determination and skills in finding ever more effective ways of developing pupils' thinking and improving learning.

Andrew Herdman, Principal Development Officer, Neath Port Talbot Education Authority, a leader of deep integrity and principle.

Jayne Sawtell and Joanne Clarke for everything they do for us that makes it possible for us to do what we do!

Simon Roberson at Dark Haven for his patience and expertise in keeping us on-line, up to date with our technical equipment and making sure everything works! We appreciate how many times you have gone the extra distance for us when we've needed your help.

Liza Parry, a wise counsellor and excellent acupuncturist who keeps us calm and helps us to maintain a healthy balance.

The education visionaries and leaders who have encouraged and supported us in recent times: Mick Waters, Gavin Bolton, John West Burnham, Clive Harber, Iram Siraj-Blatchford, Alistair Smith, Guy Claxton, Bill Lucas, Mike Hughes, Jenny Mosley, Ian Gilbert, Christine Skelton, Simon Cooper-Hind, Patrice Baldwin, Jane Davies, Pam Walker, Tony Witte, Jonothon Neelands and Anthony Gregorc.

A special thanks to Dorothy Heathcote who has been described as one of the greatest teachers of the last hundred years. She showed the world the potential of drama as a learning medium and defined its core practices. Now in her eighties, Dorothy remains an inspiration and model, not just to drama teachers, but to all who take true education seriously. She holds to a way of teaching that challenges the current orthodoxy but which is, once again, slowly, returning to the fore. We are proud that she has endorsed our work.

Contents

Foreword

The schools that Sharon and Paul are concerned with, and the teachers they are anxious to help, are at a stage that T.S. Eliot neatly, and disturbingly, sums up in his *Journey of the Magi*: '[We are] no longer at ease here in the old dispensation'. Planners, teachers, business managers, parents and, as they get older, young people themselves, are considering the need for change. There is dis-ease about the way we run schools, organise the curriculum and teach. We want to provide time and experiences for young people to widen their knowledge, to understand their culture and the world's variety of patterns of association among its peoples, to explore skills and to acquire the tools of getting, mending and processing. Through writers, painters and artists of many disciplines, we want students to encounter, in lots of ways, what it means to be human.

We see the dilemma. Far away there is a horizon of what just possibly might be. Between this close view and that possibility is a no-man's landscape as yet lacking definition: hopes for great happenings, but no clearly defined strategies. *Covering the Curriculum with Stories* begins to map this interim territory.

The book assumes that the reader will want to:

- find bridges between previously divided subjects
- provide experiences that will attract, stimulate and challenge individual children in the classroom
- support children in feeling valued and realistically competent as learners and thinkers
- help them work alongside each other in understanding a wide variety of situations, dilemmas and resolutions
- exercise children's ability to think and communicate in a variety of ways for a range of purposes.

The authors write to their title very precisely and without unnecessary embellishments. People who use the ideas in the book will feel that every care has been taken to address the position of the teacher who is seeking help in using stories as a kind of 'universal joint' from which to start 'getting things together' rather than simply providing a curriculum based on 'bits of this and that'.

The deep play aspects of children's behaviour are related unpedantically to the ancient power of stories to organise and pattern human behaviour. A guide, clear and unpretentious, is then created to enable many levels of engagement to flow from the stories that have been crafted.

Young teachers entering the profession frequently feel they neither know enough stories, nor have had, via their own schooling, experiences that enabled them to penetrate the layers of motive, information and dilemmas that quality stories provide. Sharon and Paul explain clearly that a story becomes a 'universal joint' only when participants are invited to *identify themselves with the people and dilemmas the story contains*. Thereby, the gate is opened for dramatic involvement and points of view.

'Point of view' is at the heart of this book. Being required to take a point of view shifts a child from merely hearing a story to identifying herself within it. 'Point of view' changes how time and the summoning of knowledge operate in the learning process. Children come to realise 'what they now know' at unpredictable moments, stimulated by looking at circumstances from different points of view and from different points in time. This is a kaleidoscopic process. Subject-based schooling operates in what E.T. Hall[1] calls monochronic time – clocktime, divisions of time, agreements about the times of events. Stories as used in this book invoke sacred time – polychronic or diachronic time – the time of *being in events*, driving and participating in the flow of encounters, problems, resolutions and reflections upon those aspects of life that the stories open for consideration.

---

[1] Hall, E.T. (1996), The Dance of Life, Anchor, New York

This book will provide a guide for those who feel unskilled and uneasy about sharing power with their classes, and who feel they might lack the imaginative ability to invent meaningful, progressive tasks that involve the basic element of drama: being in role. It does not bring the radical and far horizon shifts that eventually our education system must embrace, when it ceases ducking and diving and tinkering round the edges. Rather *Covering the Curriculum with Stories* helps those prepared to give it a try to break the current pattern of 'dummy runs' and disconnected activities that children are expected to get interested in and submit to teacher scrutiny. It also sets out the first steps of a journey towards engaging children, so they bring what they already know to a situation in which they want to know more, a process through which they will eventually become confident, decently behaved, social individuals.

Dorothy Heathcote, Hon DLit (Newcastle), Hon DEd (Derby)

What is *Covering the Curriculum with Stories?*

Covering the Curriculum with Stories is the first in the *Play Write* series of books.

As literacy involves much more than a set of technical exercises, the *Play Write* series is designed to provide structured opportunities for the emotional and imaginative engagement that is required for pupils' future development as readers and writers. *Play Write* does this through creative activity using dramatic techniques to explore a selection of stories.

Covering the Curriculum with Stories provides six story-based projects (with two additional projects available on a Supplementary CD, *Covering the Curriculum with Stories: Supplementary Projects for Foundation and KS1*). The book will also help you deliver much of the Foundation and KS1 curricula in ways that the pupils will find meaningful, enjoyable and memorable.

You will find tales of adventure and daring (*The Incredible Shrinking Machine* and *The Quest*), of comedy (*Mrs Hope's Shop*), of unleashed and uncontrollable supernatural forces (*The Magic Book Adventure*), of dilemmas in outer space (*The Remedy Rocket*) and of complex life-threatening problems (*The Big Factory and River Trouble*).

Each project has a central story that is used as the starting point to develop a range of activities that cover many areas of the curriculum. The stories are brought to life through the use of the teacher and pupils working in role. Each project has detailed guidance notes that suggest how the activities can be developed to deliver cross-curricular material, literacy skills, thinking skills, as well as emotional intelligence and the foundation of independent learning.

All you need to know to teach the projects successfully is explained in the project sections. At your fingertips, for each project, you have:

- a clear overview with precise learning outcomes
- simple, clear, step-by-step instructions
- in some cases, the very words to say
- details of pupil activities, including Optional Extras
- lists of resources (some of these resources are on the Resources CD inside the back cover)
- worksheets (also on the Resources CD)
- references to QCA programmes of study.

References to the worksheets and other resources on the Resources CD are given in the text. In addition, the original artwork by Sue Hagerty is available in a Poster Pack and Artwork set, available separately, so that you can easily make your own customised paper-based or hi-tech resources to extend project activities.

The projects cover a lot of the curriculum but not all of it. Not every potential cross-curricular link is pursued with activities; if we'd tried to do this the book would have run into several volumes! The Optional Extras within the projects give you examples of activities you can carry out to cover additional curriculum content and a table at the back of each project gives you further pointers so that you can create more opportunities of your own.

So, the complete set of resources for *Covering the Curriculum with Stories* comprises:

- this book, with the worksheets and other classroom resources on the Resources CD inside the back cover

- a Supplementary CD, which can be bought separately, containing two further projects complete with resources: *Little Bo Peep* (for 3–5 year olds) and *The Giant Pet Escape* (for 5–7 year olds)

- a Poster Pack containing posters of the original artwork and illustrations that can be used as visual aids for all the projects and an Artwork Memory Stick containing all the artwork that you can then print, customise and project onto your whiteboard to your heart's content. This set can also be bought separately.

Covering the Curriculum with Stories is in three parts.

Part 1 provides the rationale for the methodology and explains the teaching techniques you will need.

Part 2 presents three outstanding story-based projects for children aged 3–5:

- **Mrs Hope's Shop** Customers tidy up Mrs Hope's disorganised shop as a surprise for her, but find that the surprise is on them! What will they do when she doesn't react as expected?

- **The Incredible Shrinking Machine** Mrs Leszczyk's friends are shrunk to the size of ants and have fun and adventures in the garden with a giant-sized spider and an enormous caterpillar. Can they outwit the spider and save the garden from the giant caterpillar?

- **The Magic Book Adventure** In a dusty tower, the King's new cleaning staff discover a magic book that no one has opened for a very long time. The book can make good things happen, but at a very high cost to the local villagers. What should they do?

Part 3 provides a further three original projects for children aged 5–7:

- **The Remedy Rocket** When a rocket full of newly-trained astronauts and boxes of medicine is forced to land on a strange planet, there are issues to be faced. Should the local inhabitants be trusted? Should the astronauts share their resources? What are they prepared to sacrifice to care for others?

- **The Quest** The people of The Pastures must wake the Queen of Golden Towers who has been put into an enchanted sleep. Time is running out. The great monster of Bad Land is about to break through the Great Wall and threatens to spoil everything in Good Land for ever. What can they do?

- **The Big Factory and River Trouble** Factory workers are making a special secret medicine that will stop worldwide disease for all time. The trouble is that people who live near the factory keep getting sick. Is there a connection? What should they do?

Two more projects can be found on the Supplementary CD:

- **Little Bo Peep** (for 3–5 year olds)
- **The Giant Pet Escape** (for 5–7 year olds).

By following the *Play Write* series, you will provide your young students with a curriculum that is personalised, flexible and creative. You will be astonished at how much material you cover through these story-based projects. They will take you away from fragmented, subject-based teaching towards thematic, cross-curricular, integrated schemes of work of the kind currently favoured by the Qualifications and Curriculum Authority (QCA) in England and the Department for Education, Lifelong Learning and Skills (DELLS) in Wales. You will embed literacy within a variety of contexts, just as you are being encouraged to do by 'the powers that be'. In other words, your methodology will be completely up to date.

Across the UK, teachers and policy-makers are in the mood for creativity and for active, play-based experiential approaches that deliver essential skills. Through *Covering the Curriculum with Stories*, your pupils will become good authors, good thinkers and good learners; they will become personally aware and socially skilled. Along the way, they will have lots of fun and will lay down important conceptual frameworks in readiness for the 'heavier' content of Key Stages 2, 3 and 4. In fact, you will have built for them a true foundation for life-long learning.

Part 1

Reasons, Benefits and Teaching Tools

Why Work Like This?

The books in the *Play Write* series provide teachers and their pupils with a creative approach to the Foundation and KS1 curriculum. They show you how to cover a great deal in a short time through cross-curricular projects. As a teacher, you can achieve lots of learning outcomes by following these step-by-step project plans. In addition to this, using *Play Write*'s fiction-based approach will provide pupils with a series of coherent and engaging contexts that will help them to make more *sense* of the curriculum. Being engaged in enjoyable physical and imaginative learning will give them the motivation and confidence to do some challenging thinking.

As this book's title suggests, *Covering the Curriculum with Stories* is designed to help you teach much of the current curriculum, particularly literacy and thinking, entirely through stories. This is in line with the trend for more thematic, as opposed to fragmented, teaching.

Your children can achieve learning outcomes beyond those generally expected at Foundation and KS1. They can reach levels of skill, levels of personal and social awareness, and depths of conceptual understanding that go well beyond the standards to which we have become accustomed. All of this is achievable with young children by following some relatively simple guidance. The methods advocated in this book are the result of 20 years of classroom experience. Everything has been tried and refined several times over. Nothing is conjecture.

A prime aim of this book, and the others in the *Play Write* series, is to meet the growing demand from teachers, and government, for effective ways to teach literacy that are creative and embedded, and simultaneously develop the qualities of thoughtfulness and independence. Here you will find an approach that sits comfortably alongside more formal techniques. The *Play Write* series focuses on the art of *story making* (and as children get older, *story writing*) and *story reading*. It shows you how young children can understand the literary qualities of stories, and can create their own genuine literature with artistic merit.

Delivering the power of play through drama

'In play, children are given the chance to imagine and recreate experience. As they explore situations, events and ideas … they improve their competence with language through social interaction … As they play, children will practice doing and saying things that they are not really able to do, such as making a journey in space. They can capture their actions in drawing, early writing or painting, and retell events to friends, practitioners and parents. They are learning that pictures and words are symbolic ways of presenting meaning.'

(QCA Curriculum Guidance for the Foundation Stage)

'Children learn through first hand experiential activities with the serious business of "play" providing the vehicle. Through their play, children practice and consolidate their learning, play with ideas, experiment, take risks, solve problems and make decisions individually, in small and in large groups. First hand experiences allow children to develop an understanding of themselves and the world in which they live.'

(Jane Davidson, Welsh Assembly Government's Education and Lifelong Learning Minister)

All children are innately driven to play and in playing their learning develops naturally. Imaginative play is such a powerful tool for learning because it allows children to go beyond the limitations of their physical world. In imaginative play, they can be who they want to be: adults; other children; superheroes; even villains!

The medium of imaginative play allows children to practice attitudes, skills and speech patterns that they don't use in 'real life'. For example, their play activities might involve being a fearless adventurer with lots of running, shouting, jumping and fighting. It's common for children to import into imaginary situations the language and behaviours that are modelled in ordinary scenarios around them. In a game, children will use fragments of speech, or styles of speech, that have been overheard in the house or come from the TV or story books. This copying helps them to work out what words and registers mean, as well as what effect they have in certain situations and, therefore, when it's appropriate to use them.

Likewise, children often copy the behaviours of the grown-ups around them (we all know how embarrassing this can be!) as they test out more sophisticated ways of going about things. They watch, they copy and they project what they see and hear into their own fictional contexts. In particular, they examine 'cause and effect' in relationships; they observe what seems to make people happy, sad, furious and stressed – and watch how these situations are handled. Then they replay them back to us with telling accuracy.

The use of drama at Foundation and KS1 is very closely related to play, so please do not feel that using drama with very young children is beyond them. In following the projects in this book, you will be adding a degree of structure and challenge that will guide and enrich the play experience.

Dramatic fictions deliver further benefits. Nowadays, there is some consensus about the kind of qualities (sometimes called 'attitudes', 'dispositions' or 'attributes') that learners need to 'learn how to learn' in order to move towards genuine independence. Conveniently, they all begin with R!

Conflating these ideas from Alistair Smith, Bill Lucas and Guy Claxton, the qualities can be summarised as:

- Resilience
- Reciprocity
- Resourcefulness
- Responsibility
- Reflectiveness
- Responsiveness.

The *process* of devising a drama will, sooner or later, confront children with the need to demonstrate these various qualities. They will be required to co-operate in groups and make democratic decisions (Reciprocity); to work things out for themselves and explore alternatives when things don't work (Resourcefulness); to keep going when it gets tough (Resilience); to draw on their (limited) experience, making connections with real life and reflecting on the process once it's finished (Reflectiveness).

The *content* of many dramas (the fictional situations pupils find themselves in) also provides opportunities to further their senses of Responsibility and Responsiveness, in that they are often asked to make tough decisions and face the consequences, as well as to monitor and evaluate situations and react to changing circumstances. The building of these 'learning-to-learn' dispositions is a key feature of personalised learning and goes to the heart of true transition.

In addition, devising stories collaboratively and taking part in dramas provides the foundations of good citizenship:

- first-hand experience of team-work
- experience in managing personal emotions and behavioural choices
- practice in deferring gratification
- being required to listen to and value other people's viewpoints
- a chance to practice collaborative decision-making, compromise and conflict-resolution
- increased awareness of the impact of one's own behaviour on others.

However, some teachers fear that pupils might get carried away by drama, leading to facts being exaggerated, distorted or ignored. It is true, sloppily done classroom drama might result in material being compromised. However, if the teacher is prepared to learn the conventions and strategies that create dramatic discipline and rigour, this will not be the case. Please read *Dramatic Conventions: the tools for the job!* (Page 27).

You will also note that the projects in *Parts 2 and 3* have *Optional Extras* that punctuate the action with opportunities for the pupils to engage in tasks out of role. In some cases, the knowledge the pupils acquire out of role informs their thinking when they are back in role. Other suggested *Optional Extras* are fringe to the story; for instance, pupils taking part in *The Remedy Rocket* might enjoy researching the NASA space projects, which is material that is interesting in itself but not essential to furthering the drama. Using these activities to slow the drama and to stop and start acting-out sessions helps to deepen learning and allows curriculum content to be readily absorbed.

How stories can develop learners

We are all familiar with the universal appeal of stories being created, read and told for escapism and entertainment. We also know that throughout history societies have also used them for instruction. What do stories offer today's young children growing up in the 'modern world'?

1. Use stories to expand pupils' personal horizons

Stories can teach children about themselves, and their families, along with the workings of human relationships and the world in general.

A young child's natural curiosity about the world is boundless. Stories feed that curiosity. The young mind is capable of expansive thought; stories help children to move beyond their limited real-life experience into new situations in their heads.

Through stories, young children learn about language, about choices, about family life, about relationships in general, and so they can begin to construct a model of what people are generally like. They begin to note that all human beings are the same in some fundamental ways and yet have different personalities.

Beyond this, stories can teach children about society, giving them broader views than they can get from their young world, and an awareness of bigger issues – political, environmental, economic, national, international – through small-scale, close-to-home fictional contexts.

Stories can offer children a view of the world *outside the familiar settings* of home and school. Children naturally learn about this 'world beyond' from the imaginary play they conduct for themselves and from listening to stories read to them. However, *Play Write* aims to enhance this learning through skillful adult intervention; the story-telling is developed through drama, which allows the teacher to share their experiences of the world with the class.

The *Play Write* world of stories provides a place to explore new civilisations, different kinds of people, and unfamiliar customs and cultures.

For example, in the project called *The Big Factory and River Trouble*, the class are in role as workers who are invited to be part of a project to create a new medicine. The workers discover that the medicine may be damaging the environment and harming the local community. As the drama unfolds, the children face questions such as:

• Is it sometimes necessary for leaders to keep secrets?
• Is it ever right to lie or deceive people?
• Is any product worth wrecking a community for?
• Is it selfish to look after yourself and your own family and ignore the needs of others around you?
• Is it right to break a promise (to keep your work secret) if you know the promise is harming others?
• Is it fair to trade the lives of local people (who have no choice in the matter) for the lives of others who will benefit from the new medicine?
• Is it OK to accept bribes?

These questions are alive and 'real' in the drama, arising naturally as the children play out the scenario. Working in role alongside the pupils enables a teacher to inject questions and suggest issues from inside the story. The teacher can also manipulate the action of the story to make it more tense and therefore more exciting and help the pupils to see connections with their real-life experiences. In the factory drama, pupils are likely to relate to people making and breaking friendships as they do it themselves every day. These connections help to 'hook' them into thinking about universal issues such as survival, acceptance and fairness.

Such issues are also big national and international concerns and as adults we can immediately think of examples of each of them in current affairs. It is unlikely that the children will be aware of the connection between what they've done in class that day and the news on TV that night, although with older children it is possible to make these explicit links. It is enough for younger children that they have faced the situation, they have subtly built it into their developing life-experience and have tested out some ways of tackling such dilemmas. They have done all this within their own world of play, with a story that thrilled and absorbed them to the point where they will remember it clearly many months later.

So, stories open up a world of possibilities and build up in children's minds an understanding of what it is like to live through all kinds of situations – situations that they have not yet experienced personally. Bit by bit, over time, different stories and dramas are connected up and an understanding of quite complex social issues develops. As they get older, pupils are then able to project the issues that they worked on in small-scale stories, into 'real' social contexts. For instance, they can more easily understand the causes and consequences of certain scientific discoveries, of breakthroughs in engineering, of war, of colonisation, of business ethics, of global climate change, of natural disasters and so on because they have experienced the issues in different, but parallel, fictional circumstances. *Covering the Curriculum with Stories* lays down an important conceptual foundation for KS2 and beyond.

2. Use stories to develop children's thinking skills

Fiction, in the hands of a skilled teacher, will automatically require children to think in a variety of ways. Take the questions, 'Can you imagine ...?' and 'What if ...?'. These are the starting point for any story, as they are for any scientific enquiry. Such questions are the springboard of creativity. As Einstein famously said, *'Imagination is more important than knowledge.'*

As children gain experience of story making, they learn to think laterally and make interesting connections. For instance, one of our favourite fiction-writing sessions with young children begins with a battered old suitcase full of objects: a hat; a pair of binoculars; an unopened letter; some photographs; a map; and a pair of shoes perhaps. We use the items to stimulate a range of questions: Who might these have belonged to? Where do you think they've been? What happened? Intuition, reasoning, analysis and logic are all involved as children connect these initially random objects. Eventually, the strands of thought are brought together into a coherent set of characters and events. In Benjamin Bloom's famous *Taxonomy of Educational Objectives* this is called synthesis.

At some point in the process, problems and tensions need to be introduced. Without these, stories will inevitably be flat, dull, sequential offerings in which this happened, then that, then something else and then it was the end. A good story always has a problem and a tension, as you will see in the *Play Write* projects. In creating good stories, the injection of twists immediately throws the children into problem-solving mode, requiring analytical and creative thinking, where they suggest and evaluate options until a resolution is finalised.

Stories also provide opportunities for empathetic thinking, particularly as the fiction is developed 'live' through drama in the classroom when pupils and teacher are in role (see *Dramatic Conventions - the tools for the job!*, Page 27). To be able to portray characters reasonably and suggest what they would do in a given situation, children must think empathetically. Becoming empathetic can be a demanding process: it requires thinking in action, thinking on your feet.

The story-based projects in *Play Write* may feel like play to pupils but they are designed to promote reflective thinking so that pupils expand their perspectives and develop a degree of objectivity. In this way, *Play Write* helps to lay the foundations for the future development of children's thinking skills. Remember, children in early years are at a concrete stage of development. Just as they learn maths by using apparatus, they also learn thinking in concrete ways. The apparatus of thinking skills at this age is drama.

3. Use stories to teach children facts, concepts and skills that accelerate their learning in a number of curriculum areas

Teachers using *Play Write* will find that they are able to cover many areas of the curriculum in depth. The story-based approach provides contexts for many learning outcomes.

Once an emotional connection with the story has been made, children are likely to want to know more about related matters. Their curiosity is aroused and they have a meaningful context within which further facts and concepts will make sense. For example, *The Big Factory and River Trouble* is a drama about a medicine factory, similar in character and secrecy to Willie Wonka's chocolate factory. In role, the pupils are workers who are on the verge of making a ground-breaking medicine that will cure all illnesses. However, they realise that the waste from the factory might be poisoning the local river, which is causing real problems for the local village where the workers live. They are faced with a dilemma that foreshadows issues to be tackled in the curriculum in the future at KS2 and KS3. This is very much in tune with the aims for the Foundation stage: to provide a curriculum that fosters and promotes the children's knowledge and understanding of the world. A fiction-based approach to the Foundation and KS1 curricula creates conceptual frameworks and emotional hooks for later learning and so makes a major contribution to transition.

Here are some further examples of how the other stories can provide teachers with opportunities to cover the curriculum: *The Incredible Shrinking Machine* helps to establish the concept of scale (maths) and introduces aspects of flora and fauna (science); *The Quest* lays down the fundamentals of maps and plans (geography) and examines leadership and the concepts of 'nation' and international conflict (history); *Mrs Hope's Shop* is largely about accepting differences between people (PSHE); *The Remedy Rocket* is packed with science: outer space; gravity; the atmosphere; illness; medicine; the composition of air. Some of these curricula links are explored through the *Optional Extras*.

Brain research has provided us with a more scientific understanding of how children learn. It seems that learners thrive on relevant, complex and multi-sensory tasks. Human beings, however young, appear to enjoy having novel and mind-stretching problems to solve. We now understand why most of us don't like doing tasks simply for the sake of it: we are geared to learn in context. Therefore, we can assure ourselves that children are not necessarily lazy or disaffected if they don't readily knuckle down and follow orders to complete any old piece of work set by the teacher. They might simply be unmotivated or unmoved by the task they are given, which is not the same as being 'naughty'. Engagement, attention and success generally flow from feeling that the learning task will be useful and meaningful. Where children are provided with appropriate support and resources, they will often take on serious levels of intellectual challenge … as long as they feel *moved* to do so. Some sort of emotional connection with the material is the key.

Also, we know that teaching techniques are most effective when they are inclusive and conducted in a learning environment that is 'safe' on many levels: physically; emotionally; socially; culturally; and spiritually. Teaching at Foundation and KS1 has traditionally been very good at creating these conditions. In fact, for most primary school

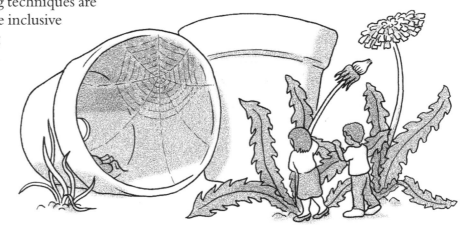

teachers it is instinctive. Stories provide safe environments for learning in that they deal with real-world issues, some of them quite sensitive, but within the artificiality of a fiction. Children are distanced and therefore protected from the force of the issues because they are only 'playing' with them – the circumstances, the choices and the consequences are not real. However, they mirror reality and provide children with essential practice and, perhaps, a degree of healthy inoculation.

If young children's learning is to be successful, it is also critical that students' diverse approaches to learning are honoured. For example, the well-known work of Professor Howard Gardner on multiple intelligences has taught us that children have distinct, personal intelligence profiles. In crude terms, the rank order of a child's intelligences – her in-built aptitudes and dispositions – will determine what she is naturally good at, what she will struggle with, what motivates her and what she will resist (see Appendix A for more detail). Doctor Anthony Gregorc's Mind Styles™ Analysis, probably the best of the cognitive models, gives us a powerful way of understanding how children naturally perceive and organise information in hugely different ways (see Appendix B). Therefore, the challenge that faces and excites many teachers is this: how can we create a curriculum; and how can we design classroom techniques; that cater for the diverse intelligence profiles and learning styles of all learners and 'hook' each of them at a deep enough level to sustain motivation? This is especially important when it comes to learning that is 'tough'. For many pupils, reading and writing are 'tough'. Stories tend to engage with 'intrapersonal' and 'interpersonal' intelligences and excite 'random' ways of thinking. Drama majors on 'kinaesthetic' and 'spatial' intelligences and 'concrete' Mind Styles, so the methods presented in this series work well for students who naturally struggle with the more 'sequential', 'abstract' and 'logical' processes that have sadly dominated primary school teaching in the past few years.

4. Use stories to explore, enjoy and teach about language

'Children are more likely to write as part of purposeful play'

(QCA Curriculum Guidance for the Foundation Stage)

Dramatic fictions can be used to create this kind of motivation and therefore make teaching the formalities of language easier.

Play Write provides dramatic fictional scenarios that engage the pupils emotionally and *also* contain the need to write. The QCA Curriculum guidance advocates *'Children will learn about the different purposes of writing by seeing practitioners write for real purposes.'* The *Play Write* stories contain many contextualised opportunities for writing to be done by Teachers and Pupils in Role: messages; reports; instructions; directions; warnings; letters; invitations; labels; signs; applications; notes; recipes; diary entries and so on. Pupils can have a go at writing within the drama, while they are motivated. Later, the writing can be looked at *out of role* and technical matters can be addressed either with individual pupils or with the whole class.

Dear Palace Servants

We are sorry to trouble you with this request, but we have heard how good and hard-working you are. We hope that you will be willing to help us.

Yesterday our grandmother called Razi went missing. We have looked everywhere we can think of, but we have not found her. Her grand-daughter is very sad and worried. Please would you search the palace to see if she has wandered inside and got lost?

From

Razi's family

The pupils' motivation usually carries over from the drama to the technical sessions, because the writing is important to them. They want to get it right. The skill of the teacher is in knowing when to stop and examine the technicalities.

The same principle applies to reading. Secret messages, letters that have been found in a suitcase, a long-lost diary, directions to a destination, a recipe for a secret potion, writing on a map, labels in a shop, lists, signposts, are all examples of texts that can have added value in the eyes of the children when they are significant details in a story. Presenting pupils with the texts to read within a drama provides the motivation to tackle the reading. The drama also provides contextual cues that help the pupils to decode the text and understand its meaning. The multi-sensory nature of drama is of enormous help to all learners, not just those who have kinaesthetic or concrete learning preferences.

Young learners can even begin to appreciate some advanced literary devices, for example, in the way characters are described. By using dramatic strategies such as *Acting Out*, *Hot Seating*, *Still Image and Forum Theatre (see Dramatic Conventions: the tools for the job!* Page 27*)* pupils can grasp how and why characters respond to given situations. They begin to appreciate the relationship between a character's outward behaviour and their internal qualities and motives, and pupils start to build a vocabulary to go with it. They are able to get under the skin of a character and go beyond physical description. Without actually using terms like metaphor and simile, pupils can nevertheless begin to appreciate how figures of speech can add meaning to the development of textual ideas. For example, 'her eyes sparkled like sapphires' does not just tell us that the character's eyes are blue, but suggests that she possesses a rare and pure soul.

5. Use stories to develop many aspects of emotional intelligence

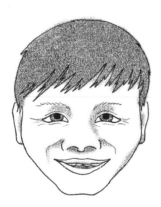 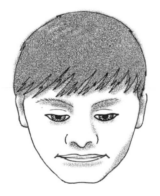 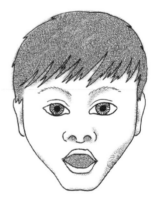

Fiction can make direct and deep contributions to the development of children's emotional intelligence, to use the phrase and concept popularised by Daniel Goleman. Stories provide:

- personal awareness: what I am like in comparison to others; they hold up a mirror to oneself
- an understanding of how relationships function – what builds them, what destroys them and how they might be repaired
- models of behaviours, both good and bad, in a whole range of situations as characters react to widely ranging circumstances
- an understanding that all behaviours are choices and all choices have consequences – this is the foundation stone of a personally responsible approach to life
- a view of how communities (such as families and friendships) operate – the importance of give and take, of social responsibility, of agreed rules and of routines

- insights into major human themes, such as conflict, trust, betrayal, loyalty, justice, greed, honesty, power, love, hate, guilt, happiness and sadness – the list is almost endless
- a catalogue of recognisable and named emotions and feelings
- the beginnings of a wide world-view and an incipient understanding of human nature.

Why bother?

So, what's in it for you? Why bother to move outside your comfort zone and start working like this? When you use the projects in this book, you will:

1. Teach thematically and embed literacy, exactly as Government agencies are asking you to. You will use the experiential, play-based approaches that are being officially encouraged across the UK.

2. Find yourself covering many areas of the curriculum in considerable depth simultaneously. Your pupils will achieve multiple learning outcomes in one fell swoop. This represents a very efficient use of lesson time and planning time.

3. Feel satisfied that you are making three major contributions to the transition agenda, helping your children to enjoy a successful and smooth school career:

   - The job of Foundation and KS1 is to provide a sufficient understanding of the way the world works so that pupils, when they are older, can make sense of the material they are being asked to learn. So much school work seems pointless and tedious to older pupils simply because they don't see its relevance or significance in the real world. It is critical that broad conceptual and social frameworks are built in young minds, so that future learning can be 'placed' easily. Future levels of achievement absolutely depend on this.

   - By the end of primary schooling, children can have grasped the art of storymaking and story-writing. They can have understood the literary art form. In KS3, they can then move rapidly beyond the idea of stories as a series of events (currently, many students never get beyond this point) and start to manipulate story structures in creative ways for themselves. They can become genuine authors. This is a far cry from the mundane and shallow approach by which children are taught that all stories have a beginning, middle and end. Young children are, absolutely are, capable of creating stories with basic elements of good literature, but they need

to have modelled them, discussed them and lived them through drama first. This process begins in Foundation and KS1.

- The beginnings of thinking skills, emotional intelligence and the dispositions of independent learning are all developed in the Early Years. These are the skills that underpin success later on. Without them, pupils will struggle to work in groups, to carry out research, to manage their relationships, to resolve conflicts peacefully, to solve their own problems, to be disciplined, to tackle difficult work, to manage time and deadlines, to speak out, to think independently and creatively … and so on. The incremental, systematic development of these generic skills and dispositions from Foundation to Post-16 education is crucially important in our hi-tech, information-rich and communication-rich society. This is the basis of life-long learning. Transition starts in Nursery.

The *Play Write* Framework

The teaching methodology advocated in the *Play Write* series has two underlying 'big ideas' or principles:

- We can use stories to develop in children the disposition to understand, appreciate and ultimately create and write good literature, as opposed to technically accurate but dull stories.
- All children, even very young ones, can learn through classroom play that is enhanced by the teacher's strategic use of dramatic techniques.

The first point is explored in this section. The second point is developed in the next section, *Dramatic Conventions – the tools for the job!*

Putting literature into literacy

If we define literacy as 'being able to read and write', then we are dealing only with the basics and not with the art of using language. Pupils who only learn the basic skills will struggle to appreciate literature, and a lack of understanding of literature will impede the development of finer writing skills, particularly story-writing skills, as children mature.

To young children, stories are as natural as breathing. In the introduction to his excellent book *The Seven Basic Plots – why we tell stories*[1], Christopher Booker says:

> *'So deep and so instinctive is our need for them that, as small children, we have no sooner learned to speak than we begin demanding to be told stories, as evidence of an appetite likely to continue to our dying day.'*

And he continues to point out the ongoing significance of stories in our lives:

> *'We spend a phenomenal amount of our lives following stories: telling them; listening to them; reading them; watching them being acted out on the television screen or in films or on a stage. They are far and away one of the most important features of our everyday existence.'*

He is describing everyone's instinctive ability and desire to use imagination. This drive is so strong and universal that young children bring into class the innate motivation to engage with fiction and therefore with literature. What they lack, but can learn, are the tools to deconstruct stories and to work out why some stories are better than others.

All good stories have 6 components:

Plot	This is the skeleton of the story, its basic shape.
Setting	The time (or times) and place (or places) where the story happens – the location(s).
Characters	The beings in the story – these might be people, animals, fantasy creatures, aliens, cartoon creations or inanimate objects given life.
Problem	A difficulty that the characters have to deal with. It cannot be avoided. The problem drives the story forward and creates interest for the reader, viewer or participant. To become good story-makers, children need to understand that a story generally revolves around the way in which characters react to a problem.
Tension	A complication that makes the problem more difficult for the characters to deal with. Tensions create excitement and suspense.
Ending	The way the story is concluded.

[1]Booker, C (2005, 2), The Seven Basic Plots, Continuum International Publishing Group, London.

Through doing the projects in *Parts 2* and *3*, your young pupils will become familiar with all of these components of stories. These will be learned experientially through the stories being acted out. It is, of course, important that you reflect on the dramas with the children afterwards and bring the components out into the open. Of course, familiarity with these ideas will only be built up over time; one project won't be enough.

In your discussions with the pupils, connect this 'literary formula' with their experience of picture books and story books that you (and parents) use with them. The various features and components can be pointed out and discussed. The more this happens, the more the fundamental ideas will be consolidated.

Once pupils have understood that these are the essential ingredients of good stories (literary *deconstruction*), they can then be taught that the story-making process weaves these components together (literary *construction*). As they become more experienced, pupils can begin to manipulate the ingredients in interesting and flexible ways – which is exactly what famous and critically acclaimed authors do.

With a good number of stories under their belts, and a little more maturity, pupils can begin to appreciate that there are different *types* of:

Plots – in sophisticated stories, the main plot is complemented by sub-plots that contrast with the main plot (for the seven basic plots, see Page 22).

Settings – options include: real-life; fantasy; past; present; future; on the earth; inside the earth; on a space station; on a distant planet and so on.

Characters – in children's stories, there are various character forms: cartoon characters; fantasy creatures; talking animals; humans of various ages and backgrounds; mythological creatures; aliens; living objects (like railway trains in *Thomas the Tank Engine*). Also, different characters have different degrees of status. Stories generally have main characters, supporting characters, fringe characters and background groups.

When depicting characters, their outward appearances are ultimately less important than their inner qualities. These inner characteristics are revealed in a number of ways, but particularly through the characters' actions and especially the way they deal with the story's problem and tensions.

Problems – classic problems include: accident; someone or something getting lost; being trapped; needing a resource; not being allowed to go somewhere; fire; something important being stolen; flood or other natural disaster; taking something that changes you; being kidnapped; someone promises to turn up but doesn't; mistaken identities; being framed; being made to look foolish; a deal that goes wrong; having made an agreement that will cause difficulty; illness; having to face a foe; not knowing vital information; a threat to life; being tricked; war; a friend or loved one needs rescuing; being hunted; hunting something or someone; being pressured to do something that is wrong; someone goes missing; forgetting to do something important; losing something precious; becoming invisible; being invaded; releasing an uncontrollable force.

Tensions – classic tension generators include: secrecy; lack of knowledge or expertise; greed; lack of skills; betrayal; fear; knowing something that others don't; not knowing something that others do; the group splits up; morals; trust; loyalty; religious rules; having power over others; social and cultural rules; lack of time; wanting something very deeply; waiting; a change of plan; running out of a resource; running out of energy; a change in the weather; bad luck; an altered state of mind; being put on the spot; being threatened with unwanted consequences; being outnumbered; being treated unjustly; being slowed down.

Endings – classic endings include: a happy event; a problem is solved at the last moment; people are rescued or reunited; a problem is resolved in an unexpected way; a problem is left unresolved; someone gets their comeuppance; it all ends badly; the characters are given another task to do; characters think their task is complete when suddenly …; the world, planet or solar system is saved; the characters will be friends for ever because of their experiences; an evil character is beaten; a bad character turns out to be a good character; a good character becomes a bad character; a character learns from the experience she has been through; a character finds a better place or way to live; someone is vindicated; the ending is unclear and the audience is left to make its own mind up.

These are the variations on the six components that effectively form the author's palette. Then there are the skills needed to combine them and convey them to an audience. The author has a number of 'writing devices' upon which she can draw as she unfolds her story to the reader. How skilfully these are chosen and how well they are committed to paper (or celluloid) will determine the quality of the final work. The devices include:

* narrative
* description
* dialogue
* monologue
* flashback
* flash forward
* dreams
* self-talk (musing to a mirror for example)
* asides
* documents
* reportage (TV and radio broadcasts, for example)
* interviews.

Finally, there's the question of genre. Currently, there's a lot of confusion about this with many commentators and teachers' manuals mixing genres with plots. In our view, a story's genre is created by making selections from each of the six component categories and putting them together. For example, an Overcoming the Monster plot, that takes place in a remote forest (setting), with inbred maniacs (characters) hunting (problem) innocent passers-by (characters) who run out of petrol (tension), have no means of communication (tension), no weapons (tension) and are tricked (tension) gives you a classic horror story (known as the *Texas Chainsaw Massacre*). Horror is a genre, so is romance. Others include: science-fiction; fantasy; detective; animal; western; war; melodramatic; autobiographical; biographical; political; historical; and supernatural … stories. Sometimes genres are combined. Incidentally, as we see it, 'mystery', 'thriller', 'adventure' and 'epic' are not genres. These are words that describe the total product. They are wraparound definitions that can be applied to a variety of genres and plots and describe the 'feel' of the story from the reader's or viewer's position. However, there are overlaps and different 'experts' have different views.

As long as pupils have substantial experience of these diverse components and genres when they are young, they will develop the internal reference points to become good writers later on. In their ordinary play, at home, in the play corner and in the playground, children operate instinctively and spontaneously. Sometimes a good story develops by chance. The aim, however, is for them to become, in time, conscious and deliberate in the way they choose and use the variables in order to fashion a story that is not just fun to take part in, but engages an audience. Ultimately, pupils will be excited by the artistry of writing.

This process of skilled story-writing is described in detail in *Stepping Stones*, the third book in the *Play Write* series.

Incidentally, everything that has been said about classroom dramas and books applies equally to films, plays, children's cartoons and soap operas – they are all fiction and therefore made of the same stuff. This means that an understanding of how stories 'work' should make for an enhanced viewing experience throughout life! There is one final point, crucial to citizenship in our media-driven and commercialised world: there is power in understanding stories and the images they create. The population's ability to analyse fiction means that it will be less open to suggestion and indoctrination, to cultural colonisation by super-powers, to victimisation by commercial interests, and to being stupefied by entertainments designed to distract from what is really happening politically and economically in our world. Someone who is practiced in the deconstruction of fiction is also likely to be able to deconstruct media-manipulation and political spin. These aptitudes are vital to the preservation and regeneration of democracy, along with the protection of human rights and civil liberties, which are becoming major issues in the Western world and will intensify over the next couple of generations.

The seven basic plots

Informing the *Play Write* series is the idea that there are just seven basic storylines. This concept is becoming increasingly accepted in literary circles thanks to Christopher Booker's work: *The Seven Basic Plots – why we tell stories*. The plots have been repeated and re-worked in various forms from earliest times. You'll find them in Greek mythology, Shakespeare's plays and films. Most soap operas are made up of several plots occurring simultaneously and the action cuts from one to another, keeping the viewer's interest. Once you get into it, plot spotting is great fun. A night out at the cinema will never be the same again!

Knowing these seven plots will enable children to deconstruct any short story, novel, film, play, musical, opera or soap opera for the rest of their lives. This knowledge will also help them to write with much more variety and depth as they get older.

The seven basic plots are simple. They are driven by human desires and fears. Even very young children can relate to most of them; in fact, most of them can be found in well-known fairy stories.

Here they are:

1. **Overcoming the Monster**
2. **Rags to Riches**
3. **The Quest**
4. **Voyage and Return**
5. **Comedy**
6. **Tragedy**
7. **Rebirth**

In this first book, you will only come across four of the plots; *The Quest,* Voyage and Return, Comedy and Tragedy. The other plots will be introduced in *Covering the Curriculum with Story Books* (Book 2), and in *Stepping Stones* (Book 3) you will be shown how to help children write stories based on the plots.

Sometimes two plots are integrated with each other – for example, *The Magic Book Adventure* is a straightforward Tragedy if looked at from the point of view that Reema is the central 'flawed' character. Reema (played by the teacher) is spurred into action by an object of desire (the magic book), using her authority as chief servant she persuades the other servants to keep the discovery and use of the book a secret. Soon things slip out of her control and her reputation as a loyal and trustworthy servant would be destroyed at the end if this were to be a true Tragedy (optional ending numbers one and two). However, there is an optional happy ending, which would make the plot feel more like a Voyage and Return story for the pupils because the benevolent character of Prince Aten puts everything right and the servants escape from the situation with their reputations undamaged.

In this case, from the pupils point of view, the servants enter the palace of the King as if it were a strange new world, they enjoy their first encounter with Reema and the excitement of their new jobs but soon they become aware of a threat. The biggest threat the servants face is being found out and 'told off' and so once that has been dissipated by Prince Aten (optional happy ending) they can escape back to what they were at the start of the story; well-behaved new employees of the King!

Likewise, in *The Big Factory and River Trouble,* because there are options for the ending of the story, the pupils could find themselves in a Tragedy or in a plot that feels more like a Rags to Riches tale.

Here is a summary of each basic plot along with a few examples …

Overcoming the Monster

- The characters become aware of a threat or monster (real, psychological or symbolic).
- The characters prepare to sort it out.
- The characters come face to face with the monster.
- There is a battle and it looks like the characters will lose.
- The characters win the battle and everyone celebrates.

Stories that conform to this plot include:

Classic: *George and the Dragon; Dracula; War of the Worlds; The Day of the Triffids.* There are elements of Overcoming the Monster in Shakespeare's *The Taming of the Shrew* and *The Tempest* (though both of these are generally regarded as Comedies).

Film: *Merry Christmas Mr Lawrence; Star Wars Episode IV; The Last Samurai; King Kong; The Descent; The Cave; The Ring; The Thing; Erin Brockovich; Jaws; The Terminator.*

Children's: *Jack and the Beanstalk; Little Red Riding Hood* (but not the early versions as they don't have a happy ending!); *Not Now Bernard* by David McKee; *Wolves* by Emily Garvett.

In this book, there are no examples of Overcoming the Monster.

Rags to Riches

- The main character is at home in a lowly and unhappy state and then something makes the character leave his or her home.
- After the main character leaves home things go well. The character is happy.
- Then there is a crisis and everything suddenly goes wrong. The main character is very unhappy and feels powerless.
- The main character faces a final test of some kind and finds new inner strength to deal with it.
- The main character is rewarded and usually lives 'happily ever after'.

Stories that conform to this plot include:

Classic: *Jane Eyre; David Copperfield;* the story of Joseph in the Bible (Genesis); *Oliver Twist.*

Film: *Working Girl; Shrek; My Fair Lady; Joseph and the Amazing Technicolour Dreamcoat.*

Children's: *Aladdin and his Enchanted Lamp*; *Dick Whittington*; *Cinderella*; *The Ugly Duckling*.

The Big Factory and River Trouble has elements of a Rags to Riches story.

The Quest

- The heroine or hero lives in a place that has become oppressive and intolerable and realises that matters can only be rectified by making a long difficult journey in order to reach a goal.
- The heroine and companions set off on their journey; it is a difficult journey and the party face life-threatening ordeals. Between ordeals, the heroine and her companions receive hospitality, help or advice often from 'wise old men' or 'beautiful young women'. The heroine may have to make a 'journey through the underworld' where she comes into helpful contact with spirits from the past who give her guidance as to how to reach her goal.
- The heroine is within sight of her goal but a series of new and terrible obstacles have to be overcome before the goal can be achieved.
- The heroine has to undergo a last series of tests (often three in number). There is a last great battle or ordeal.
- The heroine achieves her goal and the prize, whatever it may be, is won. A good life is promised thereafter, stretching indefinitely into the future.

Examples include:

Classic: *Jason and the Argonauts*; *The Odyssey*; *The Lord of the Rings*; various quests for the Holy Grail; *Pilgrim's Progress*; *Watership Down*; *Around the World in 80 Days*; *Moby Dick*; *Treasure Island*.

Film: *Raiders of the Lost Ark*; *Kingdom of Heaven*; *Troy*; *Conan the Barbarian*; *Battlestar Galactica*; the whole *Star Trek* series.

Children's: JK Rowling's *Harry Potter and the Philosopher's Stone*; *The Snow Dragon* by Vivian French.

In this book, the Quest story is called, believe it or not, *The Quest*.

Voyage and Return

- Characters leave the security of their home and end up in a strange new world, unlike anything they have ever experienced before.
- The characters enjoy the sense of adventure and explore the new world.
- The mood of the adventure changes as the characters realise there is a threat. The threat becomes increasingly alarming.
- The threat is so great that the characters fear they will not survive.
- Just as the threat closes in on the characters, they make their escape from the other world, back to where they started.

Examples include:

Classic: *Alice in Wonderland*; *Peter Pan*; H.G. Wells's *The Time Machine; Journey to the Centre of the Earth*. Elements of Voyage and Return are found in Shakespeare's *The Tempest*, *A Midsummer Night's Dream* and *A Winter's Tale*.

Film: *The Wizard of Oz*; *Jurassic Park*; *The Beach*; *Pirates of the Caribbean*; *Jumanji*.

Children's: *Where the Wild Things Are* by Maurice Sendak; *The Tunnel* by Anthony Brown; *Night Pirates* by Peter Harris; *Molly Moon's Hypnotic Time Travel Adventure* by Georgia Byng; Maurice Jones's *I'm Going on a Dragon Hunt.*

In this book, the Voyage and Return stories are *The Incredible Shrinking Machine* and *The Remedy Rocket.*

Comedy

Basic Comedy involves:

- A character (or characters) who is living a life in which he or she deludes themself that everything is as it should be, when it clearly is not. This causes increasing amounts of confusion, uncertainty and frustration.
- The state of confusion gets worse until everything seems to be in a nightmarish tangle.
- The characters see the truth and, once their perceptions of the world are changed, the whole situation is transformed and becomes harmonious and joyful.

The basic plot looks so simple, but the subtleties of dialogue and timing make Comedy the most difficult type of story to write well.

In the TV series *Keeping Up Appearances*, the lead character Hyacinth Bucket believes that she can make people regard her as upper class when she clearly is not. Confusion and frustration are caused as Hyacinth does her best to maintain the illusion. Things get into a tangle when Hyacinth's working-class family gets mixed up with her 'society events'. When Hyacinth is forced to confront the realities of her family background, she has to accept what happens with the best grace she can muster.

The children's book *Bad Habits* by Babette Cole is a typical Comedy. Lucretzia thinks she can carry on behaving badly and no one can stop her. Her behaviour is so awful that her parents make a secret plan to show her what she is really like from the point of view of other people. Confusion and frustration escalate as a band of nasty-tempered monsters with very bad habits gate crash Lucretzia's birthday party. Lucretzia is forced to see the effects of bad behaviour and is dramatically changed into a nice little girl. Everyone is happy.

Further examples include:

Classic: Shakespeare's *The Comedy of Errors, Much Ado About Nothing, As You Like It, The Merry Wives of Windsor, Love's Labour's Lost.*

Film: *The Pink Panther; Snatch; About a Boy; Two Weddings and a Funeral.*

Children's: the whole *Katie Morag* series by Maria Hedderwick; *Paddington Bear* by Michael Bond; *Thomas the Tank Engine* by W. Awdry; *Jamil's Clever Cat* by Fiona French.

In this book and the Supplementary CD, the Comedies are *Mrs Hope's Shop, Little Bo Peep* and *The Giant Pet Escape.*

Tragedy

- The hero is dissatisfied with life and wants more from it. The hero is spurred into action by some object of desire or by a course of action presenting itself to him.

- The hero becomes focused on his course of action and there is a symbol of his commitment, such as the signing of a deal, or a deed that can't be undone. All seems to be going well and the hero believes that he will get what he wants.
- Things begin to go wrong. The hero is frustrated and is compelled to do a 'dark' deed that locks him into different courses of action. A 'shadow figure' often stands in the hero's way, making his tasks and deeds even more difficult.
- Things slip out of the hero's control. The hero has a mounting sense of threat and despair. Forces of opposition and fate are closing in on him.
- Either by the forces he has roused against him, or by some final act of violence, the hero is destroyed.

Stories that conform to this plot include:

Classic: Shakespeare's *Macbeth, Julius Caesar, Anthony and Cleopatra*; Christopher Marlowe's *Dr Faustus*; Emily Bronte's *Wuthering Heights*; Arthur Miller's *The Crucible*.

Film: *Bonnie and Clyde; Collateral; Bladerunner; West Side Story; One Flew Over the Cuckoo's Nest*.

Obviously, this is not a favourite for young children's literature! In this book, the tragedies are *The Magic Book Adventure* and *The Big Factory and River Trouble*.

Rebirth

- A hero or heroine (often young) falls under the shadow of a 'dark power' of some kind – an unkind or evil person or regime (natural, supernatural or psychological).
- The hero or heroine copes and all seems to go well. The threat from the 'dark power' seems to have receded.
- The 'dark power' approaches again in full force and the hero or heroine are imprisoned in a state of 'living death'.
- This state of living death goes on for a long time and it seems the 'dark power' has triumphed over the hero or heroine.
- There is a miraculous redemption of the situation. If the imprisoned person is female, it will often be a male hero figure who will rescue her. If the imprisoned person is a male, he may be saved by a young woman or a child.

Stories that conform to this plot include:

Classic: *A Christmas Carol; Peer Gynt; Silas Marner*.

Film: *A.I. Artificial Intelligence; Gladiator; In the Name of the Father; Kiss of the Spider Woman; Minority Report*.

Children's: *The Snow Queen; Sleeping Beauty; Beauty and the Beast; The Frog Prince;* Frances Hodgson Burnett's *The Secret Garden*.

There is no Rebirth story in this book, but there is an example in Book 2: Madonna's *The English Roses*.

Happy plot spotting!

Dramatic Conventions – the tools for the job!

Remember the basic premise: all children, even very young ones, can learn through classroom play that is enhanced by the teacher's use of dramatic techniques.

The projects in *Parts 2 and 3* use technical terms that refer to key teaching strategies, all of which are explained in this section. These dramatic techniques are collectively known as *Conventions* – they are standard ways of going about drama and are well-known across the UK. Many of them are drawn from methods used to train actors, others were developed by the great Dorothy Heathcote and most of them have been defined by Jonothan Neelands, who is currently Programme Director for the Drama Education and Cultural Studies MA course at Warwick University Institute of Education (see his recently re-published book *Structuring Drama Work*[2]).

In effect, these conventions are the building blocks, or the nuts and bolts, of the project lessons. You will probably want to keep referring back to the explanations in this section as you work through the material in *Parts 2 and 3*. Please note that the conventions have been explained with the whole *Play Write* series in mind, so you will find that some of the points made apply more to Books 2 to 5 than they do to this book.

In the projects, you are told exactly what to do and when to do it. The development of each project is spelled out for you. As you gain more experience and confidence, though, you will want to be more inventive. You will want to customise the projects – to do things differently by using different conventions at different times and taking the stories off in new directions. Eventually, you will be able to build entirely original dramas from scratch with children. The conventions will be your tools. Here they are …

Pupils in Role (PIR)

This simply means pupils pretending to be people (or sometimes animals, fantasy creatures or things) other than themselves.

This is the basis of all classroom drama. Every pupil in the class is asked to operate in pretend mode. This is not performance drama, in which some pupils are actors and the rest are audience; this is collective drama in which everyone works in role simultaneously. With young children, everyone usually plays the same role at the same time (for example, they are *all* villagers, or they are *all* servants, or they are *all* customers, or they are *all* travellers). However, pupils don't spend their whole time in role. In the projects, 'time out' to reflect, discuss and carry out associated tasks is an important part of the whole learning process. Indicating to pupils when to go into role and when to come out of role is a key function of the teacher.

The good news is that young children instinctively spend a lot of time pretending; they are naturally inclined to operate in role, so it's not difficult to get them to do this. When playing spontaneously, they create imaginary situations and take on various characters as their 'game' develops. However, when engaging in a whole-class drama, there are specific skills, disciplines and terminologies to learn. In free play, individuals are able to 'live in a world of their own' and choose how much to interact with others. In whole-class drama, pupils are required to talk to each other and to build belief in a *shared* imaginary world. Listening, discussing, accepting and rejecting contributions, empathising, campaigning for viewpoints and reasoning, all become necessary when working as a group.

---

[2] Neelands J, Goode T (2000). Structuring Drama Work, Cambridge University Press, Cambridge

Although young children are keen to play-act (which makes it easy for us to do drama lessons), they are not usually very disciplined (which can make drama lessons challenging). They tend to drift in and out of the story as their concentration waxes and wanes, or as spontaneous thoughts and sudden interests take over. This is perfectly acceptable and is easily managed by using some of the other dramatic conventions in this section, especially Teacher in Role. Pupils have different levels of engagement with a story at different times, depending on how the context touches their emotions and connects with their life-experience. Sometimes it is easy for a child to believe in the fictional context and empathise with the characters and sometimes it isn't. Of course, it requires mental discipline to accept roles that are 'given' rather than chosen, and to play those roles within the circumstances laid down by the teacher. But such discipline can be acquired, with regular experience of working like this.

The teacher manages PIR by deploying the other conventions. In order to maintain a good pace to the projects, it is a good idea to teach these conventions (along with their technical names) directly to the children. This way, the teacher doesn't have to explain in tedious detail, every time, exactly what the pupils have to do. Also, knowing the conventional ways in which imaginary experience is structured and manipulated is a necessary foundation for pupils' understanding drama as an art form later on. As pupils become more experienced dramatically, they can begin to suggest for themselves which conventions to use at various points in a fiction. In this way, the Early Years teacher is supporting the development of pupils' independence and is laying solid foundations for high quality drama in KS2 and beyond.

Teacher in Role (TIR)

This means the teacher acting alongside the children.

Teacher in Role is not just *a* tool for managing learning through dramatic experience, it is *the best* tool, and therefore needs the most detailed explanation. It does not mean you have to be the world's greatest actor, but it does mean pretending to be someone else. TIR fulfils several important functions simultaneously:

1. **It is the prime way of intervening in a drama without interrupting the flow of the story.** The teacher is a participant rather than a director, manipulating the action from the inside. Taking a role within the drama allows the teacher to:

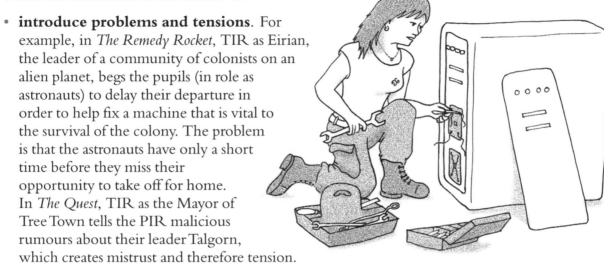

   - **introduce problems and tensions**. For example, in *The Remedy Rocket*, TIR as Eirian, the leader of a community of colonists on an alien planet, begs the pupils (in role as astronauts) to delay their departure in order to help fix a machine that is vital to the survival of the colony. The problem is that the astronauts have only a short time before they miss their opportunity to take off for home. In *The Quest*, TIR as the Mayor of Tree Town tells the PIR malicious rumours about their leader Talgorn, which creates mistrust and therefore tension.

   - **remove easy solutions**. For example, in *Mrs Hope's Shop*, TIR as Mrs Hope is not happy with what her customers have done to her shop and a simple apology is not enough to repair the relationship. It would be easy to have Mrs Hope accept what has happened to her and receive the apology graciously, but this would not make the point that she deserves respect for her way of seeing things as much as anyone else. Another example: in *The Magic Book Adventure*, TIR as the King asks the PIR to face up to the fact that they cannot put things right after they discover that some of the older villagers have gone missing. TIR as the King confronts the PIR with the consequences of their actions.

   - **add detail and depth.** If an individual pupil or a small group seems to be lost for things to act out, TIR can help by making suggestions as a natural part of conversation. For example, in *The Big Factory and River Trouble*, TIR as the gate guard suggests items that the PIR might have had stored in their private lockers. TIR might say: *'Oh, I'm really sorry about this. I hadn't realised that the security guards had made such a mess of your things. Is this someone's photograph? Are these your socks? Someone's watch is on the floor over there. I've just trodden on a hair brush! Is this your note book? Who owns this red towel? I think this must be your chemical protection suit.'* This gives the PIR some ideas to work with so that they can act out gathering their belongings together.

   - **ask questions to prompt deeper thinking**. For example, in *Mrs Hope's Shop*, TIR as Katie Kind asks the PIR as customers (who have let themselves into Mrs Hope's shop at night to tidy it up as a surprise for her) what they can see, hear and feel as they act out fumbling around in the dark trying to find the light switch. Then, before the light is put on, TIR asks the PIR whether it is a good idea to put the light on and to consider what might happen if someone outside in the street sees it. TIR challenges the PIR to propose other solutions by not knowing what to do for the best and presenting counter-arguments. Another example: in *Little Bo Peep* (on the Supplementary CD), Bo's mum asks Bo's friends for advice after they have all played a trick on her daughter. The mother feels that she has 'blown' her relationship with her daughter and wants to know how she can repair the damage.

- **hold the group together, ensuring that everyone stays in the same story**. In free play, pupils are able to act out their own stories, go off on their own tangents and develop their own narrative. Classroom drama is different. Everyone is expected to stay focused on the same story with just enough room for individuals to develop their own belief and excitement. For example, in *The Incredible Shrinking Machine*, TIR keeps the party of adventurers together by leading them through a series of events that eventually causes them to be trapped in a tunnel (worm hole) by a (giant) spider. Well-timed 'scenes' keep everyone moving, and moving in the same direction – there isn't the time or space to go off on personal adventures. The benefits for the pupils is the excitement of all class members being involved in, for example, running and hiding from the spider.

- **manage pace**. For example, in *The Quest*, Pupils in Role have to decide whether to trust the Mayor of the town or Talgorn. TIR tells them that they are not safe where they are and have to move on quickly, so they have to make a decision within the next two minutes. Another example: in *The Incredible Shrinking Machine*, TIR as the owner of the shrinking machine varies the pace of the adventure part of the story by:

  - spending a good amount of time on the introduction to the shrinking machine
  - demonstrating how to use the machine in detail
  - telling pupils about the possible dangers
  - leading the expedition (physically being at the head of the line of students, walking them round the classroom among the imaginary giant blades of grass)
  - timing the appearance of a scary spider
  - determining how long the group stay in hiding (by acting as look-out and telling them when it's safe to come out)
  - deciding when it's time for everyone to run back to the shrinking machine and make themselves big again.

2. **It tells the children how serious the drama is** – so serious that even the teacher is prepared to get involved. When the teacher starts working in role, belief in the story is built very quickly and commitment to the drama is immediately deepened.

3. **It provides a model of role-play**, showing children how to act, how to take part, when to give way to others and how to hold a role.

4. **It alters the teacher-pupil relationship and breaks down the usual barriers**. The pupils are relieved of the usual need to please the adult in charge. Consequently, pupils have a wider range of responses available to them. Working in role, pupils can test out different attitudes to people, take on more adult responsibilities, challenge the ideas of others, take control of situations, allow feelings to be fully expressed, declare uncompromising opinions and disagree with authority figures. Many of these modes of behaviour are regarded as undesirable in the ordinary classroom situation. In addition, when teacher and pupils are in role together, shy children tend to speak more. The general atmosphere of the classroom is improved, even after the drama is finished, and children are usually more willing to complete tasks associated with the drama, including writing … all because there is a new sense of comradeship with the teacher.

Role functions

To understand how TIR can be used effectively, you need to know about 'role functions'. A character's role function is the reason for that character being in the story. When deciding on what kind of character you are going to play, ask yourself:

- **What impact do I want my character to have on the other characters** (for example, raise their awareness, challenge their perceptions, make them more informed, deepen their thinking, rouse their emotions, spur them to action)?

- **How do I want my character to change the situation** (for example introduce a problem, introduce a tension, remove certain solutions, open up new possibilities)?

- **How do I want my character to influence the direction and pace of the story** (for example, slow things down or speed them up, or take everyone off to a new setting)?

The teacher's role is selected to perform one or more of these specific purposes and to stimulate particular responses from the PIR. The role function determines the way TIR will behave, what TIR will say and how TIR will say it. The role function dictates whether the character stands or sits, whispers or shouts, swaggers or shuffles, for example. Some preparation often helps: the more the teacher believes in the role, the better the pupils will respond.

There are some useful questions that you could ask yourself as you prepare a role. These revolve around what happened just before the scene in which you will introduce your character. Ask yourself:

- **What place has my character just come from?**
- **With whom has my character been speaking?**
- **What is my character wearing?**
- **What is my character's mood?**
- **Who else knows what my character is up to?**
- **What is my character's attitude to the other characters in the story?**

Role functions you can choose from include:

Authority

… a person in charge, with responsibility; for example, a captain, a boss, a police officer, the King, the Queen. This role is generally useful for getting the pupils in role to do things: *'Now go off and …'*

But there are different types of authority role functions:

1. The **benevolent** authority figure, such as the King in *The Magic Book Adventure*.
2. The **hapless** authority figure who ends up with responsibility but doesn't really want it, such as the farmer in *The Giant Pet Escape* (on the Supplementary CD).
3. The **sinister** authority figure who has some power over other characters in a story, such as Grimlac in *The Quest*.

Messenger

… a person bringing or taking information. Messenger roles are mainly used to get the pupils in role to speak about a character or a situation or to explain what has happened. This role function can also be used to raise tension.

There are three messenger role functions:

1. **delivering information** on behalf of someone else (indirectly involved). This is a useful role as the messenger is simply doing a job and can take a neutral stance about any reaction the PIR might have. For example the messenger might say, *'Look, I was sent to tell you … it has nothing to do with me'*. Tension can be raised when the role is used to increase a sense of frustration. For example, in *The Magic Book Adventure*, TIR receives, and reads to the PIR, a letter from the villagers asking if the palace staff have seen Grandma Razi.

2. **witness to an event** who is 'spreading the word' (directly involved). This role is often trying to persuade or convince people of a point of view. For example this role might say, *'I don't want to alarm you, but …'*, or *'I have seen the most incredible thing …'* Tension can be raised by providing information that conflicts with what the pupils in role think they know. For example, in *The Giant Pet Escape* (Supplementary CD) the farmer tells the PIR as the villagers that he has seen the giant in the woods at the bottom of a big hole with a broken leg, which means that the Growlabeast has not yet been captured.

3. **gathering information** that will be relayed to someone else. Typically, this role might be a news reporter, an inspector, or any person in the middle between the PIR and a person in authority. This role asks questions: *'What happened?'*; *'Why did you do that?'*; *'Can I tell her Majesty that all the jobs are done?'*. Tension can be raised by asking questions that the pupils in role don't want to answer, for example, the TV presenter in *The Big Factory and River Trouble*.

Victim

… a person requiring help, usually in the form of information, ideas or skills. This is good for building empathy and for getting the pupils to suggest what action needs to be taken.

There are three victim role functions. A character who needs:

1. **advice** … this could be a character with some authority or high status, such as Eirian, the leader of the colonists on the alien planet, who asks for advice in *The Remedy Rocket*. Again, another example is Little Bo Peep's mum who asks advice from her daughter's friends (on the Supplementary CD).

2. **practical help** … this is a person who needs some practical help to build, fix or explore, such as Mrs Leszczyk who needs help with her garden in *The Incredible Shrinking Machine*, or the giant who needs help to look after his pet Growlabeast while his broken leg mends in *The Giant Pet Escape* (on the Supplementary CD).

3. **rescuing** … this is a person in trouble, someone who is being badly treated, or is trapped somewhere, or who has a life-threatening problem, such as the Mayor's daughter in *The Quest* who is being held to ransom in Castle Grimlac. And there is the Giant who needs rescuing from his lonely isolation on the fringe of society in *The Giant Pet Escape* (Supplementary CD).

One of the gang

… this person has equal status with the roles being played by the pupils. It is useful for getting pupils to take responsibility for decisions and actions. The TIR being 'one of the gang' creates a sense of 'being a team' and generates a helpful feel-good factor. Consequently, PIR are more motivated to solve problems and to be more rigorous when weighing the consequences of proposed actions. Pupils can speak on equal terms with TIR and can therefore test out registers that they don't normally get chance to exercise. TIR can play devil's advocate easily as the equal status makes it possible for pupils to disagree or argue other points of view with the teacher's character.

An example of this role function is Katie Kind in *Mrs Hope's Shop* who, like the PIR, is a customer. Katie suggests tidying the shop up, but quickly shares the responsibility for what happens next with the pupils. Another example: in *The Quest*, Talgorn is one of the gang at times, such as when the group is making joint decisions.

You can of course mix these role functions together depending on what you want to achieve. Imagine, for example, a messenger who doesn't really want the job of delivering the message. In this case, 'Messenger' would be mixed with 'Victim' to create an interesting character. Such a character might need advice from PIR because she believes that the information she has been told to pass on is incorrect, but she doesn't want to upset her boss (who is given to fits of temper and shouting) by suggesting he is wrong. There are endless possibilities for developing interesting roles to play!

General rules for using TIR

Whenever possible, choose a role that you will enjoy playing and can be enthusiastic about. Pupils will feel safe if they are sure that you are comfortable and will quickly commit themselves to the drama if you 'hold' the role well (this means that you stay in role no matter what people say), especially in the critical first few minutes.

The following practical rules will be helpful if you are unfamiliar with the use of TIR:

1. **Inform pupils.** Tell them that you are going to work in role. Before you start, let them know who you are going to be and what situation the person is in. For example, *'I am going to be the King's Chief Housekeeper and I am going to show you around the palace.'*

2. **'Sign' the role.** Be clear with pupils about when you are, and when you are not, working in role. Use a simple piece of costume, such as a hat or shawl, or carry an item, such as a clipboard, a bag or a walking stick to

'sign' your role. For example, you might say, *'When I put this hat on, I will be the Gate Guard and when I take it off and put it on the chair, I will be myself again.'*

3. **Use body language.** The ways in which you sit, stand and move give pupils important clues about the type of role you are trying to portray. This doesn't require acting skills, just a little enthusiasm and commitment to the role you are playing. Preparation also helps; you will find the attitude and physical body language easier to create if you are clear about what you want the role to achieve (role function).

4. **Plan the use of the space you will be working in**. Decide on the best place for TIR to stand or sit so that all pupils can see you, hear you, and are not distracted by anyone or anything. Consider the potential benefits of using staging equipment; for example, standing on a stage block to speak when taking on an authority role.

5. **Be prepared for anything!** Some pupils may get carried away and respond strongly to TIR, which is usually a sign of their commitment to the drama. If anything happens that makes you feel too uncomfortable, simply stop the drama, take a break and judge whether the situation was acceptable or not. Restate your rules if necessary before starting the drama again.

Meetings

Gathering pupils together in role.

Meetings occur frequently in the projects in *Parts 2 and 3*. They are part of TIR's staple diet. Meetings have multiple benefits: they are a convenient way for TIR to give information to PIR; they provide a forum for controlled discussion; they keep the whole class bound together; they can re-focus attention; they can be used to slow the action down if it's getting too frenetic; they can re-establish discipline if things are getting too loose.

Meetings can be used to introduce problems and tensions *('I'm afraid I have to tell you that …')*, they can be used to move a story on *('Good news everyone, I've just heard that we have been given permission to …')*, they can remove easy solutions *('What a shame, the … is broken. We will have to think of another solution. Anybody got any ideas?')*. All in all, meetings are one of the main ways (with younger children, perhaps *the* main way) in which TIR structures the drama.

The good news is that young children (unlike adults!) love meetings. For them, it is very 'grown up' to be invited to attend a meeting. So, meetings usually increase pupils' commitment to the drama and add to their motivation and excitement.

There are different kinds of meetings that TIR can use and you will find all of them in the projects:

The formal meeting

This kind of meeting is called by an authority figure. For example, Talgorn calls a meeting to explain the mission at the beginning of *The Quest*. In *The Big Factory and River Trouble*, the Human Resources Manager calls a meeting to explain the new jobs that the workers are about to undertake. The best example of a formal meeting in the projects, though, is at the end of *The Big Factory*, when the bosses assemble to discuss their options.

A formal meeting is characterised by a clear distinction between the higher status of the leader (main speaker) and the lower status of group members. There is often a ready-made agenda. Pupils may be asked to sit in a way that suggests formailty, such as around a 'board' table or in rows. There may be a Ritual of some kind to mark the opening and closing of the meeting: for example, if the meeting is led by a member of a royal family, participants might bow; if it is an elected leader, participants might shake hands with each other or use some kind of salute.

The formal meeting is a good device for giving PIR information and for setting a serious tone. It can have the helpful by-product of calming everyone down!

The informal meeting

Called by 'one of the gang' in order to get an event organised. For example, Katic Kind calls an informal meeting in *Mrs Hope's Shop*. The informal meeting usually begins by TIR saying something like, *'Come on, settle down everyone, I'd like to know what you think about … /there's something we need to do/something we need to discuss/something we need to plan …'* This meeting is characterised by a feeling of 'we're all in this together'. There is often a lot of free-flowing talk as all members of the group have more or less equal status. The leader of the meeting usually asks participants lots of questions rather than giving them lots of information. Another example of an informal meeting: when PIR as friends arrive at Mrs Leszczyk's house, they sit down, have tea together and decide what jobs they are going to do in the garden.

The informal meeting is a good device for discussing situations, characters and plans with pupils. It gets pupils thinking and involved.

The urgent meeting

This is what it says, an urgent gathering of the group. The urgency is driven by the need to make a quick decision because of an imminent threat. TIR might say something like, *'I haven't got a clue what to do and we're running out of time.'* or *'Quick, we've got to decide. We've only got two minutes before …'* All members of the meeting have equal status because of the situation they are in, so even a King will be 'one of the gang'.

New leaders may emerge as options are discussed. There is usually lots of energy and lots of quick-fire pupil talk in these kinds of meetings. In *The Quest,* the adventurers have to decide whether to take the pathway through the cave. In *The Incredible Shrinking Machine,* there is an urgent meeting when PIR and TIR have to decide how to get back to the Machine before the approaching spider gets them. In *The Giant Pet Escape* (Supplementary CD), another urgent meeting takes place when the PIR see the beast escape from the giant's house into the woods. What should they do to protect themselves?

The urgent meeting is a good way of getting pupils to take responsibility for decisions and to exercise leadership. It gets them to face up to situations, think quickly and be decisive.

The spontaneous meeting

This is needed when pupils spontaneously invent a new character or decide to take an unexpected course of action. This kind of thing can happen when a group of pupils get a really strong idea of the way in which the story should develop, and a spontaneous meeting is required so they can explain what is happening (in *their* heads) to the other members of the class.

For example, in a lesson (not in this book) set in a castle, the pupils go off in small groups to explore different rooms. One group comes rushing back with a tale about meeting a dragon keeper who needs help to get his poorly animal to the dragon doctor's. The teacher calls a spontaneous meeting and sends off the excited group to round up the other pupils. In the meeting, everyone agrees to help the dragon keeper and the first task is to (pretend to) make a stretcher big enough to carry the dragon on.

TIR will usually lead the spontaneous meeting, but will be a questioner and sceptic, asking for clarification and doubting that the proposed course of action will work. This gives the pupils with the new ideas maximum opportunity to be understood by everyone as they have to explain themselves fully. Unless there is good reason not to go with the pupils' proposal, TIR will eventually come round to accepting whatever the pupils are suggesting and will shape up the next part of the drama accordingly.

The spontaneous meeting is a good way of getting pupils to communicate *their* ideas about what is happening to everyone else. As their ideas are taken seriously by the teacher, this type of meeting encourages pupils to take more and more responsibility and to put forward further creative ideas in the future.

The gathering

This is used whenever TIR wants to make sure the class is focussed. A gathering is not a full meeting, it's more of a 'checking in' with each other. TIR might just gather PIR together to remind them of something, *'Don't forget that we have to have this task done by …'*, or to tell them something, *'I have just seen the lights go on inside the shop …'*, or to ask a question, *'Should we all chip in together to buy some food for the journey?'*. For example, in *The Giant Pet Escape* (Supplementary CD), TIR as one of the village elders reminds people of jobs that they have to do to prepare for the party that will be held later that day. In *The Magic Book Adventure*, TIR as Reema the palace housekeeper might bring PIR back together to check which cleaning jobs have been completed.

The feeling of a gathering is that 'we're all in this together' and sometimes it can have a conspiratorial purpose. A conspiratorial gathering involves sharing information that is being kept from a character, such as a group of servants who are trying to hide a mistake from their Queen. TIR might gather the pupils together to whisper that the Queen is on her way, that she has forgotten her glasses and that one of the pieces of broken vase is on the floor near her throne.

The gathering is a good device for binding pupils back into the action, by giving them juicy bits of information or by prompting them to redirect their energy. It is also a device for managing pace; the teacher can give information and ask questions that deliberately slow things down (*'I'm sorry, I found out we can't go in there yet. The caretaker won't arrive for another five minutes. We might as well carry on doing our jobs.'*) or urge them on (*'Come on, we don't want the King to think we are lazy do we? He'll be here in a minute or two.'*).

Scene Drawing

Drawing the place where the drama occurs.

Scene Drawing creates a visual depiction of the story's setting. It can be done as:

- **a whole-class activity.** Several large sheets of paper can be taped together and laid out on the floor. Pupils and teacher sit in a circle around the paper. The teacher quickly draws the main features onto the paper with a large felt pen. The class contribute further ideas and either the teacher draws, or selected pupils are allowed to draw, the details that are suggested.

- **a pairs or small-group activity.** Pupils are given a large sheet of paper to work on and asked to draw a picture that contains their joint ideas.

- **an individual activity.** Drawing can be done on any sized paper, but it works particularly well if pupils are given large sheets of sugar paper. This may be because the large paper signals the importance of this task; it also suggests a more substantial art activity than the typical illustrative drawing that pupils usually do. The larger pictures can also be useful should you want the pupils to share their work with the class.

Scene Drawing can be used for a number of purposes:

- to **start** a drama by creating a shared visual image of the place where the story will occur. When it is used for this purpose, it is vital that the image is created by everyone together. The teacher draws a rough outline, then conducts a 'visual brainstorm'. This fires the pupils' imaginations and the resulting 'ownership' of the setting provides the children with enough 'belief' to get going in role. It also helps everyone to stay focused on the common agenda rather than drift off into imaginary worlds of their own.

- at the **start** of a piece of story-writing, to give pupils a visual stimulus to work from. Once the picture has been created, pupils can write words onto the picture. Later, when they have the necessary skills, they can write sentences about the picture and when they are older still, they will be able to write full descriptive narrative.

- **during** a drama or story-writing session, to give pupils time to think about details. For example, drawing the laboratory equipment and ingredients they will be pretending to use in *The Big Factory and River Trouble*, or the messy collection of things for sale inside Mrs Hope's shop, or the various stalls and activities in the market scene in *The Quest*. Paying attention to this kind of detail usually deepens pupils' involvement in the drama, makes their role-play more precise and fleshes out their descriptive writing.

Some pupils, whose imaginative abilities may not be strong, truly benefit from seeing the setting drawn out. It gives them equal access to the drama alongside those pupils who can fantasise more readily.

Map and Plan Making

This is the same as Scene Drawing, except that it is the bird's-eye view of the place where the story occurs.

Again, either a whole class can sit with the teacher and draw the map or plan onto a large piece of paper, or small groups or pairs or individuals can be given large pieces of paper to prepare their own.

Maps and plans only show features that are fixed, such as houses, rivers, roads and parks; they do not contain pictures of animals, humans, cars and so on. A map of an area provides information about the main features, but does not need to show the detail. So, for example, in *The Quest,* pupils create a simple map of Good Land and Bad Land. On the map, buildings are represented with rectangular shapes, and main geographical features such as rivers and mountains are drawn along with roads and pathways. At this point, there is enough information for the pupils to work in role as people of The Pastures.

Typically, as a next step, pupils will be asked to choose a location on the map where they are going to be when the drama starts. They might be working on a farm or in a shop or in the hospital (it depends what the pupils have put on their map). The pupils act out doing jobs in that location as a way of starting the drama.

It is important that the teacher does not draw too much onto the plan and that pupils are allowed to expand the detail. For example, in *The Quest,* small groups can draw what they think the building that houses the Shining Crystal looks like. They can then compare and contrast different visions of the place, perhaps picking out any stereotypical features of special buildings (such as churches, temples, palaces, town halls). Or, you can ask different groups to take responsibility for different areas of the map or plan. One group goes off and draws the details of the farm, another group draws the local shop, another group the hospital.

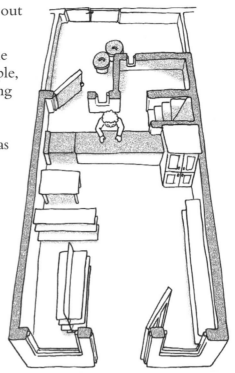

Young pupils find plans of interiors (such as the rooms in the tower in *The Magic Book Adventure*) quite difficult to understand to begin with, but with practice and experience they soon begin to get the idea. In fact, using drama helps pupils to understand the concept of maps and plans because they use them physically (in the acting out) once they have been made.

Drawing and Writing in Role

This involves recording ideas from the perspective of a role, done as part of the drama.

Young pupils naturally use drawing as an easy way to record their ideas. Sometimes, it is hard to see from a drawing alone what a pupil intended, but with a little prompting they can usually explain what they meant. Of course, older pupils can write. One benefit of Drawing or Writing in Role is that it gives pupils additional thinking time. Stopping to draw or write slows the pace of the dramatic action while keeping everyone in acting-out mode.

Here are some examples of drawing tasks that PIR might be asked to do:

- draw the cleaning equipment they will need to take with them into the Tower in *The Magic Book Adventure* or what they will pack into their bags before they go into space in *The Remedy Rocket.*

- draw what their characters can see, such as what the Tower looked like before it was cleaned so that the King will be able to see the difference (*The Magic Book Adventure*) or drawing pictures of what the characters can see on their journey to Tree Town in *The Quest*. Such drawings are the equivalent of 'photographs'.

- draw labels for Mrs Hope so that she knows where to put things in *Mrs Hope Shop,* or for the market stalls in *The Quest,* or for the laboratory in *The Big Factory and River Trouble.*

- draw a character who has been encountered in a drama, such as the creature from the giant's house in *The Giant Pet Escape* (on the Supplementary CD), or the monster that they have heard about but never seen in *The Quest*, or the giant spider or enlarged caterpillar in *The Incredible Shrinking Machine*, or the mysterious colonists led by Eirian in *The Remedy Rocket*.

- draw signposts to help people get around the garden in *The Incredible Shrinking Machine*.

Examples of the kinds of things that pupils might write (even if their writing is at a very early stage and rather ill-informed and inaccurate) in role include: letters; notes; reports; diary entries; labels; guides; instructions; signs; postcards; captions; leaflets; adverts; menus; posters; passports; visas; witness statements; tickets; timetables; programmes; agendas; minutes; emails; text messages; newspaper headlines; directions, shopping lists, prescriptions; recipes, application forms …
Generally, pupils are more motivated to write when they are in role than when they are not; their imaginations are fired and the writing is purposeful, sometimes urgent. These writings can later be used as notes and drafts from which more extended pieces can be composed out of role. With older children, they can be woven into full, written versions of the story.

It is important to remember that these drawing and writing activities are not done outside the drama, they do not take 'time out'. Rather, they are undertaken as part of the flow of the story, as natural tasks for the PIR within the situations they find themselves in.

Role on the Wall

This is a way of either creating a character from scratch or adding detail to an existing character.

An outline figure is drawn on a large sheet of paper, usually a gingerbread person. It represents a body with no bias towards age, class, gender or ethnic origin and can be human, fantasy, alien, animal or whatever you want. The paper is placed where everyone can see it and someone agrees to be the note-taker (usually the teacher in Foundation and KS1). Anyone can contribute suggestions to build the character, such as: she's a mum who works in the Big Factory; she's not got much money; she loves her children. The note-taker will generally take the first comments as true, quickly writing them onto the image, and will ask the group to decide between any contradictory ideas that are put forward. It is important for the process to remain pacey so that children spark ideas off each other.

By the end of the exercise, the group should have a description of what the character looks like, some of the character's life history, a name and age and some words to describe his or her attitude or personality. The sheet can be put on the wall as a reference point and can be brought to life through Hot Seating, Forum Theatre or acting out, or used as a prompt for writing a character description. Also, different attributes can be recorded in different colours, such as red for appearance, blue for life history, green for personality traits. This allows the teacher to manage how a character is written about. Pupils can be asked to write, for example, three sentences about the character's appearance, two

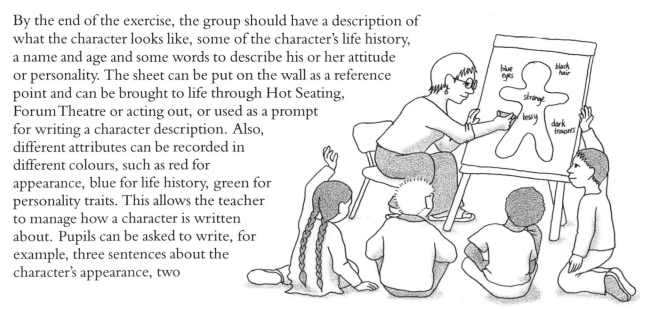

sentences about life history and two sentences that describe personality. Pupils can use the colours in their writing, too.

Once the drama has moved on a bit and the character has been Hot Seated, or has been involved in some acting out, it is often interesting to return to the original Role on the Wall to see if there is new information to add.

Hot Seating

This means asking a character questions.

Someone (teacher or a pupil) takes on the role, sits in a chair and is questioned by the rest of the class (who are out of role). This device can be used in several ways to explore and develop a character:

- a new character that has been made using Role on the Wall (see above), Costuming or Still Image (see below) can be deepened through Hot Seating. Either a teacher or a pupil answers questions in role as that character in order to find out more about her or him. For example: What does he like and dislike? What family and friends does he have? What are his possessions and favourite things? What does he like to eat? What places has he visited? What interesting things has he done? What makes him angry? Where does he live? What would he do in such-and-such a situation? What's he scared of? Does he dream about something he would like to do or someone he would like to be? … and so on.

- the action of a drama can be stopped so that questions can be asked to a particular character at that particular moment. Typically, these would be questions about her feelings there and then, her thoughts about the situation she's in, or she might be pressed for her secrets, plans or motives. This is the kind of Hot Seating that you will be most likely to use in the projects in this book. In this kind of Hot Seating, the character often reveals 'inside information' that can then be used by pupils to make decisions in role, or to discuss issues out of role. For example, it would be fascinating to ask Prince Aten in *The Magic Book Adventure* about his journeys and how he came to be able to control the magic of the book. Also, Lord Grimlac in *The Quest* could be examined about why he made a deal with the Bad Landers.

- a character from a story book, poem or play can be questioned to get his or her views or to get more background information.

- a role can be researched and then played either by pupils or the teacher as a way of sharing information about a topic. For example, the role could be one of Florence Nightingale's nurses.

- a character from a photograph, painting or picture can be questioned. For example, in an L.S. Lowry painting there are lots of visual clues to help a pupil answer questions about the life of a factory worker.

Initially, especially with younger pupils, it is important for the teacher to model the process by being Hot Seated first. This way, the procedure becomes self-explanatory and the pupils understand what is required of them. Also, pupils might not be used to asking good questions and will need some help. In this case, either the teacher can model questioning skills by reversing the process – *she* questions *the pupils* in a mass collective Hot Seating. Or the teacher can give pupils in small groups some time to come up with a few questions, then these can be discussed and refined before the formal Hot Seating begins.

It usually helps to sit the Hot Seated character on a special chair (the teacher's chair perhaps) and for the rest of the class to sit round on the floor in a horseshoe.

Costuming

This means developing a character from assortments of clothes, pieces of cloth and accessories.

Children call this 'dressing up'. Clothes and accessories can be used to create a character from scratch or they can be used to deepen an existing character. Inevitably, this means that the teacher has to raid charity shops and beg discarded items from colleagues and parents. It's important to have an ample assortment of clothes, old pieces of fabric, and lots of accessories, such as umbrellas, walking sticks, bags, clipboards, purses and wallets, briefcases, wigs, photographs, jewellery, toy weapons, back packs …. You can use them in a variety of ways:

- present pupils with a bag or suitcase of clothes and ask the pupils to create the character who owned them. Help pupils by asking questions such as, 'What kind of person do you think would wear clothes like these?' This can be done as a whole-class activity or different bags can be given to different groups.

- in groups, give pupils a few minutes to choose a few items of costume and an object from a random pile in the middle of the room. Ask each group to come up with a character based on the bits they have chosen. Prompt them with questions like, 'What does this tell us about the person?'

These first two strategies, which create characters from scratch, can easily lead to Role on the Wall or Hot Seating in order to develop the new character's personal details further. In fact, when young children are in the Hot Seat, they find it much easier to be in role if they are wearing the character's 'official' costume.

- reverse this: take a character that has just been created through Role on the Wall and/or Hot Seating and ask the pupils to 'dress' it. This will consolidate their understanding of the character and perhaps add further details.

- ask pupils to select a costume for one or more of the characters that has already become established in the drama they are doing. For example: What do you think Talgorn wears? Can you select some clothes for the Mayor of Treetown? And what about Grimlac? How did Mrs Hope look? What things has Mrs Leszczyk put on today to do the gardening? How would we recognise the farmer? How does the factory guard dress differently from the professor? What does the giant put on in the morning? The suggestions that pupils make, and the Costuming they choose, can be used to discuss their understanding of the character's job and personality. The teacher might want to challenge them: Are you sure she would wear that? Is that what all cleaners wear? Would the King wear this every day? Is this posh/sensible/pretty/cheap/warm/big enough?

- use clothes to generate a new character or to illustrate an existing character while the pupils *are in role*. For example, in a drama pupils find clothes in a room they are searching and have to either work out what kind of person they belong to. Or, they find that an umbrella has been left behind and they have to suggest whose it might be.

- ask pupils to choose just one item of clothing or one object that can be used to identify a character; for example, an apron for the King's chief housekeeper in *The Magic Book Adventure*, a belt for Talgorn, a clipboard for the professor in *The Big Factory and River Trouble*, a gardening glove for Mrs Leszczyk in *The Incredible Shrinking Machine*. This item becomes symbolic. Whenever the teacher or a pupil plays this character, the item is worn or held. In effect, the pupils are choosing how the role will be 'signed'.

Naturally, all these visual embellishments help pupils, when they come to it, to write full and interesting character descriptions. The more pupils are used to their characters being physically 'dressed', the more they will get into the habit of working with such detail in their heads.

Freeze Frame

This involves holding the action at a significant moment.

This device is like pausing a video. It creates a frozen moment, the equivalent of a still photograph. During the acting out, the teacher shouts 'freeze' and everyone just stops, in whatever position they are in at that split second. They stay stock still and say nothing. In this way, moments of particular intensity can be logged. The teacher may ask the PIR to hold the Freeze Frame for only a few seconds in silence, just long enough to let the significance of the moment sink in. Or, the teacher might want to make some comments about the meaning of the scene, or draw out acting issues to do with body language and position. When pupils are older, the teacher can use Freeze Frame to point out technical matters, such as the use of space and levels, and the impact of symbolic gesture and contrast.

Here are some examples of points where the teacher might usefully freeze the action in the projects: during the tidying up of *Mrs Hope's Shop*; while PIR ride on the water-boatman's back in *The Incredible Shrinking Machine*; making the potion in *The Magic Book Adventure*; the moment when the mysterious scientist reveals her identity in *The Big Factory and River Trouble*; when PIR are driving their space cars in *The Remedy Rocket*; watching the Lady of The Lake rise out of the misty water in *The Quest*.

An additional benefit of Freeze Frame is that it slows the action down, which can be useful if everything's getting a bit frenetic. What's more, it gives a moment's thinking time for both teacher and pupils as they work out what to do next.

Two good ways to introduce this convention to pupils are:

- play the party game 'Statues', a favourite with most children
- display a picture or photograph and ask the pupils to turn it into a Freeze Frame. To make it a bit more exciting, they can then create the picture of what happens next or what had happened just before the photograph.

Still Image

This involves identifying, portraying and examining a significant moment in the drama.

To create a Still Image, everyone takes up a position in a tableau that represents a significant moment in the story. There is no movement and no speech. Still Image is a step on from Freeze Frame: a Still Image is deliberately and thoughtfully composed and is designed to 'say something'. This is quite different from just freezing the on-going action. A particular moment within the drama is chosen for its importance. It may be the moment when PIR realise they have a problem, it may be the climax of a tension, it may be a crucial moment of choice, it may be a potential conflict, it may be the ending.

For example, in the projects, Still Images could be created around:

- families realising that their elder relatives are disappearing (*The Magic Book Adventure*)
- formal photographs of the proud astronauts arriving for their initial training (*The Remedy Rocket*)
- the returned adventurers of Green Town looking up at the star in the night sky (*The Quest*)
- the situation in Red Houses two years after the factory closed (*The Big Factory and River Trouble*).

With young children, Still Images will be realistic rather than symbolic. A realistic Still Image involves the *actual* characters presenting a moment of the *actual* action from the drama. A symbolic Still Image is more sophisticated and involves (older) pupils devising a representation of an issue within the drama, for example: conflict; freedom; remorse; forgiveness; fear; hope; victory; duplicity; and so on. Therefore, the Still Image may be stylised or figurative, it may involve 'things' rather than people, it is likely to use symbolic devices to express abstract ideas (for example to a group of pupils holding each others' raised hands to convey 'solidarity').

When a Still Image (particularly a realistic Still Image) is presented, it can be analysed through Hot Seating (see above) or Thought Tracking (see opposite) to allow the participants to express the feelings and opinions of their characters. The convention of Still Image is often used in theatre performances to make sure that the audience has really got a particular point or has deeply understood an issue. In classroom drama, these effects can be amplified by scrutinising the characters and through follow-up discussion. Still Image is therefore a great aid to Reflection. What's more, one Still Image can lead to another. Pupils might be asked to present an Image that looks at what happened at some point in time before the original (to examine causes) or at some point after (to examine effects). Again, pupils might be asked to present alternative versions of the same Still Image (to examine the options and choices available to characters).

Thought Tracking

This is a means of releasing characters' thoughts and feelings about specific issues.

This convention (sometimes referred to as 'Shoulder Tapping') works very well with Still Image and can also be used with Freeze Frame. Once a Still Image has been set up, the teacher taps one of the participants on the shoulder as a signal for her or him to vocalise, briefly, the thoughts and feelings of that character at that moment. The teacher then taps the other players in turn, so everyone in the Image has a chance to speak out.

With younger, inexperienced pupils, their responses might simply be to say who they are. As pupils become more used to this convention, they might give a more sophisticated insight into their character's attitude and intentions. Once the initial round of Thought Tracking is complete, the teacher might then invite the class to ask questions to specific characters to find out more. Again, early on, the teacher will probably need to model this process. Beware: there is a danger in asking questions that are too open, such as 'What do you feel now?' These are usually too unfocused and overwhelming to elicit a good response from inexperienced pupils. More appropriate questions might be: What do you think should happen next? or Why do you think the person said that to you? Teachers can judge the level of complexity that their pupils can manage, remembering that much of the excitement of these techniques comes from PIR having their thinking challenged.

Forum Theatre

This is a dynamic means of creating and/or re-working and refining pieces of action.

The students sit facing a small acting area – usually the centre of a circle. A specific scenario is chosen as the focus and a few pupils volunteer to act out how they think it would go. For example, a bully meets his or her victim in a quiet alley on the way home from school. The improvised work is spontaneous and there is no rehearsal. The teacher controls the action by stopping and starting the scene at intervals and by prompting the audience to provide advice and guidance to the role players. In the bullying example, the audience would suggest what the victim should say and do to handle the situation. A couple of the suggestions are played out by the actors in the middle. The teacher might then stop the action, wind the scene back and try out a different suggestion from the audience.

Once the pupils have got used to the idea, any member of the audience can shout 'stop' at any time in order to pause the action. This might be done in order to make a new suggestion or to question one of the actors, or to give the audience time for discussion. Any member of the audience can also ask to swap places with an actor and take over the role in order to try out their own way of dealing with the situation. Scenes can be rewound, fast forwarded and edited, by the audience and teacher working together, just like a piece of videotape.

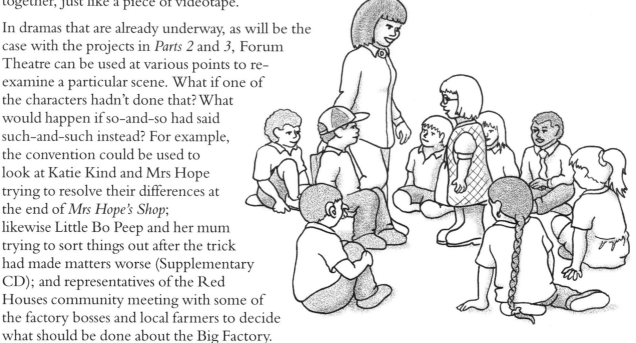

In dramas that are already underway, as will be the case with the projects in *Parts 2* and *3*, Forum Theatre can be used at various points to re-examine a particular scene. What if one of the characters hadn't done that? What would happen if so-and-so had said such-and-such instead? For example, the convention could be used to look at Katie Kind and Mrs Hope trying to resolve their differences at the end of *Mrs Hope's Shop*; likewise Little Bo Peep and her mum trying to sort things out after the trick had made matters worse (Supplementary CD); and representatives of the Red Houses community meeting with some of the factory bosses and local farmers to decide what should be done about the Big Factory.

When it's working well, Forum Theatre is a powerful analytical tool. It allows the class to examine choices, the consequences of actions, and issues of motivation and intent. Forum Theatre can be used with other conventions. For example, within Forum Theatre, characters can be Hot Seated, action can be Freeze Framed, Still Images can be composed and players can be Thought Tracked, all in order to understand more deeply what's going on.

Soundscape

Creating atmosphere, and illustrating a story, with sound.

Culturally, we are very familiar with Soundscapes: the background music of a film; sound effects on the TV and radio; the music in shops; the ambient sounds of the countryside when out walking; the CD we play in the kitchen while cooking. Sounds help to create mood and atmosphere, they affect our emotional state and often stimulate particular thoughts and memories.

Sound can be used in story making to have the same effects. Well-chosen sounds can underline the mood of a character or moment, can help to put the audience into a particular state (you always know in a film that something bad is about the happen because the music darkens), or can illustrate a key moment (such as a drum roll to emphasize the entrance of an important character).

Pupils can use voices, musical instruments, pieces of recorded music, sound-effects CDs, in fact anything that makes the right kind of noise. Making Soundscapes can be a whole-class activity. Pupils sit in a circle, a scene is acted out in the centre and selected pupils in the circle are given instruments and asked to create a spontaneous accompaniment to the drama. Alternatively, small groups can create Soundscapes for a given scene and then compare their various interpretations.

In the projects, pupils are asked to devise Soundscapes to accompany the demonstration of the machine's operation in *The Incredible Shrinking Machine* and to accompany the PIR's entry into the mysterious house where Talgorn first introduces herself in *The Quest*. Other scenes that readily lend themselves to 'Soundscaping' include: the whirlwind in *The Magic Book Adventure* when the first spell is cast; the other-worldly sounds of the alien planet in *The Remedy Rocket*; the perpetual, nagging noise of the wall being broken down in *The Quest*. Soundscapes can play an important part in rituals (see below) and a good example is the Rule Ritual at the beginning of *The Quest*.

Soundscapes can become quite sophisticated. For example, the initial attempts can be recorded, replayed and then refined. Or various pieces of commercial music can be researched until just the right one has been found. Or pupils can compose Soundscapes consciously rather than spontaneously, with plenty of discussion and the trialling of various ideas. When pupils are old enough, they can work out a way of writing the Soundscape down, using symbols of some kind, so that the 'score' can be re-performed.

Ritual

Pupils in Role come together formally to mark a significant cultural, social or religious moment.

Rituals might be held within a drama to celebrate an event (such as a victory), to honour a person (such as a heroine), to remember a significant moment in the community's history (such as a narrow escape), or to respect a natural phenomenon (such as the arrival of the Spring). They can involve bowing, curtseying, shaking hands, raising a hat, a moment of silence, chants, prayers, meditations, songs, dances, anthems, special clothes, special foods and so on.

When a Ritual is called for, the usual first step is for pupils to discuss and devise it *out of role*. This might involve some research into the kinds of rituals people hold for real in various societies. A Soundscape might be created to accompany the Ritual. Once all the details have been worked out, there might be a rehearsal or two before going into role to perform the Ritual 'for real'.

Rituals tend to make proceedings more official and formal. Their binding effect helps to sustain pupils' belief in the fictitious community to which they belong in role. Finally, a Ritual can make a powerful ending to a story.

Role Reversal

Pupils first play one set of characters and then play an opposing group of characters.

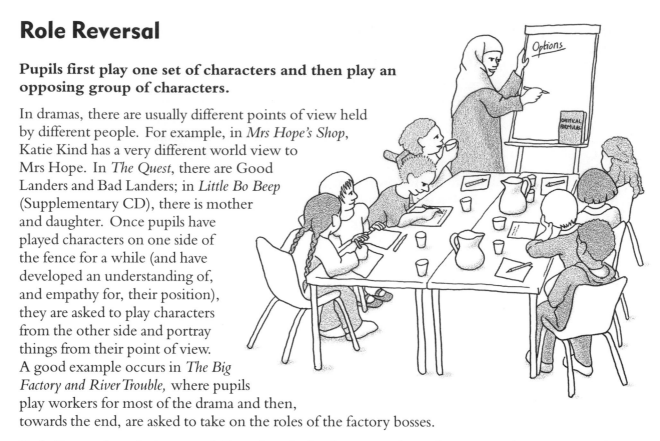

In dramas, there are usually different points of view held by different people. For example, in *Mrs Hope's Shop*, Katie Kind has a very different world view to Mrs Hope. In *The Quest*, there are Good Landers and Bad Landers; in *Little Bo Beep* (Supplementary CD), there is mother and daughter. Once pupils have played characters on one side of the fence for a while (and have developed an understanding of, and empathy for, their position), they are asked to play characters from the other side and portray things from their point of view. A good example occurs in *The Big Factory and River Trouble,* where pupils play workers for most of the drama and then, towards the end, are asked to take on the roles of the factory bosses.

Role Reversal results in powerful learning. It develops empathy and promotes democracy. It also stretches pupils ability to act; it's not easy changing roles from one extreme to another.

Reflection

This is not a dramatic convention as such. Nonetheless, it is a vital part of the whole process. The teacher helps pupils to reflect on, and bring out into the open, what has been felt, understood and learned within the dramatic experience.

Reflection takes place out of role. It should always happen at the end of a drama but it may also occur at various stages throughout. The questions teachers use in Reflection sessions are important as they prompt pupils to think more deeply about the issues and subjects covered in the drama, as well as provide a vehicle for assessing the learning that has taken place. There are three important areas of learning that can be reflected upon:

Questions about the story and its components (to aid deconstruction)

Soon after the project ends, the pupils will probably want to talk about the story. Talking about the story close to the ending is akin to discussing a film as you come out of the cinema or sharing the plot of a good book with a friend or even chatting about what happened in your favourite 'soap' last week. This kind of discussion helps pupils to re-think what happened in the story and reflect on the key messages. Pupils can also identify the component parts of the story and reflect on how the fiction was constructed – the types of characters, settings, problems, tensions and the ending. This builds their understanding of good literature.

Questions about subjects such as history, maths, geography, RE, science and citizenship

Each project story provides a context for learning about various areas of the curriculum – aspects of history, maths, geography, RE, science, citizenship and so on. Additional activities, such as the *Optional Extras,* extend pupils learning of content and skills from these subjects and it is important to consolidate what has been understood by reflecting on it.

Questions about the learning process

Finally, pupils can reflect on the learning process itself: what skills they used; what activities they enjoyed and why; how they have learned; what they need to improve next time, and so on. This kind of Reflection is known as meta-learning.

The following are examples of questions you might ask pupils. We have used *Bloom's Taxonomy of Educational Objectives* to check that we have provided a good range and have included questions that prompt higher-order thinking, such as analysis, synthesis and evaluation. Reflection sessions can be spaced out over a number of days; we certainly wouldn't expect young pupils to sit and discuss all of these questions in one go!

The following sample questions are generic. In each box, the first group is phrased for the adult reader. Underneath, you will find prompts to help you to phrase child-friendly questions.

By the way, please remember that there are also suggested Reflection questions at the end of each project.

Key questions about the story and its components (to aid deconstruction):

What did we learn from the story?

What themes and issues have been explored?

What has been learned about human nature?

What has been learned about right and wrong?

What connections does the story have with real life?

Who are the characters?

What is the status of the characters? (main characters, minor characters, groups of characters)

What kind of people are the main characters?

How can we judge what the characters are like?

What settings were used?

What kinds of places are in the story?

What time is the story set in?

What was the main problem?

What were the tensions?

How did the problem make the story interesting?

How did the tensions make the story more exciting?

What kind of ending did the story have?

What kind of plot did this story have?

What genre of story was this?

What did we notice about the way the story was constructed?

Is this story similar to any other stories we know? How?

Is there anything you would change? Why?

Prompts to help you phrase child-friendly questions:

What was the most important event in the story?

What was the most exciting event in the story?

What was the main idea of ...?

Could this happen in class/school ...?

Do you know another story where ...?

Why did ... happen?

What would have happened if ...?

If ... happened, what might the ending have been?

What have you found out about ...?

How would you feel if ...?

Why do you think that ...?

What are your reasons ...?

Is there a different point of view ...?

What is the difference between these views/ideas ...?

What is the possible solution to ...?

Can you explain ...?

Are you a ... person? Why do you think that?

Can you give an example?

How do we know that ...?

What was this similar to ...?

What do you think about ...?

How did ... make you feel?

Key questions about subjects such as history, maths, geography, RE, science and citizenship:

How do you ask big questions of little kids? There are many possible areas of subject learning that could be drawn out of the projects and we haven't got the space here to translate them all into children's language. So, we've listed the questions (in adult language) that we think are begging to be asked on the back of the projects and we're asking the teacher to consider how and when to address them with young children through classroom conversation and questions.

What have we learned about the place of **history** in our lives?
What have we learned about chronology, cause and effect, the difference between fact and opinion, evidence, constitutions, nations, boundaries, attack and defence, government, democracy, kings, queens, followers and leaders, the development over time of technology, transport, food, clothes, buildings, occupations, communications and customs?

What have we learned about the place of **mathematics** in our lives?
What have we learned about containers, capacity, area, volume, weighing, measuring, standard measures, money, counting, calculating, estimating, sorting, sequencing, pattern and shape?

What have we learned about the place of **geography** in our lives?
What have we learned about plans, maps, symbols, scale, journeys, woods, valleys, mountains, caves, rivers, settlements, farms and farming, villages, towns, cities, transport systems, supply and demand, trade, import and export, weather, other countries, the way settlements change over time, land use, pollution, conservation of resources and the environment, economic dependency, industrialisation and post-industrialisation?

What have we learned about the place of **RE** in our lives?
What have we learned about invisible forces, the supernatural, festivals, rituals, signs and symbols, special foods, special clothing, giving, charity, generosity, self-sacrifice, risk taking, the differences between people's cultures, the different ways in which people worship?

What have we learned about the place of **science** in our lives?
What have we learned about living, non-living and once-living things, insects and small creatures, food webs, soil, ecology, the human body, water, floating, sinking, materials, plants, energy, electricity, light, reflection, fridges, freezers, fuels, space, air, gravity, light, dark, medicine, accuracy, testing, health and safety?

What have we learned about **PHSE and citizenship**?
What have we learned about communities, friendship, celebrations, rights and responsibilities, right and wrong, truth and lies, trust, democracy, conflict resolution, authority, obedience, conscience, deferred gratification, gender roles, equality, sharing?

What have we learned about **art, design and technology**?
What have we learned about colour, texture, reflection, symbolism, motifs, different types of art, structures, stresses and strains, suspension, supports, materials, building, architecture, the features of castles and palaces?

Here are some of the biggest questions that cross a number of subjects:

Is progress always good?

How should rules and laws be made?

Who should be responsible for making sure that rules and laws are kept?

Should rules and laws always be obeyed?

What have we learned about our consciences?

What makes people do what they do?

Why do some people turn out to be mainly bad and others turn out to be mainly good?

Can people change?

What have we learned about predictions, assumptions, evidence and testing?

What have we learned about nature?

What have we learned about survival?

What have we learned about happiness?

Key questions about the learning process:

What activities did you enjoy doing most ? Why?

What have you learned about the way you like to learn?

What kinds of thinking did you do?

How well did you work in a group?

How well did you work by yourself?

Which ways do you like to share your ideas best? (In a group? With a partner? To an adult?)

Did anything get in the way of you enjoying the project? What? Why?

What helped you to enjoy the project?

What new learning have you done?

What new skills have you gained?

How were decisions made?

What would you do differently next time?

Prompts to help you phrase child-friendly questions:

Can you explain ...?

Can you give me an example ...?

How does ... help?

How did you feel when ...?

Why do you think ...?

What would you change?

Is there a different point of view?

Have you used ... before?

Could you use ... in a different project?

Would you suggest any rules for ...?

How could you test to see if ...?

How could you ...?

Is it a problem that ...?

How do you know when ...?

How can we solve the problem?

What is the best solution to ...?

How will you know when ...?

What questions could we ask ourselves about ...?

Part 2

Projects for
3 - 5 year olds

How the Projects are Laid Out

All the projects in this section are set out in a common way.

Planning checklist

This lists the key organisational details: teaching time and space required; main props, equipment and resources needed; main teaching tools.

Teacher's overview

This section explains the nature of the project and outlines the reasons for doing it. It explains what children will get out of the project and how it connects to their developing life experience. The thinking behind the story is unravelled and the issues that are embedded in the story are made explicit so that the purposes of the project become crystal clear and the reflection questions make sense.

The Teacher's Overview also lists the characters in the story and summarises the plot.

When you have read the Planning Checklist and the Teacher's Overview, you will be clear about what you have to do and why you are doing it. In the body of the project, you are then given the step-by-step instructions that tell you how to proceed.

The body of the project

Each project has a series of standard phases for you to work through. These mirror the stages that all story-makers and all stories follow. Think of any film you've watched or novel you've read. The pivotal problem(s) and exacerbating tension(s) are not usually introduced until the audience has become engaged with the setting, the main characters and circumstances. The film-goers and readers have to be emotionally and intellectually hooked if the problems and tensions are to be sufficiently exciting for them. In the projects, this is achieved through the Getting Going and Building Belief phases. Therefore, they always come first.

Obviously, Finding an Ending comes towards the end!

Three other ingredients (Developing the Story, Introducing a Problem, Adding Tension) can occur, and re-occur, in any order. Think of any James Bond film or Doctor Who episode it's easy to see how these elements are woven together. They are essential to any quality fiction.

The element of Reflection turns the fiction into personal learning. In grown-up films, novels and plays, the reflective element is usually implicit (the fiction makes you think) and this can happen because the audience has the life-experience and thinking abilities to operate in 'automatic reflection' mode. With young children, however, the process of reflection has to be explicit. By pausing the drama and asking questions, pupils are being inducted into reflective habits that are not yet established. In the projects that follow, Reflection is sometimes saved up to the end and sometimes it occurs at key points throughout. It's a moveable feast. To summarise, the standard phases of each project are:

- Getting going
- Building belief

- Developing the story
- Introducing a problem
- Adding tension
- Finding an ending
- Reflection.

Potential cross-curricular learning

Each project has so many potential links with the rest of the curriculum that you will have lots of fun spotting and pursuing them. The tables at the end of the projects give you a good number of pointers to start you off.

By the way ...

Wherever you see this symbol you will find the materials you need on the Resources CD inside the back cover of the book.

Planning checklist

Subject matter	Shops and shopping
Themes	Respect for differences between people; the nature of kindness
Key resources and equipment	Costume items to sign TIR, such as a coat or jacket; and other items such as an apron for Katie Kind, and a coloured scarf and a cardigan for Mrs Hope **For the activities** Large sheets of paper Pens and pencils Ingredients and equipment for making salt dough Weighing equipment Measuring jugs and other containers Shopping Cards (Shopping Cards.pdf) **Worksheets (in folder Mrs Hope on the Resources CD)** Shop plan drawings (Shop Plan Whole.pdf, Shop Plan1.pdf etc) The End (The End.pdf) **Props include** Pictures of shops (Shops.pdf) Cleaning items such as buckets, mops, dusters Any items that might be found in a small general store that sells a number of different things. A torch
Organisation	**Time** Without Optional Extras: 8–10 hours With Optional Extras: 12–14 hours **Teaching space** A large space in a classroom. Also, a separate space large enough to lay out a plan of Mrs Hope's shop on the floor and leave it out so that it can be added to and changed as the story develops. Possible themes for the role-play area include a shop.
Main dramatic devices used	Teacher in Role Pupils in Role **Basic plot** This may not be obvious but the plot conforms to Comedy in the following way: Mrs Hope believes that her customers like the 'organic' way she organises her shop; Katie Kind believes Mrs Hope needs help to make things neat and tidy. This clash of 'ways of seeing things' results in confusion and an emotional tangle. At the end of the story, everybody 'sees the world' in a different way. **Basic problem** A secret pact is made to tidy up Mrs Hope's Shop (not knowing vital information and being made to look foolish). **Basic tensions** Mrs Hope is shocked by what happens (being put on the spot; social rules; secrecy; trust).

Teacher's overview

Set in a shop, this story is firmly rooted in the everyday experiences of young children. It is a cautionary tale of the muddle that can arise when two people see the world from very different perspectives. Mrs Hope likes her shop the way it is – messy. Katie Kind likes everything to be neat and tidy.

There is a wholesome and holistic logic to Mrs Hope's random way of thinking. Perhaps she gives Katie Kind a bunch of bananas instead of the brush she requested in order to make her stop, eat a wholesome snack and perhaps reflect on the task she is about to undertake. Maybe Mrs Hope feels that Katie needs to calm down and stop being so frantic about tidying and cleaning. Katie Kind, on the other hand, believes that everyone really wants to be neat and tidy – it's just that they don't have the skills or maybe haven't got the time. It never crosses her mind that anyone might actually *like* things to be jumbled! So, when she suggests that the shop be tidied up as a birthday present for Mrs Hope, she truly believes it is a great gift.

Like all good Comedy plots, this story has some serious issues at heart. In other words, it has a deeper meaning beyond its entertainment value. Good Comedies have characters and situations that resonate with our own real-life experiences. The characters live through events and emotions that we all understand; they deal with 'universal issues' that change very little over time. Examples of well-known TV Comedies that tackle such universals are *Dinnerladies*, *Porridge*, *The Vicar of Dibley* and *Only Fools and Horses*.

Of course, the story of *Mrs Hope's Shop* is about understanding, and being sympathetic to, differences of character. In the drama, pupils explore how such differences can be handled badly and how they can be handled well, what people might say to each other when they disagree and what to do when people are upset. The story can also be used to discuss tidiness and untidiness. Obviously, this is an important issue to address in the Early Years classroom as we endeavour to get the pupils to develop tidying-up habits. However, the intention here is not to moralise about being tidy, but to prompt pupils to think about what they need to consider if they are going to get along with other people respectfully.

At an unspoken level, the differences explored in the story relate to learning styles. According to Dr Anthony Gregorc, a person's learning style is the product of her or his fundamental Mind Style. Using Gregorc's Mind Style categories, we would say that Mrs Hope is very dominantly 'Concrete Random' and Katie Kind is very dominantly 'Concrete Sequential'. Imagine how different they would have been as pupils at school. As a result of this story, children might begin to appreciate such differences at a subconscious level. If the teacher continues to point out these sorts of style difference from time to time, pupils will be in a good position to recognise and discuss learning-style issues more explicitly when they are older. If you are interested in Gregorc's insights, see Appendix B for more details.

This project is relatively easy to teach. Pupils will be familiar with the basic Comedy plot used in many stories for young children: a character sees the world in a particular way and consequently gets into a tangle; then, after some confusion, there is a happy ending. The *Mr Men* stories, for example, tell of characters getting into and out of various 'scrapes' because of their personality traits. More sophistication is added in adult stories, but the idea is pretty much the same. In every episode of *Fawlty Towers*, for example, Basil gets himself into a pickle of some kind. For Basil, though, there is never a happy resolution, rather one predicament just leads to another. This is an 'adult' twist to the basic Comedy plot. *Spot the Dog* stories deal with a character who is finding out about the world through his experiences in much the same way as Paddington Bear does. Both get into trouble, but in the end things get sorted out. The comforting message of these stories for young listeners and readers is that it is OK to learn by experience and make mistakes along the way. Sometimes things might seem confusing and uncomfortable, but everything will work out well sooner or later.

This story isn't a television or play script, so it lacks the funny lines that would make an audience laugh. However, you may find that the pupils will add some humorous dialogue of their own. Children often have a refreshing way of seeing things!

Role-play area

This drama gives pupils a model for playing shopkeepers and customers. It could serve as a very useful introduction to a role-play area set out as a shop.

The cast of characters

- Mrs Hope, the shopkeeper (TIR)
- Katie Kind, a customer (TIR)
- Other customers (PIR)

Summary of the plot

Katie Kind has decided that Mrs Hope's shop needs tidying up, so she purloins the key. Katie enlists the help of other customers and asks them to meet her near the shop late at night. While Mrs Hope is asleep upstairs, Katie and the other customers secretly tidy everything up. It is Mrs Hope's birthday the following day, so Katie wants to get the job done as a present for her.

When Mrs Hope wakes up and comes downstairs in the morning, the 'tidying-up party' are waiting to jump out of hiding and sing 'Happy Birthday'. However, Mrs Hope is horrified when she sees what has been done to her shop; in fact, she is so shocked by the sight that greets her that she begins to cry.

Katie and the customers have to decide what to do next.

Getting going

Talk about shops and look at pictures of shops (Shops.pdf in folder Mrs Hope on the Resources CD).

Optional Extra

Play a game of 'Shop'

It takes some time to teach pupils this game, so you may want to play it a few times before starting the drama. 'Shop' is an old-fashioned parlour game that is often played at young children's parties. It requires two volunteer pupils to work out what type of shop they are 'in' from hearing other players say, shout or whisper a number of separate items that would be found in it.

Sit the pupils in a circle. Discuss with the pupils the types of shop they are familiar with. Perhaps write a list of shops the pupils can name. Then discuss other types of shop with them to extend the list. The list might contain:

- supermarket
- newsagent
- butcher
- halal butcher
- bakery
- sweet centre
- grocer
- clothes shop – sari, boutique, any of the chain stores
- department store
- chemist
- toy shop
- ironmonger
- general store
- craft shop
- florist
- card shop
- bookshop
- Chinese herb and medicine centre
- jeweller
- kosher restaurant
- shoe shop
- optician
- fabric shop
- travel agent
- computer shop
- sports shop
- mobile phone shop
- music shop.

To play the game, two pupils volunteer to leave the circle. When the two pupils are 'out of earshot' (perhaps in a corner of the room with headphones on listening to music, or in the corridor with a classroom assistant), everyone sitting in the circle collectively decides, from the list, what kind of shop the group is going to be.

Once a shop type has been chosen (for example, a grocery shop), everyone in the circle must be able to say one item that would be found there. Go round the circle asking each pupil to choose what they want to say: for example, carrots; cauliflower; potatoes; brown bags; weighing scales. It doesn't matter if two children choose the same item, but pupils should be encouraged to pick different things where possible.

The first time you play this game everyone will probably need to practise saying their item in unison. Tell the pupils that you are going to count them in, and that you want them to say their item in a normal speaking voice. It might take a couple of goes to establish what is required. It would be beneficial for them to practise whispering and shouting in unison as well. If you have a boisterous class, perhaps you'd better warn the class next door that you are going to play a game that can be noisy! Also, tell the pupils in the circle not to 'let on' to the two volunteers which shop has been chosen. It's a secret!

The two volunteers then come back and stand in the centre of the circle (it is important that they remain in the centre; they might be tempted to move over to listen to individual pupils, but this will spoil the game). The teacher explains that everyone is going to say their item at the same time. The volunteers have to listen carefully and try to make out particular items from the general noise. When they think they have heard one or more of the items, they try to work out which shop was chosen.

Optional Extra continued

With everyone speaking at the same time, it is difficult to hear individuals, but not impossible! It is unlikely that the two volunteers will get the answer after the first go. So, they can have several more attempts. After a couple of times saying it in normal voices, there can be a shouting round and a whispering round.

The volunteers can have lots of guesses at what shop they are in. If they are getting stuck, they can ask two questions to get clues. Once the shop has been guessed, two new volunteers are sought and a new shop is chosen. The game can be played as often as you wish, until the novelty wears off. The teacher can increase the difficulty of the game by asking the pupils to see if they can get it in the least number of guesses, or by encouraging the class to choose a more obscure shop.

Building belief

Ask pupils where they go with their parents to shop, what their favourite shops are, what they like to buy and what kinds of things they don't like shopping for.

Tell the pupils that you are going to play shops with them. Explain that you will be a shopper and that you want them to pretend to be shoppers too. Sign your role (perhaps with a coat or jacket) and start the drama by asking the pupils to come with you to the high street to help you buy things for a party. Your role function: 'one of the gang'.

Led by TIR, the PIR act out putting their outdoor clothes on, locking the house and travelling on the bus. Throughout, you will need to talk to the pupils to let them know what is happening.

Possible script:

'I hope the bus isn't late. Here we are at the bus stop. Is that our bus? No, it's the 32. That's no good, it doesn't go into town. Have you brought your shopping bags with you? Oh, yes, I can see. Have you remembered the lists?

'Ah! Here's our bus coming now. Get the fare ready; remember they don't give change. I've got a bus pass. Have any of you got one? Oh, that's good, you can use your bus passes, then. Here we go [act out getting on the bus, showing your bus pass]. It's full so we'll have to stand.'

Act out standing in the aisle of the bus having to keep your balance as the bus stops and starts. Get off the bus. Stop the drama.

Map and Plan Making: a high street

Out of role, sit the pupils in a group so that they can see a large piece of paper on a wall or by sitting them in a circle with the paper on the floor.

Using the illustration opposite as a guide, draw a high street.

Draw the main roads.

Ask the pupils which shops to add to the plan. Draw simple shapes to represent the shops. Draw some symbols for the shops, such as a carrot for grocery or a green cross for a chemist.

Talk to the pupils about the street you have just made together. Give the roads names.

Scene Drawing: shops

Get the pupils into pairs and give each a large piece of paper and a marker pen. Ask them to draw a picture of any of the shops in the street with as much detail as they can manage, such as the number of windows, what's on display in the windows, the size and colour of the door, any signs and notices.

Talk about the pictures the pupils have drawn, then use their ideas as you lead the pupils in acting out a walk along the streets, looking in shop windows and commenting on the displays.

Optional Extra

Communication, language and literacy

The pupils might need some more visual help with different types of shop, in which case giving them a chance to look at pictures again and to read books such as the *Mouse Shop* series by Michelle Cartlidge would be helpful.

Acting out the trip to the high street

Possible script:

> 'The samosas look nice today. I must remember to pop back and get some later. Look at that lovely material. Aren't the colours wonderful? I really do need a new iron, but I haven't got time to look today. Oh! Those shoes are nice.'

Act out crossing the busy road (properly!), pretend to carry a bag, have difficulty putting up an umbrella when it starts to rain. Dash into a shop for shelter. Tell the PIR that you got a little carried away window shopping and you need to hurry because you are running out of time. Ask the pupils if they will go to different shops and buy the things for the party and meet back here.

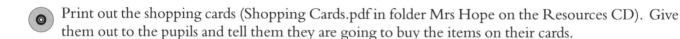 Print out the shopping cards (Shopping Cards.pdf in folder Mrs Hope on the Resources CD). Give them out to the pupils and tell them they are going to buy the items on their cards.

Items include: apples; ice-cream; party hats; birthday cake; balloons; bread; cheese; party sausages; mangos; samosas; pizza; jelly; cucumber; ham; peanut butter; milk; eggs; chocolate; chocolate cake; drinking straws; fizzy drinks; orange juice; bottled water; gulab jamun; sweets; pineapple; chicken jerky; pakora; rice; yams; apples; grapes; bananas; candles; biscuits; tomatoes; noodles; plantain; butter; lettuce; and yoghurt.

Ask the pupils to act out buying their items. As you are handing out the cards, check with a few of them which shop they will be going to and perhaps explain why their item is needed.

Sample script:

> 'What are you getting? Mangos – yes, they are important because I want to make mango lassi. Which shop are you going to, then? You'll have to be quick because that shop is right round the corner. See you in a little while, then.'

Send the pupils off and let them act out shopping. The acting out does not have to be very 'realistic' at this stage. Stop the drama.

Reflect on the drama

Out of role, sit the pupils in a circle and ask for volunteers to say what they have bought and where they bought the item(s) from. For those pupils who are confident and capable, challenge them to think in more detail by asking questions that stretch their imagination. Questions such as:

- How far was it to walk to the shop you went to?
- What was the door like?
- What was in the window?
- What other shops were nearby?
- What was next door to the shop?
- What noises did you hear in the shop?
- What kinds of cars were parked nearby?
- Who was in the shop?
- How did you pay (money, card, cheque)?

Ask pupils whether they 'went' to shops they know in real life, or whether they made up shops from their imagination.

Optional Extras

Knowledge and understanding of the world

- Make a wall display that shows a row of shops.
- Make Plasticine models of items that can be bought from the shops in the display.
- Show the pupils how to make doll's-house-style shops from shoeboxes.
- Make salt-dough models of fruit and vegetables.
- Discuss road safety and pretend to cross the road a few times (in the playground).

Memory games

Play 'I went shopping and I bought …'. Go round the circle building up a shopping list. Each child repeats what the previous children have said and adds another item.

Play 'Kim's Game'. Put items you might buy from a shop (such as a chemist) on a table and give pupils thirty seconds to look at them and try to memorise what is there. Cover the items up and ask the pupils to tell as many items as they can remember. Repeat the game with different shops.

Make a set of cards with pictures of items on one side and leave the other side blank. Spread the cards out on the floor with the picture sides facing up. Ask the pupils to memorise as many items as possible. Turn the cards over so that the blank sides are facing up and let the pupils see how many they can remember, and where they are.

Communication, language and literacy

Read books about foods, such as *Oliver's Fruit Salad* and *Oliver's Vegetables* by Vivian French.

Look at non-fiction books about food and find out some food facts.

Setting up a role-play area

This is a good time to set up a shop in the role-play area.

Developing the story

Out of role, tell the pupils that there is a shop at the end of the high street that sells all sorts of different things. The owner of the shop is called Mrs Hope and she is well liked by everyone. Mrs Hope calls her shop a 'general store'. Show the pupils the plan of the street again and explain where Mrs Hope's shop is located.

Sit the pupils in a circle. Tell them that you will pretend to be Mrs Hope and will invite pupils to come into the shop to buy something. Mrs Hope's role function is seen as a 'victim' (someone who needs practical help), by Katie Kind but is actually 'one of the gang'. Sign your role, perhaps with a coloured scarf or cardigan.

Using the centre of the circle as the acting space, TIR introduces *Mrs Hope's Shop* by explaining where things are and by miming how things work. For example, 'This is my cash register' (mime opening the till) 'and this is where I keep the boxes of apples so that they stay cool' (mime picking up an apple and perhaps repositioning an apple box).

Put the shopping cards that you used earlier into a pile and place the pile somewhere in the circle where the pupils can see them easily. If they get stuck when they are acting, pupils can use the cards to prompt them by picking one up from the top of the pack. They can, of course, also make up items of their own to buy.

Ask one of the more confident pupils to come into the shop to buy something. You may need to lead the talking and the action at first. When two or three pupils have been to buy from you, the role of shopkeeper along with the sign (a coloured scarf or cardigan) can be handed over to a volunteer pupil. It may not be necessary for all pupils to have a go at buying and selling. You will need to read levels of interest and concentration and judge how long this phase should be sustained.

Introducing a problem

Out of role, explain that Mrs Hope often gives customers things they haven't asked for because she can't find the item they want in her somewhat 'untidy-looking' shop. In fact, things are all over the place. Talk about clutter! One day, one of her customers, a person called Katie Kind, decided that something had to be done to tidy up Mrs Hope's shop.

Help the pupils to make a plan of Mrs Hope's messy shop. This can be made from six sheets of sugar paper onto which the teacher draws the basic layout of the shop. Use the illustration below as a guide. The four portions of the plan are in Shop Plan Whole.pdf, Shop Plan1.pdf etc in folder Mrs Hope on the Resources CD.

Map and Plan Making: the things in Mrs Hope's shop

Ask the pupils to suggest items that Mrs Hope might sell in her shop and write a list on a large piece of paper. Give the pupils a small piece of paper each and ask them to draw one thing that Mrs Hope sells. Place the drawings in no particular order around the outside of the plan.

Explain to the pupils that you are going to work in role as Katie Kind. Role function: 'hapless authority figure'. Show the pupils how you will sign your role (perhaps by wearing an apron and carrying a bag with cleaning things in it). Also, explain that the pupils will be in role as customers who use Mrs Hope's shop regularly.

Katie and the customers devise a cunning plan

In a part of the classroom away from the plan of the shop, TIR as Katie Kind gathers the pupils together in a 'secretive' manner to discuss the problems with Mrs Hope's shop. TIR must appear to be flabbergasted (cross without being

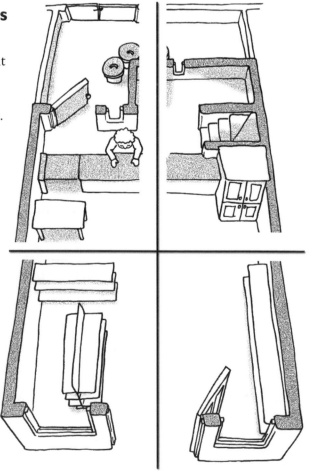

angry) and in an exasperated manner tells how the other day, when she went to buy a new sweeping brush, Mrs Hope gave her a bunch of bananas!

Possible script:

> *'Mrs Hope is lovely, but quite hopeless when it comes to sorting things out. I was in a real hurry the other day trying to tidy up my house. I needed a new sweeping brush, so I popped down to Mrs Hope's shop to buy one. I couldn't see the brushes anywhere, so I asked her if she had any sweeping brushes left and she said she hadn't, but perhaps these would do. She handed me a bunch of bananas! How on earth can I get the kitchen floor swept with a bunch of bananas?'*

Ask the PIR if things like that had ever happened to them in the shop. See if they can suggest some more examples of things that Mrs Hope had got mixed up.

TIR tells the pupils that it is Mrs Hope's birthday tomorrow and suggests that it would be a nice surprise for her if someone were to tidy up the shop and get it better organised. TIR pulls a key from her inside pocket/bag and tells the PIR she has sneakily borrowed the key to the shop. She suggests that the PIR meet her later, when Mrs Hope is asleep upstairs, to do the tidying up. During the night, the shop will be tidied and in the morning when Mrs Hope wakes up everything will be spic and span. TIR tells the pupils to go home and get some sleep because they are going to be up all night and she will meet them here when the coast is clear. She reminds the pupils that they will need to bring torches because it will be dark. (It is a good idea for you to have a real torch to hand so that you can use it in the next scene.) Oh, and they must not forget to bring cleaning equipment.

Stop the drama.

Reflect on the drama

Out of role, discuss with the pupils what is about to happen in the story. Questions might include:

- Why do Mrs Hope's customers think she needs to have her shop tidied up?
- What kind of person do you imagine Mrs Hope is (apart from untidy)?
- Is it wrong to be untidy?
- Is Mrs Hope being naughty?
- Is Mrs Hope being lazy?
- Why are people sometimes untidy?
- Do you think Mrs Hope will be pleased when her shop is tidied up?
- Is it a good idea to surprise Mrs Hope?
- Has anyone ever tidied your things up? Who? When? How did you feel about it?
- What kind of person is Katie Kind?
- Is she doing a bad thing or a good thing?

Move the story on in time. Explain to the pupils that you, and they, are about to go back into role. Later that night …

Optional Extras

Mathematical development

Money. Talk about coins and notes. Find out what the pupils know. Demonstrate some simple calculations tasks with money.

Organise counting activities using shop play items – plastic fruit and vegetables, packets of tea and cereal – or use real items that you can provide, such as potatoes, carrots, cabbages, cans of soup.

Weighing items, such as potatoes, carrots, apples.

Talk about shapes. For example, cans are cylinders. How many faces does a cereal box have? What shape are they? And so on.

Knowledge and understanding of the world

Discuss electricity – what we use it for: lighting; heating; cooking; powering household equipment; powering tools; and so on. Talk about safety issues regarding electricity.

Show pupils a simple circuit with a switch to turn a bulb on and off.

Communication, language and literacy

Make a display of interesting lamps and decorative lights. Make some descriptive labels for the display.

Investigate light and reflective surfaces including mirrors. Discuss the effects with the pupils and make a list of words and phrases to describe them.

Talk to the pupils about different types of electric light: bulbs; neon; flourescent; spot. Talk to pupils about how lights are used in shops in shopping centres. Look at pictures of lights used for cinema and theatre displays. Talk about events such as Blackpool and Walsall illuminations.

Show the pupils a theatre light, particularly the reflective surface and the lens inside the lamp.

Talk about the setting of the story. Discuss the idea of a messy shop. Make a list of words and phrases that describe the untidy nature of Mrs Hope's shop, such as:

- higgledy-piggledy
- scattered about
- all over the place
- messy
- sloppy
- disorganised
- jumbled.

Write a few sentences with the class that describe Mrs Hope's shop.

Adding tension

Acting out tidying the shop

TIR as Katie Kind gathers the PIR together and leads them to Mrs Hope's back door. TIR must use facial expressions and physical gestures that build a sense of excitement about the secret nature of the event.

Possible script:

'OK, the coast is clear and Mrs Hope's fast asleep. We'll go in through the back door. We'll have to be quiet so that we don't wake her – we don't want her thinking she's got burglars, do we?'

Act out carefully opening the back door and sneak into the dark shop using torches to light the way. If possible, TIR has a real torch, which will increase the sense of excitement. Listen carefully to determine whether Mrs Hope is snoring! If appropriate, pupils can be asked to act as if they are in the dark and cannot see where they are walking. Freeze Frame the action and Thought Track a few pupils, asking them what it is like being in the shop at night. Starter questions include:

- What can you see (if anything!)?
- Where in the shop are you standing?
- What can you smell, hear, feel, touch?

Further prompts:

- What it is like as you step into the dark shop?
- What is most scary?
- What are you most excited about?
- Is anything worrying you?
- What will you do if Mrs Hope wakes up?
- What is going to be the easiest part of the job?
- What will be the most difficult part of the job?

TIR suggests that the group look at a plan of the shop that she has made and decide where everything is going. Sneak over to where the plan was laid out on the floor with all the children's drawings around it. Using the drawings, discuss what Mrs Hope has for sale and where the various items are going to be put.

Optional Extra

Knowledge and understanding of the world

Talk about refrigerators and why they are used at home and in shops. List the kinds of food that are stored in a fridge.

Make a flask to keep things cool. Note the reflective material used in thermos flasks. There are books that have information about science experiements of this kind such as those by Neil Ardley.

Use pictures of shops to help the pupils work out the best way to store and display:

- dried foods
- cans
- cardboard boxes
- bottles
- fresh vegetables
- fresh fruit
- sweets.

Mark on the plan where everything will go. The shopping cards that you made earlier could be used as a visual way of indicating what goes where. Then go back to the 'shop' area, where TIR leads the acting out: moving items; sweeping up; dusting and wiping; counting; making lists; drawing signs and labels.

Possible script (whispered!):

'Please move the vegetables over there. They need to be carefully packed into boxes so that we don't damage them. That's right: fill that box with carrots and then we'll find another one for the onions. We'll need to have signs to tell customers where things are. Here's a piece of card. Will you draw a picture of fruit and vegetables to go above the display?'

When all the work is done, TIR announces that it's nearly morning and she can hear Mrs Hope getting up and going into her bathroom. It's time to leave. Act out sneaking out of the shop and hiding around the corner at the back of the shop so that everyone can see what happens when Mrs Hope first sees her newly tidied shop.

TIR talks to the PIR excitedly about how thrilled Mrs Hope will be.

Possible script:

> 'I can't wait to see her face! She's going to be so pleased. It won't be long now; she always opens up at 8.30 a.m. Once she's had a chance to look around, we'll jump out of hiding and shout, "Surprise!"'

Optional Extra

Practise singing 'Happy Birthday' and cheering 'Hip hip hooray!'.

Stop the drama.

Out of role, ask the pupils what they think will happen next. Discuss the pupils' ideas by probing for more extended answers. Ask why, and what makes you think that.

- Ask the pupils how they would feel if they were Mrs Hope.
- Discuss feelings: What makes people happy or sad?
- Ask the pupils whether surprises make people happy or sad.

Tell the pupils you are going to play Mrs Hope. Explain how you are going to sign the role (again with a coloured scarf and a cardigan or whatever you chose before). Your role function this time is: victim. Ask the pupils to be ready to join in the drama by shouting 'Surprise!' at Mrs Hope and wishing her a happy birthday.

When you put on your costume and start working in role, you will need immediately to look shocked and horrified at the state of your shop. You must show that you are really upset by what you see. You are upset because you liked your shop the way it was. As it becomes clear what has happened, you will be even more upset to find out it was your own customers who tidied up because you will take this to mean they didn't like your shop. You would have preferred to have been asked if you wanted help.

Mrs Hope sees that her shop has been tidied up

Possible script:

> 'Oh no! What's happened to my beautiful shop? Where are the canned foods? What's happened to the sweets? It's dreadful. Who could have done such a terrible thing?'

Pretend to cry.

The pupils might jump out of hiding and shout 'Surprise!' to Mrs Hope, but equally they might realise that her response is not what Katie Kind had in mind and choose to comfort Mrs Hope instead.

Still in role as Mrs Hope, have as much conversation with the PIR as you feel they can manage. The PIR may need some reassurance that they are still liked by Mrs Hope because the children will be worried about having done the wrong thing when they agreed to tidy up. Mrs Hope can be gracious, but in need of some comforting from the PIR.

Stop the drama.

Hot Seating Mrs Hope

Out of role, ask the pupils why they think Mrs Hope is so upset. Get them into pairs and give them five minutes to think of a question they'd like to ask Mrs Hope. Explain how the Hot Seating will work. Explain that one of them (or two pupils can be the one character if they need a little mutual support) will play Mrs Hope and everybody else will ask her questions out of role to find out what she thinks about the situation.

Check that the pupils have managed to think of questions. Help pairs to phrase questions if they are having trouble. Here are some questions and answers that you could 'feed' to the pupils if they are unable to think of their own:

- Why are you upset?
  This doesn't look like my shop. It looks like someone else's.

- What don't you like about your tidied-up shop?
  It's got no life to it. It looks just like any other shop now. I hate everything in rows so neat and tidy.

- Do you think Katie was being unkind?
  No, but I wish she'd asked me if I wanted things tidied up before she broke in and messed up my beautiful shop.

- Did you prefer your shop untidy?
  It wasn't untidy. It was the way I like it!

- Don't you think it's nice that your customers want to help you?
  I don't think my customers know anything about me or they wouldn't have done this. It wasn't a nice thing to do because I didn't want it to be tidied up, although I know they intended to be kind.

Choose a pupil or a couple of pupils to answer the questions. Place whatever costume items you used to sign Mrs Hope on a chair to represent her character and have the pupils who are answering questions sit or stand near to the chair (which is the Hot Seat). If a conversation develops between the PIR as Mrs Hope and the rest of the class, rather than strict questions and answers, this is fine, since any interaction that explores the issues will be productive.

Optional Extra

Communication, language and literacy

Discuss what kind of character Mrs Hope is. Ask the pupils to describe what they think she would look like. Make a simple Role on the Wall of Mrs Hope.

Play 'detectives'. Put five different costumes – clothes and items – into bags, such as:

Bag 1   baby clothes and a feeding bottle

Bag 2   a pair of trendy jeans, a fashionable top and jewellery

Bag 3   a smart jacket and skirt, an order book and a book with notes about what customers like

Bag 4   a uniform of some kind

Bag 5   an outdoor coat, a pair of wellington boots and a book about cows

Put the pupils in small groups and give each group a bag. Ask the pupils to open the bag and look at what is in it. Ask each group to show and tell what is in their bag to the other groups. Give the pupils time to discuss which bag belongs to Mrs Hope and to decide on two reasons to support their choice. The answer is Bag 3. This is to show that Mrs Hope has other clothes and other qualities and characteristics. Real people are not easy to stereotype and pigeon-hole. Ask the pupils to suggest whom the other bags might belong to.

Return to the Role on the Wall and add any further suggestions from the pupils about what Mrs Hope looks like. Discuss personal characteristics and add some to the Role on the Wall.

Character Drawing: Mrs Hope

With all pupils out of role, give them each a piece of paper and ask them to draw what they think Mrs Hope looks like.

Compare pictures and discuss personality characteristics: what they are and how they differ from a description of what a person physically looks like.

Finding an ending

Create a forum acting space by sitting the pupils in a circle. Remind the pupils what Mrs Hope's shop looks like now it has been tidied up and ask for a few volunteer pupils to act out being Mrs Hope. The first one gets up and has a go, then another volunteer takes over for a few moments, and so on. The volunteers follow on, one after another, furthering the action.

Start the action from when Mrs Hope wakes up, stretches and goes to the bathroom to wash her face and hands. Then she gets dressed. Ask the volunteer actors to perform what she does and says when she sees that her shop has been tidied up. Prompt pupils to perform different responses: shocked; cross; confused. Of course, you provided them with a model when you were in role as the distressed Mrs Hope a short while ago. The Hot Seating exercise added further insights.

When Mrs Hope's reactions to the tidy-up have been established, by 'playing' out the emotions several times, talk to the pupils about what Mrs Hope and Katie Kind might say to each other. Prompt the pupils to think of different reactions the characters might have to each other. For example:

1. Katie realises that Mrs Hope is not happy and apologises.

   Mrs Hope accepts the apology because she understands that Katie was trying to be kind.

2. Katie can't believe that Mrs Hope isn't thrilled and tries to persuade her that the tidy-up has improved the shop.

   Mrs Hope is upset and frustrated because Katie is making no attempt to understand her feelings.

3. Katie is cross because she thinks Mrs Hope is being ungrateful.

   Mrs Hope is cross with Katie because she is being bossy.

Ask the pupils to help you make up some script for the possible conversations that Katie and Mrs Hope might have. Write the script into large speech bubbles made of card. Lay the speech bubbles out on the floor so that the pupils can see them.

Ask for one volunteer to be Mrs Hope and another volunteer to be Katie. Let each volunteer choose a speech bubble with the dialogue that they want to use for their conversation. Read out loud to the class what is written on the chosen speech bubbles and encourage the class to join in with you. In this way, the class provide a chorus of dialogue as the two volunteers begin to act out the characters. This helps to get them started; they should then be able to add a few more lines of dialogue on their own. Once the idea has been established, other pupils might want to have a go. If they get stuck, the speech bubbles can be used to help them, or pupils in the circle can suggest lines.

If you want to improve the acting, ask the volunteers how their characters are behaving. For example:

- How would Katie come through the door to the shop?
- Would she pop her head round the door and ask Mrs Hope if she can come in? Would she barge in noisily?
- What expression would Mrs Hope have on her face?
- What expression would Katie have on her face?
- How would Katie stand? What would she do with her arms? (On her hips, or folded in front of her?)
- What gestures would Mrs Hope use during her conversation with Katie?
- Who would speak first? Why?
- When would Katie move and where would she move to. (She might sit next to Mrs Hope or keep her distance?)

Remind the volunteer actors that they can, at any time, ask for advice from the pupils who are watching them. This is an example of Forum Theatre.

Small-group play-making

Because some pupils will want to have a go at acting out the scene but will be too shy to volunteer, give all the pupils a chance to have a go at small-group play-making. Get the pupils into pairs and ask them to act out the same scene. Give them a limited time to practise and suggest to them that it would be great if they could find new things for the characters to say and do that were not done in the forum.

Let the whole class watch any scenes that look and sound particularly good. If there are still pupils who are feeling too nervous to perform in public, let everyone perform their scenes at the same time. You observe and then comment on a few of the pupils' ideas afterwards.

Resolution

Out of role, discuss with the class how the story ends. The key question to address is this: Is there a solution to the problem that has been created by Katie tidying up Mrs Hope's shop?

The pupils might have their own ideas about how the situation could be resolved, but, if not, offer them two options:

1. Katie and the other customers offer to put the shop back to how it was.
2. Mrs Hope chooses to keep the shop as it is now.

Let the pupils decide how they want the story to end.

Scene Drawing: the ending

 Give individual pupils the 'The End' worksheet (The End.pdf in folder Mrs Hope on the Resources CD) and ask them to draw the ending they would most like to have. If possible, go round and discuss and then annotate each pupil's reason for his or her choice of ending.

Optional Extras

Knowledge and understanding of the world

Compare the pupils' shop plan with a photograph or picture of a real general store. Discuss the similarities and differences.

Use a large map of the world and locate some of the countries from which food comes to the UK. A useful resource for teachers is *The Atlas of Food: Who Eats What, Where and Why* by Erik Millstone. It would also be interesting to trace where other goods, such as computers and clothing, come from.

Discuss modes of transport. Watch a film about goods arriving at the docks.

Investigate boat shapes by making (with a variety of materials) and testing boats in a water tank. Make a boat that can carry a weight. A book such as *Water and Boats* by Jon Richards would be useful as it suggests investigatory experiments.

Read *I Love Boats* by Flora McDonnell.

Communication, language and literacy

Sequence the story. Talk to the pupils about the events in the story and agree an order for them.

Identify what the setting was, who the characters were, what the main problem was and what happened at the end of the story.

Read other stories about people being messy, such as *Mr Messy* by Roger Hargraves and *Those Messy Hempels* by Brigitte Lucani. Identify the same elements of the story as above. Compare the stories with *Mrs Hope's Shop* for similarities and differences.

Final Reflection

Finally, out of role, discuss with the whole class these sorts of reflective questions:

- What have we learned from this story?
- Did Mrs Hope need help to tidy up?
- Did she want help to tidy up?
- What would have happened if the shop had been left as it was?

- Who wanted the shop tidy and why?
- What did we find out about the way people talk to each other when they disagree? Are there any important things to remember?
- If Katie had talked to Mrs Hope first about tidying the shop, would that have meant Mrs Hope would have felt differently about the situation? Why?
- Should Katie have minded her own business? Why?
- Was the shop tidying a nice surprise for Mrs Hope's birthday?
- Are surprises good or bad things? Why?
- What kind of surprise might Mrs Hope have enjoyed?
- Did Mrs Hope learn anything from what happened?
- What advice would you give Mrs Hope about her shop if she asked you for help?
- What advice would you give to Katie Kind?
- Are there really people like Mrs Hope and Katie Kind?

Potential cross-curricular learning

Here are some of the areas of the curriculum that can be linked to the story and used to design activities of your own.

Cross-curricular links	**In the Foundation Stage:** **Personal, social and emotional development** Developing respectful relationships; understanding that other people have feelings; introducing the idea of different mind styles - that people have their own unique ways of thinking and doing things; developing models of how to deal effectively with disagreements between people; working in different group sizes; presenting to others. **Communications, language and literacy** Communicating by drawing, mark making and early writing skills, physical gesture and facial expression, speaking and listening to each other and to adults; presenting to others in and out of role; learning about how stories are constructed – particularly setting, characters, problem and ending; reflecting on the meaning of the story; comparing stories in books with the dramatised story; learning about describing words and phrases; carrying out research from non-fiction books and other sources of information such as films and ICT. **Mathematical development** Introducing money concepts – what it looks like, developing an understanding of its value; performing simple calculations; developing understanding of shape – flat planes and 3D; learning about measures – volume and weight; practising counting; participating in sorting activities. **Knowledge and understanding of the world** Learning about shops and shopping, main shopping streets, towns, communities, types of shops and what they sell, types of foods; simple map and plan making – developing an early concept of scale; discussing electricity – related particularly to shop signs and displays of lights; learning about reflective surfaces – noting their use in some lights such as stage lights and in the design of thermos flasks; discussing refrigeration and why it is useful to keep things cool; learning about food and other goods from different countries; discussing the need to transport cargo with particular reference to ships that carry heavy loads. **Physical development** The active nature of drama gives plenty of opportunity for controlled movement through role-play activities and through play with toys and equipment such as Playmobil shops and houses. **Creative development** Pupils are asked to contribute their own ideas and make decisions about what happens in the story. Pupils learn how to ask and then explore possible answers to 'what if?' questions. They learn to visualise a fictional setting and pretend that imaginary events are real. They also learn drama techniques such as working in and out of role to construct a fictional scene and Freeze Frame. They learn character development through Role on the Wall, and Hot Seating.

	In preparation for Key Stage One: **Geography** Map and plan making; using geographical language; describing what places are like; learning about high street features, bus routes, different types of shops and businesses. **Science** Sc 2: Learning about food and healthy eating. Sc 3: Learning about materials and their properties – sorting and grouping objects, naming common types of material. Sc 4: General learning about electricity - a simple circuit, turning lights on and off (including environmental issues), illuminated shop signs; discussing everyday appliances that use electricity. **PSHE** Developing confidence and responsibility; preparing to take an active role as a citizen; developing good relationships and respecting differences between people.
Literacy skills	Story construction; sequencing; developing a setting and developing vocabulary to describe it; character development; physical description; learning to describe personality characteristics; choosing an appropriate ending; understanding the meaning of a story; note-making in pictorial and written form; applying labels; asking and answering questions; speaking and listening in pairs and groups; presenting opinions and ideas to others; researching from non-fiction books and other sources of information such as films and ICT.
Remember DfES thinking skills!	**Creating** Generating and extending ideas; applying imagination; looking for innovative outcomes. **Enquiring** Asking relevant questions; posing and defining problems; predicting outcomes and anticipating consequences. This type of thinking is developed through discussions about how to deal with the issues between Katie Kind and Mrs Hope. **Reasoning** Giving reasons for opinions and actions; drawing inferences and making deductions; explaining thoughts; making informed decisions and judgements. This type of thinking is developed as pupils consider the differences between Katie Kind and Mrs Hope. **Information processing** Sorting and classifying; comparing and contrasting; sequencing. This type of thinking is developed through activities which give opportunities to gather information about shops and shopping. The thinking is extended if the pupils can use the information they have gathered in their role play. Displays of the story are also the beginnings of modelling how we present information for others to see, read and understand. **Evaluating** Examining what the story means; judging the value of what you have read, heard or done. This type of thinking is developed through any activities that help the pupils to reflect on what has been happening in the story. Pupils may be able to discuss in small groups or draw or paint pictures or build models and, in the process, explain some of their thinking about what has happened to the characters in the story.

The Incredible Shrinking Machine

Planning checklist

Subject matter	Mini-beasts; gardens; ponds
Themes	Keeping the ecological balance; friendship; taking risks
Key resources and equipment	Costume items to sign TIR, such as a straw hat, a pair of gardening gloves, some clippings from shrubs, or a basket with a packet of seeds and small gardening tools in it **Props include** Targets for deciding options to escape from the spider (Option1.pdf and Option2.pdf in folder Incredible Shrinking Machine on the Resources CD) Pictures or models of insects A selection of musical instruments such as bells and tambourines A torch
Organisation	**Time** Without Optional Extras: 8–10 hours With Optional Extras: 12–14 hours **Teaching space** A large space in a classroom Possible themes for the role-play area: • a garden centre • Mrs Leszczyk's garden made large so that the pupils are small as in the story.
Main dramatic devices used	Teacher in Role Pupils in Role **Basic plot** Voyage and Return The pupils go on an adventure to a 'strange world' **Basic problem** Entering a world you are not familiar with (being trapped; having to face a potential foe; releasing a potentially uncontrollable force) **Basic tensions** Feeling unsafe (fear; lack of knowledge; lack of skills; being threatened with unwanted consequences)

Teacher's overview

One of the inspirations for this story was Sharon's Irish father's tales of the 'wee folk'. She loved hearing stories about the mischief they brought to unsuspecting people who were simply going about their business fishing or farming – her dad was from a Donegal fishing family. Many of us have a longing for a secret world and one way of entering such a place is to imagine that we are very small. Playing with models (train sets, Scalextric, Sindy dolls, toy soldiers, Sylvanian characters, Lego) is symptomatic of this (and some of us never grow out of it). In this project, the pupils play characters who are shrunk to the size of small insects. Of course, little children automatically know a lot about being small, because they live in the land of the giants every day! However, shrinking them further in the drama allows the pupils to explore the world of insects and other small garden creatures from an unusual point of view.

The story is essentially an adventure 'romp'. There are no baddies, but there is a threat posed by a spider. The scenes that involve the spider need sensitive handling, since they can be scary for young children. In fact, the spider is outwitted or outmanoeuvred (the PIR choose one of two escape plans at that point in the drama), but during the encounter the Pupils in Role get to play 'run and hide', which is exciting for them. It is important for TIR to make it feel safe. So play the role of Mrs Leszczyk (Leszczyk is pronounced lez–check) as an adventurous and confident person, someone who enjoys being in a bit of a scrape every now and then. If you look as if you are enjoying the thrill of dodging the spider, the pupils will relax and have fun with the idea too.

Before starting the project, show the pupils some short scenes from films that involve miniature worlds. This will speed up and deepen the process of building belief. Clips from the TV series *The Borrowers* would be perfect, especially the scenes where Arrietty Clock goes outside into the garden. It would also be good to show the scene from *Alice in Wonderland* in which Alice shrinks in order to get through the small door she has found. *Honey, I Shrunk the Kids* is another obvious choice. Any story that involves small creatures living in a larger-than-normal world will help to give the pupils a perspective on what it might be like to be tiny.

In the first part of the project, the pupils spend quite a long time building belief in Mrs Leszczyk's garden. Incidentally, Sharon used to play in the real Mrs Leszczyk's garden with her friend Alison when she was young, although sadly the elderly lady didn't have a shrinking machine – at least, they never found it! These first activities are important in helping pupils to visualise the imaginary setting; also, they have the added benefit of providing a context for out-of-role learning about gardens, growing things, insects and small creatures.

There are no major issues for the pupils to handle in this story (did we hear you say 'phew'?), but they do have a problem to solve and we suggest that it is worth investing time in coaching them to think systematically about it. The end of the story sees the main character having to make a difficult choice between keeping her incredible shrinking machine and doing the right thing for the caterpillar who is the wrong size.

You might want to end the project at that point, but, if you want to make the pupils aware of the serious message in the story, read on.

The big message is this: do not mess with the ecological balance of natural environments. The study of insects and small creatures begins to illustrate some of the ways in which different features of the environment (creatures, plants, water, soil and so on) exist in a state of delicate harmony. For example, worms are very important recyclers who aerate the soil and keep it turned over so that the conditions for plant growth are maximised. Worms are also food for birds and small mammals, as are insects that pollinate plants and clean up rotting vegetation and other even nastier stuff! If someone, or something, disrupts the natural balance of living things, the results can be disastrous.

> 'The world is as delicate and as complicated as a spider's web. If you touch one thread you send shudders running through all the other threads. We are not just touching the web, we are tearing great holes in it.'

Gerald Durrell, author of many books and founder of
Durrell Wildlife Conservation Trust

Take for example the introduction of rabbits into Australia. In 1859, twenty-four European rabbits were introduced onto an estate in Victoria because the owner wanted to hunt them. They bred so fast and became so problematic that in 1868 the red fox was brought in to keep the population down. Of course, foxes eat other animals when they can't catch rabbits, so they became responsible for the decline of a number of native species, some to the point of extinction. By 1910, rabbits had spread across the continent and were causing enormous damage to cereal and horticultural crops, to trees and root systems, and were competing with grazing stock for pasture. At this point, rabbitproof fences were constructed (Number 1 Fence alone was 1,834 kilometres long!). Yet rabbits are still a major pest in Australia today. This situation is paralleled in *The Incredible Shrinking Machine*, in that the giant caterpillar is artificially introduced into the garden, creating a no-win situation for the humans.

Case studies such as this are too complex for very young children, but there is no harm in explaining that scientists study animal and plant life so that we can either avoid making mistakes in the first place (preferably) or deal with problems effectively. Using an electronic whiteboard or data projector, these points can be illustrated using pictures from various websites. You can also use the Reflection sessions at the end of the story to get pupils thinking about how creatures connect with each other (food webs). Pupils can also learn about organisations that work hard to protect ecosystems: for example, the Royal Society for the Protection of Birds and Durrell Wildlife Conservation Trust. In this project, from a fantasy starting point, pupils build an interest in knowing more about wildlife, plants and nature.

The plot is classic Voyage and Return, in which a group of people set off on an adventure and find themselves in an unusual and potentially dangerous world. At first, they enjoy the exhilaration of exploring their 'new' surroundings, but then they become aware of a threat. The situation becomes difficult, so the adventurers make their way home as quickly as possible, being cunning and quick along the way. To be true to the plot type, the heroine should be changed by her experiences, gaining a deeper understanding of the world. If the pupils follow up the story with further work on conservation, zoological or ecological matters, they will fulfil this requirement!

Classic Voyage and Return stories include Daniel Defoe's *Robinson Crusoe*; H.G. Wells's *The Time Machine*; Jules Verne's *Journey to the Centre of the Earth* and Jonathan Swift's *Gulliver's Travels*. Children's stories include *The Wizard of Oz*; *Alice's Adventures in Wonderland*; *The Lion, the Witch and the Wardrobe*; *Elidor*; *Peter Rabbit* and *I'm Going on a Dragon Hunt*. We've already mentioned the film *Honey, I Shrunk the Kids*, in which there is, in fact, an incredible shrinking machine. Adults might know an old science-fiction film called *The Incredible Journey*, in which a team of scientists are shrunk in a submarine-style vessel and injected into the body of a sick man so that they can heal him. So, the plot of *The Incredible Shrinking Machine* is part of a fantastic pedigree and there are many children's stories to compare it with and borrow from.

Role-play area

The role-play area could become a garden centre or Mrs Leszczyk's garden made large so that the pupils are small as in the story.

The cast of characters

- Mrs Leszczyk, a friendly, enthusiastic and adventurous gardener (TIR)
- Mrs Leszczyk's friends, helpful, enthusiastic and up-for-it gardeners (PIR)

Summary of the plot

Mrs Leszczyk wants to make a new pond in her garden and asks some of her friends to help her do the heavy digging and planting. They arrive at her house to help with the pond and a number of other gardening jobs. While having a break, Mrs Leszczyk tells her friends about a machine she has found that shrinks people to the size of small insects. She persuades her friends to have a go and come on an adventure in the garden.

The friends enjoy exploring the garden as tiny creatures and have an adventure on the pond riding on the backs of pond skaters.

All is going well until Mrs Leszczyk gets stuck on a spider's web. Her friends help her to break free from the web, but the movement alerts the spider to their presence. The whole party hides in a worm hole, but the spider seems to have them trapped. The adventurers have to work out an escape plan.

Eventually, the adventurers make a run for it and get back to the shrinking machine. Mrs Leszczyk returns them all to their proper size. But, unknown to her at the time, a tiny butterfly egg has blown into the machine and has been made bigger. During the night the caterpillar hatches.

The next morning, Mrs Leszczyk calls her friends because she needs help to capture the giant caterpillar that is eating all the lovely plants in her garden. The friends arrive and help to put the creature into the shrinking machine, but there is no room for anyone or anything else. Mrs Leszczyk realises that she either has to set the machine going and let it shrink the caterpillar with the consequence that the machine will be too small to operate afterwards, or the caterpillar will have to stay in the garden with the consequence that it will eat all the plants. Mrs Leszczyk sadly sets the shrinking machine's controls and the caterpillar is returned to its normal size. And that is the end of the incredible shrinking machine.

Getting going

Explain that in this story the pupils are going on an adventure that involves a very interesting machine that does a most unusual job. The machine can shrink people to the size of a ladybird and also make them human size again. Discuss what the word *shrink* means. Tell the pupils that in this story they will pretend to get smaller and smaller until they are tiny. Show the pupils some pictures, or models, of insects to give them an idea of the real size of the creatures so they can understand how small they are going to pretend to be. If possible, show excerpts from films such as *Honey, I Shrunk the Kids,* or *The Borrowers,* which would give an instant impression of the perspective pupils will need in role.

Tell the pupils that the story starts on a lovely sunny afternoon in Mrs Leszczyk's garden. Explain that you are going to play the role of Mrs Leszczyk and show the pupils how you will sign the role (possibly a straw hat, pair of gardening gloves and a handful of clippings from shrubs). Explain that Mrs Leszczyk has a wonderful garden full of flowers and trees. Also in the garden are many different insects and small creatures.

Map and Plan Making: Mrs Leszczyk's garden

Sit the pupils so that they can see a large piece of paper. Using the illustration below as a guide, draw a simple plan of Mrs Leszczyk's garden. The plan will not be like the picture, it will just have shapes to represent the various features, such as an octagon to represent the summer house.

Provide a running commentary; as you draw each feature, explain what it looks like, or ask pupils to tell you what they think it looks like. If it is appropriate, briefly discuss the difference between a picture and a plan with the class.

Building belief

Ask the pupils what jobs they think Mrs Leszczyk might do to keep her garden looking lovely. Make a note of the pupils' suggestions and use their ideas in the acting out that will follow.

Jobs might include:

- mowing the grass
- trimming the edges of the lawn
- raking up the grass
- weeding
- trimming the bushes
- planting new plants
- hoeing
- taking the dead heads off the roses
- watering the plants
- filling the pond with water
- filling the bird feeder.

Pupils follow the teacher's model

In the early stages of drama work, it is important for the teacher to model acting out to the children. So, as a first step, pretend to do gardening jobs together, in a follow-my-leader manner. The pupils copy what you do.

Possible script:

'Have you all got spades ready for digging? No? Help yourself to one of these here [pick up an imaginary spade]. *These are good heavy spades and they make digging easier. Now then, the thing to watch is that you get the blade into the soil as far as you can and then turn the soil over like this* [demonstrate digging]. *Let's dig this patch here ready for planting …*

'Now, I've got several boxes of pretty plants here. What do you think of the colours? I like this pink-and-purple flower – I think these are called fuchsias. You'll need a trowel for this job. No, not the forks – one of these. It looks a bit like a small spade – that's it, you've got it. Get yourself a trowel and we'll plant these plants [act out planting].

'We'd better water them. Get one of the watering cans and come and fill it up with water from this tap. Just gently sprinkle them with water …'

And so on.

This modelling develops pupils' confidence and also gets them used to the idea of Teacher in Role. What's more, physicalising ideas, rather than just talking about them, helps pupils to visualise the setting for the drama more easily; it 'brings the story to life'.

Pupils act out their own ideas

Once the pretending mode has been established, encourage the pupils to choose their own individual gardening jobs. Then everyone acts out doing his or her chosen activity. You are still acting out too, doing your own gardening activity, but now the garden is a busy place with lots of jobs getting done at once.

If you feel that the pupils are confident enough, encourage some of them to show their acting out to the class.

Optional Extra

Mathematical development

Use differently shaped tiles to make a pathway for Mrs Leszczyk's garden. This would best be done with card 'tiles' of different shapes: squares; various triangles; circles; semicircles; quarter-circles and rectangles. Ask the pupils to work in pairs and lay out a pathway. They must try to make the edges of the tiles meet as closely as possible with the smallest gaps in between. If possible, digitally photograph the pathways 'laid' by the pupils and use the photographs to discuss the properties of the shapes.

Ask the pupils in their pairs to have another go at laying a pathway, but this time they have to make all the edges meet. No gaps allowed. They may use two or three tile shapes only. Pupils can choose the shapes. Ask the pupils why they chose those particular shapes. Ask the pupils if any particular tile shapes are easier to lay without gaps than others, and why.

You could go on to ask pupils to make a *repeating* pattern from two or three tile shapes. This is the beginning of tessellation.

Before moving the story on …

Pupils will need time to build a visual picture of the setting for themselves. The Optional Extras opposite suggest lots of activities to achieve this. You could set up a circus of tasks, which either all of the pupils visit in turn, or pupils could choose one, two or three tasks from the menu on offer.

Although we've listed lots of ideas at this point, some of the activities could be introduced later in the story. For example, planting and growing seeds would work best after the pupils have acted out being in the worm hole, because it is topical at that point to discuss soil. Developing a garden centre in the role-play area can be built up as the drama progresses.

Developing the story

Tell the pupils that, when the drama restarts, you are going to play Mrs Leszczyk and they are going to be her friends. Like Mrs Leszczyk, they too are very good gardeners. The role function for Mrs Leszczyk is 'one of the gang'. Sign your role and welcome the PIR to your house.

Possible script:

> 'Come in, everyone. I'm so glad to see you. Did you have a good journey? I'm so excited that you've come to help me make a new pond in my garden, and I'd love to have it by the bird table, if possible. I'm not sure what we'll need to make the pond. Do you have any ideas? What shall we do first, then?'

Mrs Leszczyk's friends help her make a new pond in her garden

In role, discuss what needs to be done to make a pond. Keep asking questions, such as:

- How will the water stay in the pond?
- Where is the best place to make the pond?
- How can I find out which plants to put in the pond?
- What creatures should I expect to find in a pond?

Act out making the pond by asking the PIR to do tasks, such as digging the hole, placing the pond liner in position, putting stones around the outside and planting in and around the pond. Ask the PIR if they will help make a path to the new pond. Act out getting wheelbarrows out of the shed, moving heavy stones, digging up plants and replanting them, planting flowers to make the pathway pretty, laying down crazy paving or gravel and so on.

TIR suggests that the PIR stop for a drink and a piece of cake. While the PIR are 'relaxing', talk about the insects and small creatures that you have seen in the garden. Tell the PIR how interesting they are and how they all seem to be so busy. Ask the PIR which insects they have noticed in their own gardens. Tell the PIR that you have a secret you'd like to share with them, but they must not tell anyone about it. Ask the pupils if they promise to keep the secret.

Optional Extras

Knowledge and understanding of the world

1. Pupils make a model of a garden on a tray or in a box. Making a small model scene in a shoebox or on a tray gives further opportunities to discuss size and scale. Pupils could be asked to look at pictures of gardens and identify the features they want in their model gardens. Pupils can discuss the materials they use, describe textures and learn about colours. They could collect natural objects from a garden such as twigs, soil and stones to use in their models. Items that are alive now, those that were alive once and those that have never been alive could be discussed as part of the process of selecting materials for the model.

2. Make a collage of Mrs Leszczyk's garden. As a whole class, make a wall display. Plan a garden with the pupils or use the plan you have already drawn for the drama. Make an outline drawing on a display board (at child height) or on sheets of card that can be fixed to a wall when the collage is completed. Discuss the features of the garden with the pupils. Give the pupils time to look at and handle a range of collage materials. Decide together which materials could be used to represent the garden features. Sort the materials onto tables: Table 1, pond; Table 2, lawn; Table 3, flower beds; and so on. Let the pupils choose which feature they are going to work on and sit them at the appropriate table. Help the pupils to cut, arrange and stick as they design and make their section of the garden. You could have one or two pupils operating as the 'gardeners', whose job it is to put all the features made by the table groups onto the mega-display.

3. Go and see a real garden with a classroom assistant and discuss what you find there. What are the features of a good garden – lawn, borders, flowerbeds, shrubs, trees, pond, ornaments and so on? Discuss colours, shapes, smells and sounds. Look for insects and small creatures and discuss where they are most often found. Talk about gardening equipment and using it safely. Talk about growing things and what plants need to survive. Discuss seeds, roots, sunlight, water and shade. Find objects that are alive now, some that were alive once and some that have never been alive, and discuss what they are and what living things must have and what they all do.

4. Watch a TV programme about gardening; pupils are asked to spot different jobs and how

Optional Extras continued

they are done. In fact, everyone can watch clips from TV programmes at various points during the day – for example, when having drinks. Talk to the children informally about the programmes.

5. Show a film about pond insects and creatures. To focus the pupils' attention, tell them that after they have watched the film they are going to test themselves and see how many creatures they can remember. Organise pupils to work in pairs. Give each pair two sets of cards. Set 1 has only pictures of pond creatures such as pond skaters, frogs, snails, fish, dragonflies, toads, newts, ducks, herons and so forth. This is the set that pupils will use to check their choices. Set 2 has pictures of all the same pond creatures, plus other creatures such as ants, ladybirds, dogs, cats, flies, lions, spiders, elephants.

Every pupil *must* sort Set 2 and from memory choose the pond creatures that they saw in the film. They put the pond creatures and the other creatures into separate piles.

Most pupils *should* check that they have selected the right creatures by matching the pile they have created with Set 1.

Some pupils *could* sort the creatures in Set 2 into groups. Pupils can decide the categories but must be able to explain them – such as legs and no legs; wings and no wings; four legs or more than four legs; with backbones and without backbones.

6. Use different materials to make a pond in the sand tray. How do you get the water to stay in the pond?

Set up a sand tray so that water poured into it can drain away. Give the pupils the challenge to work out how to build a pond in the sand tray that will hold water. When it's appropriate, offer them different materials to use as a lining, suggesting that they might test different ones. Help them to time how long the water stays in the pond; the chosen device could be a sand timer, stopwatch or egg timer (the water level must stay the same for at least two minutes). The task could be extended to include accurate measuring.

Discuss with the pupils which materials work best and put them in rank order. Ask the pupils to give their reasons why some materials let water through and others don't.

Plant seeds and young plants and help the pupils learn how to look after them. Read *Tiny Seed* by Eric Carle.

Communication, language and literacy

7. Read story books about insects and small creatures, such as Eric Carle's *The Bad Tempered Ladybird*, *The Very Hungry Caterpillar*, *The Very Busy Spider*, *The Very Quiet Cricket Board* and *The Grouchy Ladybug*.

8. Talk with the pupils about spiders, worms, caterpillars and butterflies and let them look through books, and on posters about them. Discuss non-fiction books, such as *Mini Beasts* by Lynn Huggins-Cooper (in the Starters series), contents, index pages and so on.

9. Visit a garden centre. Set up a role-play area as a garden centre.

Mathematical development

10. Give pupils sorting, categorising, measuring and weighing activities based on gardening equipment.

Mrs Leszczyk shows her friends the incredible shrinking machine

Whether the pupils agree to keep the secret or not (the secret is simply to add a little spice and tension to the story), gather the PIR close together and tell them about your incredible shrinking machine.

Possible script:

> *'Well! You know how much I like machines. I've found the most incredible machine. It was in the old summer house in the corner of the garden. I've no idea who put it there or who built it, but I know you will love it! I've worked out how to use it and it can shrink a person down to the size of a ladybird and make them their normal size again, too. I've tried it a couple of times and last time I almost got a chance to ride on a butterfly's back! Come on, I've got to show you because it's great fun.'*

Lead the pupils to a large enough open space for them to stand in a circle.

Say, 'Here it is. My incredible shrinking machine!' Motion towards the centre of the circle.

Act out opening the door and invite the PIR to step inside. Give an impression of the inside of the shrinking machine and where the buttons are that each user must press to be shrunk or grown back to size.

Possible script:

> *'Come in, come in, there's enough room in here for all of us. Stand by a seat. You can see the garden through that window. I've put some pictures of insects and small creatures on the wall over there. Each seat has a seat belt, a red shrinking button and a green growing button.'*

Later on in the story, the pupils will be acting out hiding in a dark place. TIR will need a torch. Therefore, before you demonstrate how the machine works, make a big issue of needing to go and get a torch from the house: *'I'm sorry I've forgotten something. Wait here. I'll just go back to the house and get it.'* (Bring a real torch back with you.)

Out of role, demonstrate how everyone is going to act out shrinking and then growing again to normal size. Your demonstration might include fastening yourself into a seat, pressing your red button, spiralling downwards, standing up, and releasing your seat belt. This is reversed for growing back.

Explain to pupils that you are going back into role and that everyone will act out shrinking. So, ready for the adventure, you can say:

> *'Strap yourselves in and get ready to press the shrinking button. I'll start the machine up properly so that we can all shrink together. Are you ready? After three: one, two, three! Press your red button now.'*

Repeat the action of spiralling downwards.

Optional Extra

Mathematical development

Use the action of spiralling downwards to talk to the pupils about scale. Ask them to estimate the fraction of their normal size they have now become. For example, one-tenth, one-hundredth, one-thousandth.

Soundscape

Ask the pupils to imagine what sounds the machine makes when it is working. Suggest that, when the machine is first switched on, there is a loud noise, and then it settles down into a quieter sound until it begins the shrinking process. Give the pupils a selection of musical instruments such as bells and tambourines and help them to play these sounds.

Next, experiment with some sounds for the shrinking process. Encourage the pupils to play the instruments and act out the shrinking at the same time, but if they can't do both things simultaneously, the group can be split so that one half play the Soundscape while the other half act out being shrunk. Then they swap over.

Put the musical instruments to one side.

'OK. We are now the size of ladybirds and we can go and explore the world of the mini-beast!'

The shrunken Mrs Leszczyk and her friends have an adventure in the garden

Act out opening the door of the shrinking machine. Tell the PIR what you can see. Imagine yourself in a wild area of the garden. The blades of grass look as big as trees and little pebbles are as big as boulders. Big stones are like mountains.

Possible script:

'Isn't this just fantastic! Look at the grass. The blades of grass look as tall as trees do to us usually. The pebbles that are so small when we are normal size are like huge rocks. The colours are so bright. There is an old brick left over from some work I was doing last week when I was repairing a wall – it looks as big as a block of flats or at least a very large tall house.'

Gather all the PIR together and ask them how they feel now they have shrunk. All answers are acceptable: no different; I feel strange; I don't like it; I wish we could do this for real …

Encourage the pupils to join you as you act out an adventure in the garden. Suggest that everyone catch a lift on a butterfly's back: *'Here one comes, jump on!'*

Act out flying around the room and jump off the butterfly's back when you get to the pond!

'Whee! Jump off, everyone. Let's go and play with the pond-skaters in the pond.'

Act out swimming and splashing around in the pond. Freeze Frame the action two or three times and ask the PIR to tell you what they are doing, how the water feels and what they can see.

Tell the PIR about pond-skaters, which can walk on the surface of the water. Set up an area with cushions that can be used as the back of a pond-skater. Get the PIR to jump onto the pond-skater's back and go for a ride across the pond. Narrate the journey.

Possible script:

'Hold onto each other because these guys go really fast. Whoo hoo! The pond looks like a big lake. Look out, there's another pond-skater heading straight for us. It's like being in bumping cars at the fair [Make movements that suggest the creature has changed direction quickly]. *Oh, no! Look out! We're going to crash. We're all going to fall into the water.'*

Act out falling into the water: *'Oops! We've got a bit wet! Never mind – we'll soon dry out.'*

Get out of the water and sit on the rocks to dry. Take shoes and socks off, wring out clothes and try to dry your hair. Encourage the pupils to do the same: *'Let's sit on this rock and dry ourselves off a bit. That was fun, wasn't it?'*

Notice a plant pot left over from planting in the pond earlier in the day. Point out to the PIR how big it is: *'Look over there at that plant pot I left here earlier today. It looks so big now I'm so small. Let's go and have a closer look.'*

Act out looking all around the large plant pot. Have a bright idea for making a house from the plant pot: *'This plant pot is big enough for us to live in. Perhaps we could make ourselves a house that we can use when we come on "shrinking adventures". That would be lots of fun.'* (Act out the moment when you realise there is something moving inside the plant pot.) *'Wait a minute – what was that?'*

Introducing a problem

Tell the PIR there is something moving in the plant pot, but you can't see what it is because it's too dark. Start to creep forward tentatively to peek inside the pot. Act out getting stuck in something. First, your feet are stuck, then your arms. Alarmed, you realise you are caught in a spider's web.

Tell the PIR what has happened. Be very frightened as you see the spider hiding at the back of the plant pot! You can't easily be pulled out of the web. Ask the PIR what they can do to free you from the web. Use the PIR's suggestions and allow them to set you free.

As you dust yourself down, you notice that the spider is moving towards you. Tell the PIR that the spider knows you have escaped her web and now she's coming after everyone. Suggest that everyone dive down a worm hole in the ground to avoid the spider. Diving down the hole can be acted out by assuming a swimming-dive position with your arms and then, turning your body round and round, walking forward and spiralling down until you are on the ground.

Possible script:

> 'Thank goodness I'm free from the web! Wait a minute, though. I can see the spider moving towards us. Oh, no! I think she can tell I'm free from her web. She's definitely coming after us! Quick, let's dive down this worm hole and hide; she won't get us while were in there.'

Adding tension

In the dark

You may want to close the curtains or blinds at this point to simulate being underground. Act out a long slide down into the 'cave'. Gather the PIR together and discuss what to do next.

Possible script:

> 'It's dark down here, I'll just put my torch on [Switch on torch]. We'll be safe for now, but we can't stay here all day [Shine torch around room]. I suppose a worm could come along at any minute. Does anyone know what worms eat? Can they see? Can they hear? Should we be frightened of them? What can we do to keep them away?'

Discuss what the pupils know about worms. Discuss what options the group might have for getting back to the shrinking machine safely. Encourage the PIR to make suggestions: 'Should we climb back up out of the hole? Do you think we'll be OK?'

If the PIR want to climb out of the hole, act out a very difficult climb; keep sliding back down. This can be acted out by walking forward slowly using your arms and hands to suggest climbing up. As you slide back down, move backwards and bend down or end up on the floor again. Complain that someone should have thought to bring a rope!

Keep climbing and sliding until you feel that it's the right time to get to the surface. Pupils often enjoy the repeated climb and fall, but there comes a point where everyone is ready to move the story on. Once at the surface, take a look around and begin to move stealthily away from the hole entrance. Suddenly, notice that the spider is coming and get everyone to dive down the hole again.

Optional Extras

Knowledge and understanding of the world

Observe worms in a wormery. Discuss soil with the pupils and talk about how worms help to turn and aerate the soil and how this helps to make good conditions for lawns and plants.

Watch a film about worms. Do a movement-and-music session: move like a worm; wiggly fingers; wiggly arms; squeezing; sliding; turning; bending and so forth. Using various instruments, make sounds and music that go with the worm movements. Make a 'Wonder Worm' wall display that includes words that describe worms and the movements they make and gives information about how they live.

Mrs Leszczyk and her friends decide how to get back safely to the incredible shrinking machine

Explain to the PIR that the spider is waiting for them to come out of the hole. Explain to the PIR that there seem to be two options:

1. dig a tunnel and a new hole up to the surface
2. return out through the same hole, but be ready to run from the spider.

Ask the PIR to think with you what the good and bad points of each option are.

Put up a large leaf-shaped piece of paper with a blank 'good-and-bad' matrix grid on it. Ideas included in the matrix grid below are just examples. Tell the PIR that you are using a leaf to write on! Shine your torch on anything you want the PIR to be able to see.

Option	Good	Bad
1	The spider can't get us underground. The spider won't know where we will come out.	We don't know where the tunnel will lead and we might get lost. There might be worms travelling through the soil and they might block our way.
2	We know which part of the garden we are in. We can think of places to hide because we know the area.	We don't know how fast the spider can move. We will still be a long way from the shrinking machine.

Discuss how you will decide which option to take:

• hands–up voting: greatest number of hands wins the vote
• deferring responsibility to someone else: one person in the group makes the choice for everyone
• putting pebbles onto two targets (Option1.pdf and Option2.pdf in folder Incredible Shrinking Machine on the resources CD), one for Option 1 and another for Option 2: the distribution of pebbles (you could use glass beads or plastic counters) on the targets determines the vote – see overleaf.

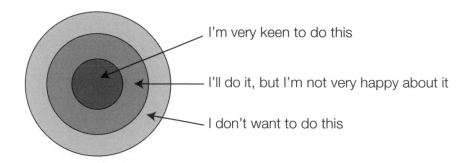

I'm very keen to do this

I'll do it, but I'm not very happy about it

I don't want to do this

If PIR choose Option 1:

Act out digging along (making a tunnel) and then upwards (making a shaft). Be excited about breaking through onto the surface and into the light. Emerge behind the plant pot (open the curtains) and run in the direction of the shrinking machine. Hitch a lift on a passing beetle. This can be done by setting up some cushions to represent the beetle's shell or using tables to sit on.

If PIR choose Option 2:

Act out a difficult climb (open the curtains) and then sneak very quietly past the spider! Make your way towards the shrinking machine, dodging from blade of grass to blade of grass to ensure that you are not seen.

Act out getting back to the machine. Climb in, fasten seat belts. Explain to the PIR that each seat has a green button for growing. Give the pupils musical instruments and ask them to create a Soundscape for the machine as it makes them bigger. Give the PIR a countdown – three, two, one – and tell them to press the green button. They all spiral upwards (as you demonstrated before).

Announce that the growing has been successful. Stop the drama.

Optional Extras

Knowledge and understanding of the world

1. Make a 'dark den' from large cardboard boxes and fabric. Get the pupils to work in construction teams of four. Each team is to make a den using cardboard boxes and old sheets and blankets (that you've collected over the last couple of weeks). For example, desks and chairs can be used to make basic frameworks, then cardboard can be leaned against them to make walls and sheets or blankets draped over them for roofs. Afterwards, discuss with the pupils what they have learned about construction materials and processes.

Give the pupils torches and objects with reflective surfaces to play with. Ask the pupils to take toys of different colours into their dens to find out which colours are easiest to see in the dark. Discuss what has been learned about light.

2. Go and look for a real spider outside. Discuss where it would be best to look for a spider and why. Pupils could go out in small 'detective teams' in turn, with the classroom assistant, equipped with magnifying glasses. Each team is to find at least one spider. If possible, look at it with a magnifying glass, be able to describe it and say where it was found.

3. Find pictures of spiders in books. Paint, draw or make a collage of a spider. Or make dough models of different types of spider – check the accuracy of the number of body sections and legs using computer games, posters or books. Or make one large model of a spider as a whole-class activity.

Reflect on the drama

Out of role, discuss the drama adventure with the pupils. With prompts, help the pupils to remember the sequence of events so far. Ask them what they have enjoyed most about the story up to now. Ask when it was easiest to imagine themselves being very small people and when it was hardest to keep believing they were very small.

Discuss the character of Mrs Leszczyk. Ask the pupils how they might describe her and make up a background for her.

Prompt questions:

- How old is she?
- Does she have any brothers or sisters?
- Does she get on well with her family?
- How long has she lived in her present house?
- What does she like to eat?
- Does she have any pets? If so, what?
- What is she good at?
- What is she not good at?
- What was she like at school?
- What is her favourite insect or small creature and why?
- Why does she like gardening?

Optional Extra

Communication, language and literacy

Ask each pupil to draw a picture of Mrs Leszczyk (character drawing). Discuss the pictures and the different ways in which it is possible to see her – for example, as an elderly or a young woman, with different hair and eye colours, wearing different kinds of clothes and so on. Let the pupils know that having different ideas is good and makes the drama interesting.

Other possible questions:

- Which small creatures were in our story?
- Were the characters in the story frightened of the spider? Why?
- Can spiders really hurt us? How do you know?
- Do you think Mrs Leszczyk did the right thing when she shrank her friends and took them on an adventure? Why?
- What could Mrs Leszczyk do to make sure her friends were safe if they ever went on another 'shrinking adventure'?
- What do you think the friends should wear on any future adventures?
- What equipment should they take?

Optional Extras

Communication, language and literacy

Prop drawing. Sit the pupils in group so that they can see a large piece of paper and discuss with them what equipment Mrs Leszczyk and her friends should take with them on their adventures next time they decide to shrink themselves. Draw the pupils' suggestions on the paper so that it can serve as a reminder of what is needed.

Prop drawing. As a final Reflection for this section, ask the pupils to work in pairs and draw what they think the incredible shrinking machine looks like. Talk to the pupils about their machines and write some of their words and phrases onto their drawings. Asking the pupils to visualise and then draw an imaginary machine of this kind is a very challenging task. Support and encourage the pupils by asking questions, such as:

- What shape is it?
- What colour is it?
- What is it made from?
- Where is the door?
- Does it have windows? What shape are they?
- What does it feel like when you touch it?
- What size is it?

Tell the pupils about caterpillars and the life cycle of a caterpillar. Read books such as *The Munching Crunching Caterpillar* by Sheridan Cain, *Tweenies*: *Caterpillar Surprise* by Siobhan Mullarky and *First Flight* by Sara Fanelle.

Finding an ending

Tell the pupils that, although the characters in the story thought the adventure was over, it wasn't!

Mrs Leszczyk needs help to shrink a giant caterpillar

Tell the pupils that the final part of the drama starts the day after the story ended last time. Mrs Leszczyk has phoned all her friends and asked them to come round to her house as quickly as they can. Everyone arrives at about the same time, and Mrs Leszczyk is at the front gate ready to meet them.

Tell the pupils that you are going to play Mrs Leszczyk again, and sign your role.

Gather the pupils in front of you and welcome them warmly. Tell them that you need their help urgently. Explain that when the shrinking machine made everyone their real size again you hadn't realised that a tiny caterpillar egg had somehow got into the shrinking machine. The egg must have rolled under one of the seats, and, as everybody in the machine got bigger, so did the caterpillar egg!

Because caterpillar eggs really are very, very tiny to begin with, you didn't notice it was there even when it had been made bigger than normal. It was hidden under one of the seats. Then, this morning, you went to clean inside the machine and when you opened the door an enormous caterpillar crawled out. Since then it has been eating all the leaves on the trees and bushes and ruining the garden. Soon it will be too big to squeeze back into the shrinking machine, so you have asked all your friends over to help you catch it and get it into the machine so that it can be shrunk back to its normal small size.

Ask the pupils if they have any ideas about how it might be caught (in the manner of a spontaneous meeting). Use one of their ideas to catch the caterpillar. If there are lots of ideas, act out using a few but always let the caterpillar get away until the last idea is being tried.

If the pupils are unable to suggest ideas of their own, ask them to help you throw a big net over the caterpillar. Send the PIR to gather the caterpillar's favourite leaves; use the leaves as bait. With all PIR helping to throw the net over the caterpillar, act out catching it and dragging it to the shrinking machine.

To help the caterpillar, Mrs Leszczyk will have to lose the shrinking machine forever

Declare that the caterpillar has already grown and there will be no room in the machine for anyone else. Therefore, tell the PIR that this can only be a one-way trip for the machine. You will have to set the machine to shrink to the right size and let it take the caterpillar back all by itself. You will of course leave the door open!

Ask the PIR if you are doing the right thing. Be upset that you will lose your machine because it will be too small to make it work again. Set the controls that operate the machine.

Ask the PIR:

- Shall I turn the machine on and make the caterpillar shrink back to its proper size?
- What will happen if I don't? Can I look after the enormous caterpillar?
- Perhaps once it has turned into a butterfly things will be easier. What do you think?
- What damage could an enormous butterfly do?
- Is it fair that I have to lose the shrinking machine?
- What is best for the caterpillar?

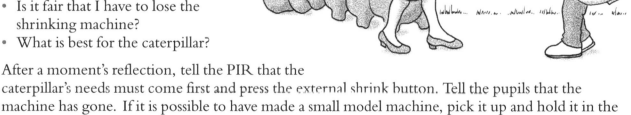

After a moment's reflection, tell the PIR that the caterpillar's needs must come first and press the external shrink button. Tell the pupils that the machine has gone. If it is possible to have made a small model machine, pick it up and hold it in the palm of your hand to show the children.

Close the story with, *'And that was the end of the incredible shrinking machine.'*

Final Reflection

Discuss whether Mrs Leszczyk did the right thing and why.

Then ask the pupils:

- How could we find out how scientists study small creatures such as insects?
- Why is it useful to know about small creatures?
- What would you most like to find out about small creatures?

Optional Extras

Communication, language and literacy

Give the pupils books, posters, films and ICT resources to find out about mini-beasts. Make a 'Facts About Mini-Beasts' board and encourage pupils to write and draw information to go on it. Review the information regularly and check with pupils where they found the facts.

Art

Look at pictures of butterflies and discuss the patterns and colours on their wings. Use a variety of different materials to make large 3D butterflies to hang in the classroom.

Potential cross-curricular learning

Here are some of the areas of the curriculum that can be linked to the story and used to design activities of your own.

Cross-curricular links	**In the Foundation Stage:** **Personal, social and emotional development** Pupils are working in role as friends and the teacher-led action provides a model for dramatic play. Pupils are invited to talk in supported discussions and encouraged to listen to the ideas of others. In part of the story the pupils are adventuring and experience the excitement of a chase – meaning that self discipline is required in order to remain aware of others. At the end of the story, pupils are asked to empathise with the teacher's role and help her to do the right thing. **Communication, language and literacy** Communicating by drawing, physical gesture, facial expression; writing labels and other appropriate mark making; speaking and listening to each other and to adults; exposure to new vocabulary; learning about how stories are constructed by actively taking part in one and participating in problem solving and decision making. **Mathematical development** Discussing shapes, size and measurements of length, area, capacity; learning colours; learning numbers and performing simple calculations using equipment. **Knowledge and understanding of the world** Discussing gardens, plants and names of parts of plants; learning how things grow and the conditions for growth; discussing soil, seeds, ponds and pond life; learning about insects and small creatures such as worms, spiders, beetles, pond-skaters; discussing animal habitats; learning about materials that repel water, also natural and synthetic materials; discussing weather conditions. **Physical development** The active nature of drama gives plenty of opportunity for controlled movement. **Creative development** Pupils are asked to contribute their own ideas and make decisions about what happens in the story. They learn drama forms such as Freeze Frame. They also learn to develop an imaginary setting using a variety of media – for example drawing, model making, collage. They learn to share imaginary events with others in role play, to respond to stimuli, both visual and verbal, to generate ideas and to turn those ideas into actions. **In preparation for Key Stage One:** **Geography** Map and plan making; using geographical language; describing what places are like; discussing physical and human features; recognising how places are linked to other places in the world through ecological issues. **Science** Sc 1: Encouraging pupils to ask questions about mini-beasts and find some of their own answers and information. Sc 2: Studying insects and small creatures; growing plants; learning about care and respect for the environment. Sc 3: Sorting and classifying – particularly building materials used in the garden; discussing living and non-living things. Sc 4: discussing light.

	PSHE Many aspects of the curriculum. In role, the teacher is helping to provide a model of leadership - speaking and listening, managing discussions fairly. This project asks the pupils to understand that humans sometimes have to make decisions in relation to the environment and that sometimes they have responsibilities for it.
Literacy skills	Story construction. Sequencing; character development; setting; including a problem; selecting a suitable ending; understanding the meaning of a story; familiarisation with a type of plot known as Voyage and Return; note-making in pictorial and written form; asking and answering questions; speaking and listening in pairs and groups.
Remember DfES thinking skills!	**Creating** Generating and extending ideas; applying imagination; looking for innovative outcomes. Taking a voyage of discovery into an imaginary world in which the Pupils in Role are shrunk to a tiny size is a challenging exercise. The pupils develop creative thinking through using their ability to imagine being a different size and through helping to find solutions to problems they encounter in the story.
	Enquiring Asking relevant questions; posing and defining problems; predicting outcomes and anticipating consequences. There are lots of opportunities for pupils to develop this kind of thinking during the drama where the Pupils in Role are discussing with the Teacher in Role how to solve problems, what the best course of action would be and what the consequences of their actions might be. TIR can easily model how to ask questions and encourage pupils to pose their own questions. Pupils can also be encouraged to find out about insects and small animals from other resources such as books and films.
	Reasoning Giving reasons for opinions and actions; drawing inferences and making deductions; explaining thoughts; making informed decisions and judgements. This type of thinking is developed during the drama where PIR and TIR discuss the best way to deal with a situation or how to solve a problem such as being trapped by the spider.
	Information processing Sorting and classifying; comparing and contrasting; sequencing. This type of thinking can be developed through displays that show the sequence of the story and through discussions about what happened in the story. Pupils can also be given opportunities to find out about gardens, insects and small animals and growing things from resources such as books, films and visits.
	Evaluating Examining what the story means; judging the value of what you have read, heard or done. This type of thinking can be developed through reflecting on the story, discussing what happened and whether the people in the story made the best decisions. The teacher can model asking effective questions and can encourage pupils to ask reflective questions too. Teachers might wish to discuss real-life incidents in which an environment has been challenged by the introduction of a creature that does not naturally belong there, such as the introduction of rabbits into Australia.

The Magic Book Adventure

Planning checklist

Subject matter	A royal home; a ruler; a magic book and an invisible power
Themes	Trust; responsibilities of authority; integrity; meddling with things you do not understand properly; self interest; guilt; manipulation; bullying; spiritual themes such as conscience; selfishness and right and wrong; lying and telling the truth
Key resources and equipment	Costume items to sign TIR, such as a caretaker's jacket or overall for Reema, a spell making robe, a crown and cloak for the King Costume items for the PIR in role as servants such as aprons **Worksheets (in folder Magic Book on the Resources CD)** The Tower Room (Tower Room.pdf) 'Dear Palace Servants' letter (Dear Palace Servants.pdf) **Props include** Cleaning items such as brushes, brooms, dusters, feather dusters, buckets Cleaning cards (Cleaning Cards.pdf) Pictures of domestic jobs (Domestic Jobs.pdf) Play tools, such as hammers, screwdrivers, saws, spirit level Kitchen equipment such as bowls, spoons, whisks, saucepans, ingredients for cooking, play food A large pot for spell making Pieces of brightly coloured cloth for draping to make furniture more interesting, such as a throne or for costumes – cloaks, wraps and so on A purple cloth for the Book Room scene Warning message in the magic book (Warning.pdf)
Organisation	**Time** Without Optional Extras: 8–10 hours With Optional Extras: 12–14 hours **Teaching space** A large space in a classroom Possible themes for the role-play area: • the palace kitchen • the kitchen vegetable garden • the throne room and King's office • the laundry room • the pet area • the King's own mechanic's garage for fixing the royal coaches or cars.
Main dramatic devices used	Teacher in Role Pupils in Role **Basic plot** Tragedy with elements of Voyage and Return **Basic problem** The characters are unaware that the magic book unleashes a devastating invisible force (not knowing vital information) **Basic tension** Struggling with conscience; the threat of being 'found out' and told off (morals)

Teacher's overview

This is a tale of ordinary folk who find themselves caught up in a strange and difficult situation through no real fault of their own. It is presented in the style of a traditional children's folk tale. The pupils' characters have to make decisions that affect the lives of other people, but they are not in control of the circumstances that generate the options. This, of course, makes the debate about right and wrong, innocence and guilt very interesting.

This is the kind of adventure that children love. It's a bit scary, but nothing really happens. The palace is a light, bright place where a happy King lives who will soon be even happier because his son is returning home after a long absence. This connection with families is one that children easily make and the domesticity of the servants' work is another link with their daily lives at home and school.

However, the story has depth. It reflects those difficult real-life situations in which people must decide how far to trust their gut instincts, how far to resist authority and when to insist on doing the 'right' thing. In other words, it explores matters of conscience: when to tell the truth; when to speak up; how to listen to 'the voice in your head'. Of course, this is a central theme of PSHE in the Early Years. Yet *The Magic Book Adventure* goes even further. It helps children to develop the skills they need to deal with the kinds of danger that could affect them at their young age: 'going with a stranger'; being bullied; being 'carried along by the crowd' into danger; even being abused. It helps them to recognise unhealthy pressure.

These are tough areas to work on and, given the age of the children, they can be tackled only in the safety of a fiction. Consequently, *The Magic Book Adventure* takes place in a fantasy setting reminiscent of many fairy stories. The characters the pupils play are not to blame for what happens and there is a happy ending for those who want one. What's more, where decisions are made that could be regarded as morally wrong, those decisions were driven either by the need to survive or a desire to do good for others.

Role-play area

The role-play area could be a palace or castle (whichever is chosen for the story) with a throne room that also contains a desk with scrolls of paper to be written on, dining room, kitchen area, kings bedroom and lots of cleaning equipment to use! The pupils could be given lists and could also make their own lists of jobs to be done, write to other kings and queens, plan parties and other events and so on.

The cast of characters

The characters are fairly familiar:

- the leader of the ruling family, who is the King in this case, but could just as well be a Queen, Prince, Sheikh, Lord, Lady or Maharajah (unnamed) (TIR)
- the returning person – someone who has been away for a long time (Prince Aten) (optional TIR at the end of the story)
- the chief servant or housekeeper who organises the staff (Reema) (TIR)
- the more lowly servants who work to orders and do jobs (PIR)

- in the background: the cook; gardener; stable-hand; chauffeur; footman; mechanic; and so on
- local villagers.

For those who are unsure about the content

Written in the form of a fairy story (or what is now more accurately referred to as a folk tale), *The Magic Book Adventure* contains, as many old tales do, scenes where magic is used. This may be something that appeals or appals. If you have a strong reaction against working with a story that involves magic, you may not want to tackle this project. If you believe that the inclusion of magic is inappropriate on religious or cultural grounds, then this project is not for you. On the other hand, you might see this dimension of the story as an opportunity to begin discussing spiritual matters with the class, particularly as the spells appear to have a beneficial effect, but are actually harmful in ways that the children's characters cannot control. There is a strong and invisible force at work. At the end, Prince Aten appears as a 'light of the world'-type character (check the meaning of his name and connections with the Egyptian Pharaoh Akhenaten) who has a 'saving' function (note the connection with Aslan in *The Lion, the Witch and the Wardrobe*). So, the story can make a significant contribution to pupils' religious development.

Furthermore, magic serves several important purposes in myths, legends and traditional folk tales. At various times it is used:

- to manipulate natural phenomena that are not scientifically understood (as was the case in early societies) – crops failing, water sources drying up, the moon disappearing, tempests and so forth
- as an easy way out of a tricky situation – a person surviving a disaster or an illness
- as entertainment – changes in fortune, changes in appearance, discoveries of treasure
- as an invitation to enter a world of fantasy – benevolent fairies and cuddly creatures
- to frighten people away from 'dabbling' in magic – magic that goes wrong
- to increase the status and power of children – children understand how to use the power better than adults and can make things happen that adults cannot
- to communicate between the heavenly world and the real world – in Greek and Roman stories the gods give gifts of magical items and magical powers, or simply make extraordinary things happen.

It could be argued that the presence of magic in our story helps children with their incipient appreciation of these literary art forms. If magic is not the problem, but you have some reservations about the seriousness of the issues raised by the story, please read on and let us explain the literary influences behind the plot and the reasons for its being 'healthy food for thought' for young children. Consider:

- the disturbing content of *Rumpelstiltskin*, which is essentially a 'deal with the devil'
- the dark threat symbolised by the wolf in *Little Red Riding Hood*
- the caged children in *Hansel and Gretel* who are to be murdered and eaten
- narcissism and the use of a potion for selfish and murderous purposes in *Snow White*.

Major, even frightening, issues are tackled in these well-known tales, but within fantasy worlds that make the stories 'light' enough for young children, despite the heaviness of the material. Actually, most of these stories originally ended violently (for example, the wolf ate both Little Red Riding Hood and her grandma; Rumpelstiltskin – a demon – tore himself in two!). In the late nineteenth and early twentieth centuries, the endings were rewritten to make them more palatable. Likewise, in *The Magic Book Adventure*, there is an optional happy ending, which you may want to use for the same reason.

While we are on the subject, there are many more modern examples of big issues that are addressed in children's literature. For instance, for younger listeners and readers see: *Gobbolino the Witch's Cat* by Ursula Moray Williams; *Beaver Towers* by Nigel Hinton; *Ms Wiz-Millionaire* by Terence Blacker. These stories contain magic and monsters and address issues such as exclusion, slavery and the consequences of accidentally giving magic powers to a bad character. These kinds of story are intended to be read and discussed with children before they are able to read them for themselves. You could say that *The Magic Book Adventure* is similar to *The Sorcerer's Apprentice*, a Disney cartoon that is often enjoyed by pre-readers.

In a different style, but with similarly 'meaty' content, are the wonderful stories of Babette Cole. *Princess Smartypants*, for example, turns a typical fairy story on its head and tackles gender issues with a vengeance. *Bad Manners* deals with social rules, manners, self-respect and self-control, and *Two of Everything* addresses separation and divorce directly. *Dinosaurs and All That Rubbish* by Michael Foreman has a strong message about how mankind is in danger of destroying the environment but uses the style of a myth to make the point.

Examples for older readers include *The Earth Giant* by Melvin Burgess, which deals with issues of alienation: the children struggle with their feelings as they defy their parents and help the giant; the parents suffer badly when they believe their daughter has gone missing.

There is also the bestselling *I am David*, by Anne Holm, which deals with displaced persons, concentration camps and the struggle to survive. Of the three projects in *Part 2* of the book, this one puts the pupils in the most challenging and therefore the most uncomfortable situation. Consequently, it needs sensitive and thoughtful handling. It will be important to debrief the experience properly and to do the suggested activities that take the pupils out of role and into more familiar territory.

Summary of the plot

Reema welcomes the new servants

A King lives in a beautiful palace and is looked after by his servants. There is no Queen in the story, but the King has a son called Prince Aten, whom he loves very much. Prince Aten has been living away from the palace for a number of years, travelling and being educated ready for his future role as King. As the drama begins, the King is awaiting the return of his son, who is coming home for good to live in the palace. The King wants him to be comfortable and to have a place of his own, so he orders the servants to clean up a part of the palace that hasn't been used for many years. It is called the Fortune Tower. This will be the new living quarters for the Prince.

A new group of servants (the PIR) have just been employed to work in the palace and the King has asked one of his trusted older servants, Reema (TIR), to look after the new recruits and show them what they have to do. Reema greets the new servants and makes sure they have the right clothes and equipment for their first task, which is to clean the Fortune Tower.

Reema tells the servants that it is going to be a difficult job because the King's grandfather had the tower locked up many years ago and, as far as she knows, no one has been in there since.

This is the first indication that something is not as it should be. The tower has been locked up for many years, but no one knows why. Later on, when the pupils reflect on the story, they will be asked to consider whether or not someone should have taken more care to pass on information about the tower. The pupils, in role as new servants, are about to be put in a difficult situation because they don't know what potential dangers lurk there.

Inside the tower

Reema leads the new servants to the Fortune Tower and unlocks the door. They all step inside the tower and into darkness. After fumbling around in the dark for a while, the servants find a light and can then see the first of two rooms they will discover. The first room is dirty, dusty, full of cobwebs, dark and dingy, and they realise they have a huge job ahead to get it cleaned up.

Reema points out that there is a strange noise that sounds like scratching coming from somewhere inside the tower. The servants search the first room, listening for the scratching sounds, and eventually uncover a door that has, up to now, been hidden. Reema thinks the scratching might be coming from behind the door, so she tries the handle but the door is locked. She asks the servants to search for a key, which they find, and it fits the lock perfectly. Reema hesitates to open the door, being somewhat afraid of what she might find on the other side. As Reema and the other servants hesitate, there is a loud roar behind them, which startles the group. In panic, Reema unlocks the door and the cleaning party hurriedly enter the second room.

This is the second indication that something is not as it should be. The door to the second room was locked, which suggested there is something in there to avoid. However, Reema and the servants were panicked and this forced their decision. If the servants had been at liberty to choose what to do for themselves, they would probably have left the tower at this point and reported what had happened to the King. However, they are low-status characters who have been sent to do a job; Reema is in charge, not the servants.

Entering the Book Room

The second room had clearly been an important room in the past. While looking around, Reema sees a large book lying on a stand. She takes a closer look and sees a warning on the front cover. Reema is intrigued and so, ignoring the fact that there is clearly some danger, opens it and realises with delight that she has found a book of spells. The spells all appear to be for good purposes such as healing and helping people with tasks.

At this point in the story, Reema is getting carried away. She has ignored the obvious signals and so leads the other servants into trouble. Had she asked herself why the book was left in the tower and locked inside the inner room, she might have been more cautious. However, before anyone can debate whether the book is good or bad, there is another creepy noise, which suggests that a monster of some kind is moving towards the servants. The noise seems to be coming from the first room, so the servants can't exit using the door. Given the emergency, Reema decides to use a spell from the book to get rid of whatever it is that is coming towards them. Quickly, she finds a spell and reads it.

Immediately, everyone is swooped into a whirling wind and spun round and round. When the whirlwind has stopped, the servants find themselves back in the first room. The whole tower is now clean, bright and sparkling. The windows are letting in the bright sunlight and everything is beautiful. Also, the monster, whatever it was, has disappeared.

A plan is hatched to keep the book

Reema is delighted and suggests that the book be kept by herself and the other servants as their secret. After all, the spells can be used to do good deeds for people in need. Reema knows she has to keep the other servants on her side or they might tell the King. Because Reema has a higher status than the servants and is trusted by the King, this leaves the servants in a difficult position. Reema knows that the King is away from the palace on business, so the servants wouldn't be able to talk to him for a while. She also knows that, if she is challenged, she can tell the servants that she has to look after the book anyway until the King returns. Manipulated through the use of Reema's higher status, her reasons and excuses, the servants find themselves being led into deceiving the King and taking property that probably belongs to him.

This is the point at which the story becomes very serious. In real life, young children can find themselves in similar situations. Adults and older siblings usually have more status and young children trust them, but there are times when it is necessary for youngsters to insist on their own views of what is right. In the reflection on the story, it is important for children to recognise that there were warning signals right at the beginning of the adventure and that Reema did not necessarily make the right decisions, despite her authority.

The servants are told to go about their business as if they were cleaning up the tower, so that no one will suspect that anything unusual has happened. Reema takes the book and hides it in her living quarters.

The servants' day off

The King returns, inspects the Fortune Tower and is delighted by what he sees. Prince Aten is due home the next day, so the King declares a two-day holiday for everyone in the palace and the surrounding area as part of the celebrations to welcome his son.

A day later, Reema and the servants are gathered in the servants' quarters. Reema congratulates the servants on their work and tells them how very pleased the King was to find the tower so clean and bright. It is unusual for the King to grant two days' holiday, so Reema points out that the servants have clearly made a very good impression on him. This is of course more manipulation by 'hooking' the pupils into feeling approved of by the King.

A problem is introduced

Everyone is discussing what they are going to do on their days off, when Reema remembers that she has been handed a letter from some people in the nearby village. The letter asks the servants if they will search the palace for a missing grandparent. Reema quickly decides to use another spell to solve the problem. There isn't a spell for finding people, so Reema comes up with an idea. Without giving the servants time to think or debate the rights and wrongs of spell casting, she persuades them to gather the ingredients needed to make a potion that will improve their sight and hearing. This, she reasons, will ensure that Grandma Razi is found more quickly.

Enough potion is made for all the servants. Just then, the King arrives, alarmed that he has just seen some elderly people disappear in front of him in a puff of smoke. The King tells the servants that he suspects someone is using bad magic in his palace. Reema and the servants are about to realise that each time a spell is cast from the book an elderly person disappears. They have cast so many spells to improve the sight and hearing of the servants that now lots of elderly people have vanished. What is more, there seems no way to bring the elderly people back!

Choosing a suitable ending

There is a choice of endings. The servants have to decide whether to tell the King the truth or cover up what they have done. The optional happy ending involves Prince Aten, who, having travelled far and wide, has become worldly wise. The Prince knows how to reverse the bad magic and bring back all the elderly people. He takes the book and hides it so that no one will ever find it again.

Getting going

Tell the pupils that they are going to act out a story that is set in a palace. Explain that it is a nice big palace with lots of rooms. Show the pupils a picture of a palace. It can be situated in any country that is culturally suitable for the class, or that connects to your 'Knowledge and Understanding of the World' curriculum.

Explain that a King (or any ruler, such as a sultan, Rajah, Sheikh, Pharaoh or Emperor) lives in the palace and he has lots of servants, but no family living with him. As the story starts, the teacher is going to play one of the King's old and trusted servants called Reema. The King has just decided to have a really big 'spring clean' and therefore some new servants are just about to join the palace staff. Tell the pupils that they are going to be the new servants.

TIR as Reema welcomes the new servants

Reema's role function is as a 'low-status, benevolent authority figure'. Possible costume to sign the role: caretaker's jacket or overall. TIR as Reema starts the drama by welcoming the new servants and helping everyone to sort out their aprons and cleaning equipment, such as dusters and sweeping brushes.

Possible script:

'Welcome, everyone. I'm so glad to see you. My name is Reema and I'm here to help get you started in your new jobs. The King is keen to get the Fortune Tower cleaned up today but nobody's been in there for years so my guess is that it's going to be really mucky. You'll need some aprons. I'm sure I had some aprons in here! [Look in an imaginary or real cupboard]. *Ah! here we are, some aprons.* [Hand out imaginary or real aprons]. *That's it, put them over your head and tie at the back* [Demonstrate]. *You'd better put these hats on, too, to keep your hair clean.'*

TIR tells the pupils the King has decided to have the Fortune Tower cleaned because his son Prince Aten will be coming home from his travels soon and he is going to give him the Fortune Tower to live in.

Explain that the Fortune Tower has not been lived in for a very long time. The King's grandfather had it locked up for some reason that has long been forgotten. It is going to be a very dusty and dirty place to clean!

Drawing and Writing in Role: gathering the equipment

TIR asks for help to decide what cleaning equipment to use. Give the PIR mini-whiteboards and ask them to write or draw the equipment they think will be useful. Use the pupils' ideas and write a list on a large sheet of paper. Use this list as you send PIR to imaginary cupboards to gather the equipment together.

Possible script:

> *'Now let's see what we can find in the palace cleaning cupboards. First thing on the list is a … [Read the item from your list]. I've sure I've seen those recently. [Mime opening cupboards and looking inside]. Here we are, plenty of … Help yourselves to what you need. I'm pretty sure the … are over there – just open the doors and take a look. Ah! Some of the things we need are in the kitchen store room. Would you go and get …, and could you get … The … are upstairs in the laundry room. The washing team used them yesterday. Would you go? That's great. Everything else must be in these cupboards here – you'll just have to look.'*

Give the PIR time to act out gathering the equipment.

> *'Have you got everything? Good. Well, it's only a short journey from here to the Fortune Tower, but we'll have to carry everything over there ourselves. I don't think there's any water over there so we'd better fill our buckets from these taps here and carry them over carefully.'*

Mime filling a bucket from a tap. Act out carrying the bucket now heavy with water.

Say, 'OK, follow me …'

Act out carrying all the equipment to the door of the Tower, unlocking the door and everyone stepping tentatively inside.

> *'Here we are. I'll just unlock the door. Goodness me! This door is very heavy. [Act out pushing the door open and peering inside] It is quite dark in there. [To the PIR] Come on let's go in and see if we can find a light inside. [Act out stepping tentatively into the darkened room, the only light coming from the open doorway] There's a lamp here on the floor, I'll light it and see if it still works, it must be quite old, it's covered in dust. Yes it works! It's not very bright but at least we can see … oh dear, look at the mess! Dust and cobwebs everywhere, everything is so dirty.'*

Stop the drama.

Tell the pupils that the room the servants have just entered is called the Tower Room. You may want to ask the pupils the following reflection questions at this point.

- Why do you think the Fortune Tower has been left to get so dirty and messy?
- If someone told the servants it was dangerous to enter the Fortune Tower do you think they would still go in? Why?

Optional Extras

Mathematical development

Print the cards showing different kinds of cleaning equipment (Cleaning Cards.pdf in folder Magic Book on the Resources CD) ready to be sorted and counted into 'sorting boxes'. You will need 10 cards for each piece of equipment so that pupils can place a group of them into a box. For example, you might ask the pupils to place four duster cards in the first sorting box and two broom cards in the second sorting box and so on.

Depending on the age and capability of the pupils, you could ask them to:

- write a number label for each box to show how many items there are in it

- make a chart to show how many items of equipment there are

Equipment	Number of items
Dusters	6
Mops	2

- ask the pupils to work out simple calculations, such as how many dusters would be left in the box if two were taken out to be used

- tell the pupils the King has given Reema some money to buy cleaning equipment and he has told her to make sure there is ten of everything. Ask the pupils to work out a shopping list so that the servants can buy the items that are needed. For example, to have ten dusters in the box the servants need to buy five and to have ten mops the servants need to buy eight.

Select a few of the printed cards to play a memory game.

First, shuffle the cards so that they are in a random order and lay them out on a flat surface picture side up. Give the pupils time to look at them and remember what they see. Then turn all the cards picture side down. Pupils now take turns to try to find pairs of cards by turning one card over and then trying to remember where there is a matching card. Once a second card is chosen, it is turned face up and if it is a match the pupil keeps the pair. If it isn't a match both cards are turned picture down again and the next pupil takes their turn. The winner is the person with the most pairs of cards at the end of the game. The game can be used as an opportunity to talk with the pupils about memory and spatial awareness.

Ask the pupils to design some new rectangular rugs for the Fortune Tower using squares, rectangles triangles and circle shapes.

Communication, language and literacy; Knowledge and understanding of the world

Play Snap with the cards you have printed. The idea of the game is to win as many pairs of cards as you can, The cards are shuffled and dealt out to the players (pairs or groups). To win a pair of cards a pupil must shout 'snap' when she sees the cards are identical.

Discuss with the pupils who does the cleaning at home and what equipment people might use in real life that we haven't used in our story yet, such as dishwashing machines, washing machines and tumble dryers. Talk about the story, how it is set in a time and place where there are no machines, and therefore why we won't be using machines to help us clean up in the story!

Give pupils cards with pictures of domestic jobs (Domestic Jobs.pdf in folder Magic Book on the Resources CD) and ask them to describe the domestic job being done on their card.

Ask the pupils to talk to a partner about the domestic job on their card. Ask them who does this job in their home. Then as a group act out the domestic jobs with the teacher leading the acting and demonstrating with as much detail as possible. For example, cleaning the windows might start with looking at an imaginary window, then opening it up, paying attention to the type of catch, walking away to collect a bucket from the cupboard and then pretending to rummage

Optional Extras continued

around in a different cupboard to find a cloth or other window-cleaning equipment, then going to an imaginary kitchen cupboard to find the cleaning liquid, filling the bucket with water, noticing that the bucket gets heavier with water in it and adding some cleaning liquid, returning to the window and having to put all your equipment down on the floor to free your hands so that you can close it. Finally, clean the window, making sure that you find there is something stuck to the window that won't be cleaned without some considerable effort. Open the window again to let the glass dry.

When the pupils have had a go at acting out doing jobs with the teacher and feel confident enough to act out in front of others, they can play a guessing game with the cards. Sit the pupils in a circle and give each child a card, which they have to keep secret. When the teacher chooses a pupil to 'act out', they stand in the centre of the circle and act out the job pictured on the card they have been given. The other pupils watch until the teacher gives a signal for the acting out to stop.

The teacher then randomly selects pupils to have a go at guessing what the job was. The pupils try to guess as many jobs correctly as they can and the teacher keeps the scores.

In pairs, pupils can also decide the order in which jobs might be done. Pupils talk together and decide what order the cards will go in; for example, they might decide first to make the beds, then do the ironing, then take the rubbish out and so on. There is no right answer to this, of course, but the pupils can be asked why they would do the jobs in that order.

Pupils could apply their knowledge about domestic jobs to tasks we have to do in the classroom to keep things clean and tidy. Ask pupils to list cleaning and tidying jobs that have to be done in class. Discussions about keeping the classroom clean and tidy could also include talking about people who help us in school such as parents, cleaners, the caretaker and older pupils.

Building belief

Sit the pupils, out of role, in a circle and place a large sheet of paper in the centre. Ask the pupils to close their eyes and remember acting out stepping inside the Tower Room a little while ago. Ask them to think about what it was like. Prompt them to imagine that they are seeing what the servants saw, hearing what the servants heard, feeling what the servants felt, and so on.

Possible prompt questions:

- When the servants got inside the Tower Room, what did they notice first?
- When their eyes got used to the dim light, what did they see?
- What colours did they see?
- What interested them most?
- What surprised them most?
- What was to their left/right/straight ahead?
- Was there a smell or a scent of any kind?
- What was in the Tower Room (furniture; a trunk; boxes; a rail of clothes; treasure)?

Collective Scene Drawing: inside the Tower Room

From the pupils' responses to these questions, begin to draw a picture of the inside of the Tower Room on a large piece of paper (on the flipchart or on the floor). Now and again, encourage individuals to come and add details such as items of furniture, spiders' webs or windows. As the picture is being constructed, point out all the jobs that will need to be done, such as taking the curtains down and washing them, clearing away the cobwebs, sweeping the dusty floor, cleaning the rusty lock, or whatever fits the setting the pupils are creating.

PIR enter the Tower Room

Restart the drama and go back to the point at which the door is opened and everyone gets their first look inside the Tower Room. TIR as Reema leads the pupils on a walk around the Tower Room with the lamp, acting out looking around and assessing the jobs that have to be done.

TIR organises the cleaning and sets the PIR to work. Freeze Frame the action from time to time and ask pupils to say what they are doing.

Further questions asked by TIR during the acting out:

- Do you think Prince Aten will like living here when it's all tidied up? Why?
- Do you think the Prince will want to change anything when he moves in? What?
- Do you think anyone ever lived here before? Why?
- What would be the best thing about living in the Fortune Tower?
- What is the biggest job that will have to be done in here?
- What are you looking forward to doing when you finish work today?
- What do you think of the King?

Adding tension

TIR as Reema creates tension by stopping the PIR and asking them if they can hear a scratching noise. TIR uses facial expressions, body language (exaggerated listening, hand cupped behind ear) and verbal cues ('Did you her that?') to generate an interest in what the scratching noise might be.

TIR leads the PIR around the tower listening for the scratching sounds. Hunting under (imaginary) cupboards and in drawers, behind curtains until eventually a door is discovered that has been hidden by a big tapestry. TIR tries the door, but it is locked and asks the PIR to search for a key. As the PIR are searching for the key, TIR reports to them that the scratching sounds are getting louder and are definitely coming from behind the door.

When the key is found (PIR will usually find the key quickly), TIR will ask the PIR what they think is behind the door. TIR leads a discussion about whether or not the door should be opened.

Further questions asked by TIR during the acting out:

* What could be making the scratching noises?
* What if we can't deal with whatever is behind the door?
* Has the door been locked by someone for some reason?
* Should we get permission to unlock the door from the King?

Stop the drama.

Narration

Out of role, move the story on a bit. Explain that a loud roar was heard by the servants. It came from somewhere behind them. Being frightened, they decided to open the door quickly and take their chance with whatever they found. As the door swung open, they could see a room with a red carpet but very little light.

Entering the Book Room

Back in role, act out the moment when the door is opened. TIR as Reema (in mime) lights some candles and everybody gets a look at the room they are standing in.

Doing whichever feels more comfortable, either:

1. you come out of role, but the pupils stay in role Freeze Frame the action and Thought Track the PIR about what they can see; or
2. you stay in role and develop a conversation with PIR about what they can see in the room.

In role, point out a rough wooden table with a large book on it. The book has a red cover and a golden clasp to hold it closed. TIR leads the PIR to the table and acts out turning the front cover to reveal a warning message. TIR reads the warning, 'This book gives and takes away. If you use it, *beware!*' The teacher could print off the inside page of the book (Warning.pdf in folder Magic Book in the Resources CD).

Developing the story

Act out turning pages and describe what you see.

Possible script:

> 'The front cover's very heavy. I wonder what it's made from. The pages have strange writing on them. It's funny, but I feel a tingle in my fingers when I touch the book. This page has a spell written on it; the writing's very odd and hard to read.'

TIR explains to the PIR that the book contains spells and magic words. The spells seem to be the kind that make good things happen, such as healing people, doing jobs and giving people gifts.

'I'm not sure we should be looking at this. I wonder who the book belonged to. The spells look as if they are meant to do good, but they could be dangerous. After all, someone left that message on the front page. What did it say again?'

Repeat the warning and discuss what it might mean with the PIR. At this point, make sure that the pupils understand that some sort of risk is involved.

While in role, convey the idea that suddenly all the candles blow out and the loud deep roar is heard again. TIR becomes frightened, gathers the PIR around her, everyone listens and the roar is heard again. This time it sounds nearer. Something is coming. What should they do?

Possible script:

'The candles have all blown out! Come here quick! Listen – shh! – did you here that? Something is padding towards us. There! A roar again, it sounds much closer to us this time. We've got to do something to save ourselves.'

Give the PIR time to make suggestions.

Start to talk in an urgent tone and look agitated. Acknowledge all of the pupils' suggestions as good ideas and then find a reason why the suggestions can't be used, such as that the door to the other room has closed and locked again; the key won't work; it's too dark to see; and so on.

In a state of near panic, suggest that a spell from the book be used to get rid of whatever it is. Act out carefully lifting the book from the table and placing it on the floor. Open the front cover. Be dazzled as the pages light up so that they can be read in the dark. Frantically look through the book, find the right kind of spell and get everyone to join in with saying it.

Possible script:

'I know! Let's use the book. There must be a spell in here that will save us. Help me lift it down onto the floor. Has anyone got a candle? [Open the front cover]. *Oh! The pages are lighting up. I can read them.* [Search for a spell]. *This one should work: it's called Making a Clean Sweep. It says, "Clean out monsters and baddies from any building and start afresh." Perfect!*

> *"Winds of change blow this way;*
> *In this place monsters and baddies may not stay;*
> *Bring fresh air to sweep them all away."'*

TIR leads acting out being blown around by a strong wind. You can make this as dramatic or as simple as you like. When the wind dies down, TIR points out to the PIR that light has returned and the room is sparkling clean and, when the party return into the Tower Room (through the door that is miraculously open again!), that is sparkling clean, too. All their work has been done for them. Walk around in amazement looking at how clean everything is. The scary noises, and any monsters that might have been there, have gone too.

Possible script:

'Look! Everything is so bright and clean. The whole tower seems to be full of light. Listen! It's absolutely quiet, no scratching sounds, no roars, no monsters or scary things of any kind. Let's go and look next door. [The door will have magically opened] *Oh! It is beautiful, everything is so sparklingly clean and shining; the windows were so dark and dirty, now they are bright and clean; the colours of the drapes are fantastic. To think, the mess this tower was in and one little spell has changed everything.'*

Stop the drama.

Prop drawing: the book

Out of role, put the pupils into pairs and give each pair a large piece of paper and a marker pen. Ask the pairs to design the front cover of the book. Give them a short time to complete the task, a maximum of five minutes.

Ask the pupils:

- What do you imagine the cover is made from?
- What would it feel like?
- What colour is it?
- Does it have a pattern on it anywhere?
- Does it have any words on it apart from the warning?
- Does it have any pictures on it?

When the pictures are finished, display them so that pupils can see each other's ideas. Discuss the book and its significance with the pupils.

Possible prompt questions:

- What is this book?
- Who do you think left it in the tower?
- Who owns it?
- Where did the owner get it from?
- Where did it come from in the first place?
- Why was it left in the tower?
- What is good about the book?
- What is bad about the book?
- What would you like to know about the book?
- What advice would you give to the people in the story about the book?

Scene drawing: the Tower Room

Give the pupils a piece of paper each and ask them to fold it in half (or use the Tower Room worksheet – Tower Room.pdf in folder Magic Book on the Resources CD). On one half, draw a picture of the Tower Room before the spell was used, and in the other half draw a picture of the room after the spell was used.

> ### Optional Extra
>
> **Communication, language and literacy; Knowledge and understanding of the world**
>
> Use the pictures of the Tower Room to discuss how a description is conveyed. Begin to identify adjectives, verbs and nouns. With the class, write a model description of the room before the spell was used. Write a list of things that changed after the spell was used. Use the list as an opportunity to explain the use of colons and semicolons. This is an ideal opportunity to begin raising pupils' awareness of parts of speech and grammar long before they would normally be introduced. It can do no harm.

A plan is hatched to keep the book

TIR as Reema wants to have the book for herself, but realises that she needs to keep the other servants involved so they don't tell anyone. She tries to persuade the PIR to take the book and keep it somewhere safe and secret so they can learn how to use the spells to help people.

Possible script:

> *'This book is marvellous! Look at what we can do with just one simple spell. Think of all the good we could do for people: we could help the old people to keep their houses clean and tidy; make people who are poorly feel well; help school children to do their homework. I bet you have lots of jobs that you would like done by magic, haven't you?'*

Let the PIR make suggestions. If the PIR raise objections and give reasons for not taking the book, TIR must work hard to persuade them to take it. TIR's reasons might include the following:

- the book has been here for many years and clearly no one wants it
- if anyone had known about it, they would have taken it away a long time ago
- we can protect it to make sure it doesn't fall into the hands of a bad person
- the King often tells me to take any unwanted items, so he won't mind.

Possible script:

> *'I suggest that we don't tell anyone about the book. Let's keep it a secret or people will keep asking us to cast spells for them. We'll just use it when we think we can be really helpful. Where shall we hide it?'*

Let PIR make suggestions. If the PIR continue to object strongly, TIR can tell them she will keep the book for only a day and then give it to the King as soon as he gets back. TIR tells the PIR that the King is away from the palace at present on business, so she has to keep it safe until he returns.

TIR might 'distract' the PIR from this issue by engaging them in more action.

Possible script:

> *'OK, let's pretend we're cleaning, because we don't want people to get suspicious. It would have taken us all day to clean up in here without the spell. It must look as if we're emptying dirty water from our buckets and fetching more cleaning cloths. Don't forget to tell everyone you meet how hard we've had to work.'*

Act out the 'pretend' cleaning. Stop the drama.

Reflect on the drama

Out of role, get the pupils to talk about the following questions:

- What has just happened in the story?
- What have you found out?
- Why do you think that Reema wants to keep the book?
- Do you think she has good reasons for keeping the book?
- What advice would you give to her if she was willing to listen?
- What advice would you give to the servants?

Explore with the pupils issues such as:

- whether the other servants (PIR) are being 'led astray'
- how far you trust your feelings

- how far you stick up for what you think is right
- the extent to which the servants can, or should, say no to Reema, who has more authority than they do
- the difference between reasons and excuses.

Possible questions include:

- Is it OK for Reema to keep the book if she intends to do good with the spells?
- What do you think will happen if the King finds out that Reema has taken the book out of the tower?
- Would the King think there are good reasons for what Reema and the servants did?
- How did the servants feel about keeping the book a secret for Reema?
- What do you think would have happened if the servants had refused to go along with Reema's plan?
- How much freedom do you think the servants have to choose what they want to do?
- What have you found out about Reema?

The immediate playground connection is: doing something because your friend told you to, even though you feel it is wrong or you know it is likely to get you into trouble. More broadly, any situation where a person with responsibility puts innocent dependants in jeopardy. This situation also has parallels with bullying, when someone who has, or is certainly perceived to have, more authority persuades others to do and say things that they really shouldn't do and probably don't want to do.

Narration

Still out of role, move the story on in time by telling the pupils that it is the next day and the King has arrived back at his palace from his business trip.

Explain to the pupils that the King is very pleased with how well Reema and the new servants have cleaned the Fortune Tower. He is very excited about having his son Aten back and, as part of the homecoming celebrations, the King declares a two-day holiday for everyone in the kingdom.

Optional Extra

Mathematical development

Make some cakes or biscuits for the King to celebrate the return of Prince Aten. Use the making process to practise weighing and measuring and to develop a vocabulary for weighing and measuring.

Map and Plan Making: the servants' days off

Help the pupils (out of role) to think about what the servants would do with their two days off by drawing a map of the area around the palace. Naturally, the facilities for leisure and recreation will depend on where the palace is located.

Draw a basic map and ask pupils to suggest the details. Either you can draw these onto the map for the pupils, or you can invite pupils to draw their ideas onto the map themselves.

Details might include:

* woods and forests
* pools
* roads
* special buildings such as temples, churches, mosques
* parks and gardens
* play areas.

Tell the pupils that, when the drama starts again, the servants are sitting together in their quarters talking with Reema about what activities they are going to do on their days off.

Sign your role as Reema (as before) and sit down with the PIR. Praise the PIR for their hard work yesterday. Remind them what a good job they did and tell them that the King was so pleased with what they had done that he has granted everybody in the land a two-day holiday. The two-day holiday will also be a celebration for the return of his son Prince Aten. Speculate what the Prince might be like: will he be handsome, kind, a good master and so on? Discuss with them how they will spend their time during the two holiday days.

Possible script:

> *'The King is so pleased with you. It's unheard of to have two days' holiday given to us. All the other people in the kingdom have heard about our good work and know that they have two days' holiday all because of us. It will be so good for the King to have his son Prince Aten at home. Of course, the two-day holiday is part of the celebration for the return of the Prince. I wonder what Prince Aten is like now. When he went away, he was just a little boy; I wonder if he's a handsome young man. I hope he will be a good master to work for like his father the King. What are you going to do on your days off?'*

Discuss with the PIR what they want to do during the holiday.

Introducing a problem

The servants are just about to learn that an elderly person from the nearby village has gone missing. The news comes in a letter sent from a village family. The letter is seeking help from the palace staff to search for the missing person (Dear Palace Servants.pdf in folder Magic Book on the Resources CD).

Possible script:

> 'Oh, dear me! I nearly forgot! We've had a letter from a family who live in the village. It's addressed to all of us, so let me open it and read it out to you.'

You may wish to have the letter on a large sheet of paper so that the pupils can follow the words as you read it. Alternatively, project it onto your whiteboard.

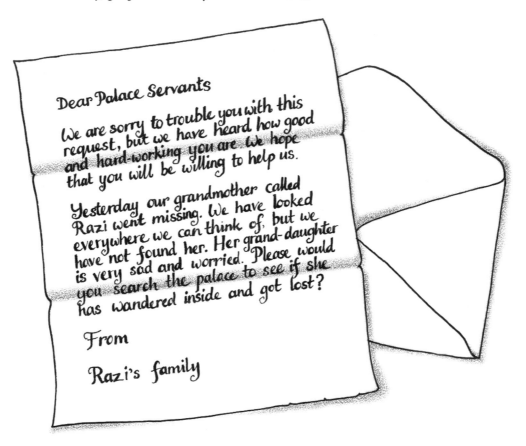

Dear Palace Servants

We are sorry to trouble you with this request, but we have heard how good and hard-working you are. We hope that you will be willing to help us.

Yesterday our grandmother called Razi went missing. We have looked everywhere we can think of, but we have not found her. Her grand-daughter is very sad and worried. Please would you search the palace to see if she has wandered inside and got lost?

From

Razi's family

TIR immediately suggests the use of the spell book to help find Grandma Razi. After looking through the book, TIR announces that there isn't a 'finding spell', but there are spells to improve the senses. TIR suggests that, if everyone in the palace is made to hear and see better, then it will be more likely that Grandma Razi will be found.

Possible script:

> 'This is a perfect example of when the book can be useful. Poor Grandma Razi must be found. She will be frightened and hungry by now, so there is no time to lose. I'll get the book.'

Act out bringing the book down onto the floor and let the PIR gather around it. Mime turning the pages and pretending to read some spells. Look disappointed when you can't see a spell that will find Grandma Razi.

Possible script:

'There isn't a finding spell, but look: this one here can improve people's senses. You know what they are – seeing, hearing, touching, tasting and smelling. If we cast a spell that makes everyone in the palace hear and see better, then, surely, Grandma Razi will be found much more quickly!'

Casting the spell

Staying in role, be very excited about casting the spell to help Grandma Razi.

Possible script:

'We need to make a potion and some of the ingredients are going to be hard to find. Who can run fast? Good. Please run to the nearest well and climb down to collect the blue moss plant. Will someone please go and find a ring-a-ling ting-a-ling bell. We also need something that feels soft to touch and something that tastes nice. You [choose an eager-looking PIR] can choose whatever you think will taste nice from the kitchen store cupboard. I'm going to need a big pan, some firewood, lots of little pebbles, three kettles of water, some purple material and a feather. Finally, we must have the nicest-smelling flower from the garden. Quick, off you go and get the ingredients – there's no time to lose!'

Let the pupils act out running around finding and collecting the ingredients. Mime setting up a fire and all the equipment you will need to make a potion that will be used to cast the spell.

Tell the PIR that they are going to have to make lots of the potion because all the servants need to drink some. Explain that you are going to make a 'test' potion first and then the PIR will get together in groups and make their own.

This is a means of demonstrating what to do in role so the pupils can act it out for themselves with confidence.

Act out making the spell:

- sit the PIR in a circle
- put on a 'spell-making' robe or cloak
- use the centre of the circle as your acting space
- get a large heavy pot
- mime making a fire and putting the pot on the fire
- open the book and read out the ingredients
- get PIR to help you add the ingredients to the pot
- get the PIR to stand up
- say the spell.

Suggested spell:

'Hands that touch,
Eyes that see,
Five senses that belong to me.
A tongue to taste with,
Nose to smell,
Ears to hear,
Now serve me well.'

TIR stirs the potion and then carefully pours it into a glass and drinks some. Explain to the pupils how good you feel and that you are sure you can see better and your hearing is greatly improved.

You might say:

> 'I can see everything so clearly, all the little insects and all the veins in the leaves of the plants … I can hear the cook snoring in the kitchen and the gardener whistling a tune as he works …'

Declare that the potion is safe and tell the PIR to gather up the ingredients they need to make their own potions. Let the PIR form groups and act out the potion making.

When the potions have been made and drunk, Freeze Frame the action and Thought Track a few pupils about what it is like to have improved senses. Prompt the pupils to think about what it would really be like to have 'super' sight, hearing, touch, smell and taste.

TIR declares that everyone is ready to search for Grandma Razi. But, before the search gets underway, TIR notices that the King is on his way to the room where the potions have been brewed. TIR tells the PIR to tidy up quickly, since it wouldn't be good for the King to find out what they have been up to before they can prove themselves to be skilled in using the spells.

Direct the process of tidying up, all the time adding tension by frequently telling the PIR the King is nearly here.

When the PIR have finished the tidying up, TIR tells them to get their cleaning things so that they look like 'normal' servants. Stop the drama.

Teacher changes role

Explain to the pupils that you are going to change your role. You are going to play the part of the King. Sign the role with appropriate costume, perhaps a stick as a sceptre. Role function: benevolent authority figure.

Finding an ending

At this point in the story, the King doesn't know about the book or that the servants have been using it to cast spells. The servants don't know that casting a spell has a very serious consequence. In actual fact, every time a spell is cast from the book an elderly person from the village disappears!

The King is unaware of what has been going on in the servants' quarters, but has just witnessed the disappearance of several people himself, and so he is quite sure someone somewhere nearby is using magic. Remember, it's important that the number of people who have disappeared must correlate to the number of potions that the PIR have made. So, if there have been six groups of pupils making potions, six elderly people will have disappeared.

Adding tension

Start the drama with TIR as King saying how pleased he is to see the servants. The PIR as servants bow to the King. Explain that there is a real problem.

Possible script:

'Someone in the palace is using magic to make people disappear! Just minutes ago [use the number of groups who made potions] elderly people disappeared right in front of me. I was in my royal chamber talking to some elderly people who are worried about a friend of theirs, a grandmother who had gone missing, when suddenly there was a puff of blue smoke and they all disappeared! Before they disappeared, they told me that the grandmother's family had written to you to ask if you would look for her in the palace, so I thought I'd come and see you first. Does anyone know what is going on?'

Give the PIR time to think and speak. The PIR may choose to lie and try to keep the book a secret, or may choose to explain what they have been doing.

This is what you do if:

Option 1: the PIR tell the King they have no idea what is going on, or make up a lie of some kind to cover up what actually happened;

Option 2: the PIR tell the King the truth about what happened.

Option 1

TIR as the King will believe the servants and ask them to help him find whoever is using bad magic to make the elderly people disappear. The King will say how glad he is to have the servants working for him because they are so trustworthy.

The teacher will change role to become the servant Reema again (remember to change your sign). Reema will try to persuade the PIR to blame (frame) other people, possibly the cook and the gardener. If the PIR object to this action, Reema will ask them to pretend they have looked everywhere for the people who have been using magic, but have found no clues as to who it might be.

The King will invite the servants to his royal chamber. Act out getting dressed in best clothes. Build a sense of expectation that the King is going to reward the servants for being loyal and hardworking.

Set up a scene where the PIR meet TIR as the King. As the PIR enter the royal chamber, get them to bow, then sit down. TIR as the King will be holding a scroll. You can rehearse this opening few seconds of the scene to capture a feeling of pomp and ceremony.

TIR as the King explains that, while he was helping to search the palace for Grandma Razi, he found a special scroll in a large cupboard in one of the rooms in the Fortune Tower. The scroll is very old and tells the tale of how, many years ago, the Prince who lived in the Fortune Tower was given a book of spells as a gift from a Queen who lived far away over the sea.

The King should ask the PIR if the story 'rings any bells' for them and if they know anything about a book of spells.

The tale is continued by telling the PIR that at first the Prince thought the book was the most wonderful of all gifts because the spells seemed to be written to do such good deeds. The Prince had his most clever servants try out the spells and paid a terrible cost. For he soon discovered that, every time a spell is cast or a potion made, an elderly person disappeared. As it happens, the Prince's own father, the King, being an elderly gentleman, disappeared that very day and he never saw him again.

The Prince was heartbroken and tried to destroy the book, but it would not burn and it could not be chopped up even with the biggest, sharpest axe the Prince could find. So, he put it in the Fortune Tower and left a warning so that anyone who found it would know that it was dangerous.

He wrote this account of what happened and left it so that others coming after his time would know about the book. Then the Fortune Tower was locked and no one was ever allowed to go in there again.

The King will then let the servants know that he has found out what they have been up to.

Possible script:

> *'The only people who have been in the Fortune Tower for hundreds of years are you! You cleaned the tower from top to bottom and yet you didn't mention that you found a book with spells in it. You took that book, didn't you?'*

Allow the PIR to respond. Then:

> *'I trusted you and you lied to me and stole a book from my palace. What do you have to say for yourselves?'*

Allow the PIR to respond. Stop the drama.

Reflect on the drama

- What do you think the servants are thinking?
- What are they feeling?
- What do you think they should say to the King?
- How is the King feeling?
- Will it help to tell the truth now?
- Will anything mend the relationship between the King and the servants?
- Could the servants have made better decisions at any point in the story?
- What might the consequences be for the servants?
- Who is responsible for the decisions the servants made? Why?

Option 2

TIR as the King will listen patiently to what the PIR have to tell him. The King will feed back what he has been told. The King will then explain all about the scroll as above.

The King will be most disappointed, but not angry, with the servants. The King will ask the PIR questions to prompt them to reflect on the consequences of the decisions they made.

- What did you think when you first noticed the warning on the front of the book?
- Whom did you think the book belonged to?
- What did you think I would feel if I found out you had taken the book?
- When did you first start to think that the book could be dangerous?
- How do you think the families feel about the disappearance of their grandparents?
- Would you be happy for them to know the grandparents disappeared because of you?
- If you could change any of your decisions, what would you have done differently?
- What do you think I should tell the families of the people who have disappeared?
- What have you learned from this experience?

Finally, the King will ask the PIR what should be done now the truth is known. Do not allow the pupils to attempt a magic answer! The King has banned the use of magic and spells and, in any case, spell-casting leads to loss of life.

PIR can:

- choose to tell the truth to the families of the grandparents who have disappeared
- apologise publicly
- apologise privately
- not tell, but find ways of helping the people who have lost grandparents
- any other positive solution (that doesn't involve punishment) that the PIR can suggest.

Reflect on the drama

- Why wasn't the King angry with the servants?
- How would you describe the way he behaved towards the servants?
- Do you think he handled the situation well? Why?
- What do you think the servants felt when they realised what they had done?
- Is there any way of making the end of this story a happy one?
- Would it help to apologise to the families of the people who disappeared?
- Do you know of any real situations in which people end up feeling the way the servants did in this story?
- Ask the pupils to draw the most important moment in the story. Ask each pupil to say why they have chosen that moment and annotate the drawing.

The optional happy ending

Play the story as far as the King's entry into the servants' quarters to speak to the servants. Have the King explain how the elderly people disappeared in front of him. Allow the PIR to have some thinking time to decide what they are going to tell the King (by having the King leave the servants' quarters to attend to an urgent message).

Tell the pupils that you are going to play Prince Aten. Tell them that the Prince seems to know exactly what has been going on and can bring the old people back. Sign your role with a sash or cloak. Role function: benevolent authority figure. The PIR bow as the Prince enters. He seems so impressive, full of goodness and authority.

Possible script:

> 'Good day to you. I am Prince Aten. I understand you have found the Magic Book and tried out some of its spells. The book plays a naughty trick, you know. Have you guessed what the trick is?'

Allow the pupils to explain if they can.

> 'Quite right! The book makes one elderly person disappear every time a spell is cast. When you cast your first spell, the one to help you escape from the tower, Grandma Razi disappeared. When you made the potions intended to help you find Grandma Razi, the elderly people who were here in the palace talking to my father disappeared. My father was very upset. One minute he was listening to them tell him how their friend Razi had gone missing and then in a puff of smoke they had vanished too!

> 'The book is a bit of mischief, but you were not to know that and I believe your hearts are good. Thankfully, I have learned many things on my travels and, with your agreement, I will make everything right. I will bring back all the elderly people who have disappeared and then take the book and hide it in a place where no one will ever find it again. Sit with me in a circle.'

Get the PIR sitting in a circle with TIR. Ask everyone to hold hands.

Narration

Talk as you take off the costume that signs your role. Tell the pupils that Prince Aten did indeed put everything right. He brought all the old people back. Everyone was relieved and happy. In time, Prince Aten became the King and was a very wise ruler and everyone in his kingdom lived happily ever after.

Final Reflection

- Is the book a force for good or evil?
- Was it wise to lock the book up in the tower?
- Were the servants good or bad?
- Was Reema good or bad?
- What kind of person is Prince Aten?
- Where has he been on his travels and what has he learned?
- Can you think of a better way of dealing with the book so other people aren't caught out?

Potential cross-curricular learning

Here are some of the areas of the curriculum that can be linked to the story and used to design activities of your own.

Cross-curricular links	**In the Foundation Stage:** **Personal, social and emotional development** Discussing the nature of trust and responsibility between persons of higher rank and those they are responsible for (parents, teachers, older friends and older siblings who might encourage children to follow their lead); understanding that some actions, however well intentioned, may have serious consequences; considering the effects of being involved in events that cause other people to be upset; recognising right and wrong. **Communication, language and literacy** Communicating by drawing, physical gesture and facial expression; speaking and listening to each other and to adults; learning about how stories are constructed. This story has a basic folktale plot and structure and, in common with many well known fairy tales, the main characters learn a lesson from the events. **Mathematical development** Discussing size and measurements of length, shape and space; carrying out activities designed to run alongside the fiction - for example, the King could ask for several new rugs to be made for the tower, which pupils could measure onto paper and then make a pattern with shapes to decorate; practising counting – using the cleaning equipment; weighing and measuring - especially if the PIR make cakes or other foods for the King as part of their work. The authority figure of the King could set the PIR a variety of tasks. **Knowledge and understanding of the world** Depending on where the story is set (a palace in India, Pakistan or the United Arab Emirates, or a castle in France, the United Kingdom or Romania, for example), pupils could learn about a country and its people and compare their own homes with homes elsewhere. There are also basic domestic jobs being done in the story that could be used as the basis for a discussion about routines at school and at home. **Physical development** The active nature of drama gives plenty of opportunity for controlled movement. A music and movement session could be based on the scene where the servants get blown around the tower. **Creative development** Pupils are asked to contribute their own ideas and make key decisions about what happens in the story. They learn about drama techniques such as Freeze Frame and Hot Seating. They learn to imagine a setting in a land different from the one in which they live. They contribute to the development of characters and work with others to create a shared imaginary experience. **In preparation for Key Stage One:** **Geography** Map and plan making; using geographical language; describing what places are like; studying life in a different country. **History** Studying famous people from the country the story is set in. **Science** Sc 3: Using the cleaning equipment for sorting and grouping objects; naming common types of material; using spell making to explore and describe the way in which everyday materials might change when they are heated or cooled. Sc 4: Discussing items that use electricity, such as a vacuum cleaner, kettle, iron;

	discussing light and dark, including sources of light.
	PSHE and citizenship Developing confidence and responsibility; recognising what is fair and unfair; learning from experiences; preparing to take an active role as citizens, such as taking part in discussions and making collective decisions; recognising options and the difference between right and wrong; developing good relationships and respecting the differences between people; recognising how our behaviour affects other people.
	Design technology Building towers with everyday items – stones, building blocks, empty boxes - with support structures such as a central core or using X-shaped braces.
	Art Studying designs from the country the story is set in; using the designs to inspire pictures – using specific colours, patterns and so on.
	Music Listening to music from the country the story is set in.
Literacy skills	Story construction; sequencing; character development; setting; including a problem; selecting a suitable ending; understanding the meaning of a story; understanding the folktale genre; familiarisation with the plot types Tragedy, and Voyage and Return; note-making in pictorial and written form; asking and answering questions; speaking and listening in pairs and groups.
Remember DfES thinking skills!	**Creating** Generating and extending ideas; applying imagination; looking for innovative outcomes. In the drama pupils are asked to imagine a range of events from the very ordinary cleaning activities of the servants to the much more fantastical scenes that involve the magic book. Pupils are asked to think about and act out events that are caused by the magic book. Pupils help to develop characters who are both in the drama and played by themselves or TIR. They are also asked to imagine the character Prince Aten, who is only briefly met at the end of the story but has a very important role to play in sorting out the difficulties the servants have got themselves into. Pupils can be encouraged to think about why Prince Aten has the ability to put things right when others cannot.
	Enquiring Asking relevant questions; posing and defining problems; predicting outcomes and anticipating consequences. This type of thinking is developed through discussions with TIR about what is happening in the story and about what course of action to take. The whole story is also a tale of what might happen if people do not ask enquiring questions. The palace staff find a resource (the book) and choose to use it without understanding how it works and what the consequences of using it might be.
	Reasoning Giving reasons for opinions and actions; drawing inferences and making deductions; explaining thoughts; making informed decisions and judgements. This type of thinking is developed during the drama when pupils discuss what the palace staff should do to solve their problems. At the end of the drama, PIR have to present their case to the King and TIR can prompt deeper thinking through questioning.
	Information processing Sorting and classifying; comparing and contrasting; sequencing. This type of thinking can be developed through discussion about the sequence of the story and systematic recording of the story, which can be displayed on a wall board or as a class book.
	Evaluating Examining what the story means; judging the value of what you have read, heard or done. This type of thinking is developed through the questions that get the pupils to reflect on the story. Did the pupils do the right things? If they could turn the clock back, would they do things differently?

Part 3

Projects for 5 – 7 year olds

How the Projects are Laid Out

All the projects in this section are set out in a common way.

Planning checklist

This lists the key organisational details: teaching time and space required; main props, equipment and resources needed; main teaching tools.

Teacher's overview

This section explains the nature of the project and outlines the reasons for doing it. It explains what children will get out of the project and how it connects to their developing life experience. The thinking behind the story is unravelled and the issues that are embedded in the story are made explicit so that the purposes of the project become crystal clear and the reflection questions make sense.

The Teacher's Overview also lists the characters in the story and summarises the plot.

When you have read the Planning Checklist and the Teacher's Overview, you will be clear about what you have to do and why you are doing it. In the body of the project, you are then given the step-by-step instructions that tell you how to proceed.

The body of the project

Each project has a series of standard phases for you to work through. These mirror the stages that all story-makers and all stories follow. Think of any film you've watched or novel you've read. The pivotal problem(s) and exacerbating tension(s) are not usually introduced until the audience has become engaged with the setting, the main characters and circumstances. The film-goers and readers have to be emotionally and intellectually hooked if the problems and tensions are to be sufficiently exciting for them. In the projects, this is achieved through the Getting Going and Building Belief phases. Therefore, they always come first.

Obviously, Finding an Ending comes towards the end!

Three other ingredients (Developing the Story, Introducing a Problem, Adding Tension) can occur, and re-occur, in any order. Think of any James Bond film or Doctor Who episode – it's easy to see how these elements are woven together. They are essential to any quality fiction.

The element of Reflection turns the fiction into personal learning. In grown-up films, novels and plays, the reflective element is usually implicit (the fiction makes you think) and this can happen because the audience has the life-experience and thinking abilities to operate in 'automatic reflection' mode. With young children, however, the process of reflection has to be explicit. By pausing the drama and asking questions, pupils are being inducted into reflective habits that are not yet established. In the projects that follow, Reflection is sometimes saved up to the end and sometimes it occurs at key points throughout. It's a moveable feast. To summarise, the standard phases of each project are:

- Getting going
- Building belief

- Developing the story
- Introducing a problem
- Adding tension
- Finding an ending
- Reflection.

Potential cross-curricular learning

Each project has so many potential links with the rest of the curriculum that you will have lots of fun spotting and pursuing them. The tables at the end of the projects give you a good number of pointers to start you off.

By the way ...

Wherever you see this symbol you will find the materials you need on the Resources CD inside the back cover of the book.

The Remedy Rocket

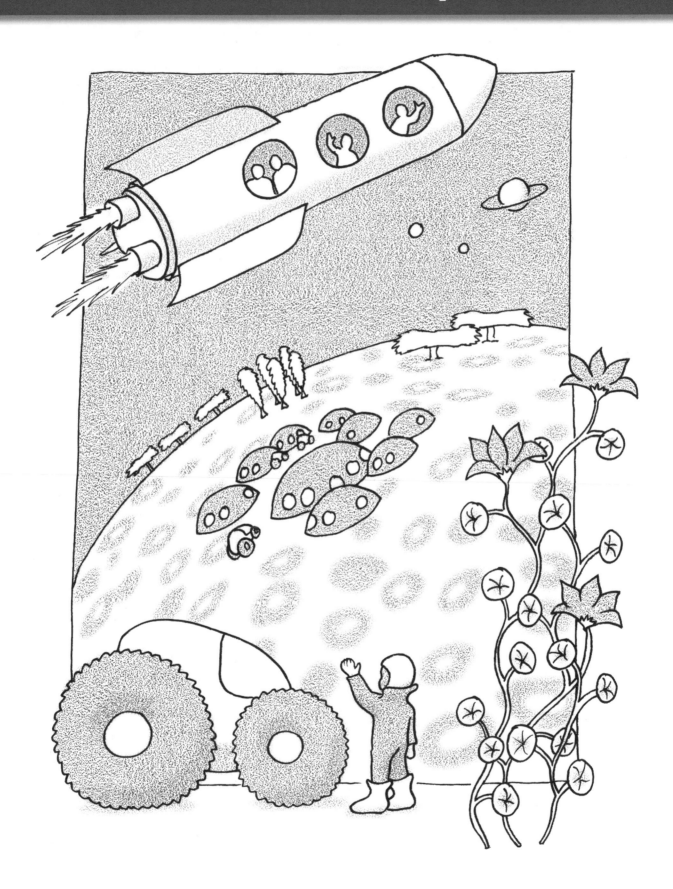

Planning checklist

Subject matter	Space rockets; space travel; planets; illness; medicines; hospital
Themes	Helping others; responsibility for others; sharing; cooperation; negotiation
Key resources and equipment	Costume items to sign TIR as Pilot Llewellyn, such as a body warmer, boots and tools (screwdrivers, hammers and so on) Costume items to sign TIR as Eirian such as a cloak, shawl or long coat **Props include** Pictures of space and planets (Spacepics.pdf) in folder Remedy Rocket on the Resources CD Illustrations of faces with different expressions (Expressions.pdf) Illustration of a spacesuit (Spacesuit.pdf) A biological picture of the human body (Body.pdf) Digital camera Cardboard boxes Lengths of fabric Sand tray Pebbles and stones
Organisation	**Time** Without optional extras: 8–10 hours With optional extras: 12–14 hours **Teaching space** A large space in a classroom Possible themes for the role play area include the inside of the rocket with tools, equipment and first-aid box for the pupils to play with
Main dramatic devices used	Teacher in Role Pupils in Role **Basic plot** Voyage and Return. The pupils go on a journey to a 'strange world' **Basic problem** Encountering the unexpected (an accident, not knowing vital information, strangers, illness, needing a resource) **Basic tensions** Being asked to share a precious resource (a change of plan, waiting for information, running out of time, being put on the spot)

Teacher's overview

There had to be at least one science-fiction story in the mini-projects because Sharon loves the genre, and here it is! This story is set in a future that is probably closer than we think. Although the TV puppet series (and more recently the film) *Thunderbirds* had a big influence on this tale, the inspiration for the space rocket actually came from the NASA space shuttle. When the children are asked to name the rocket in the story, this is in line with reality, as each shuttle has its own name. Incidentally, we have used some facts and figures from the NASA website (www.nasa.gov/home), including the speed at which the shuttle travels. Should you wish to do further research, there is plenty of information about the space programme there. There is also a section of the website 'for kids', which has lots of activities, stories, art and games.

This story is a rescue adventure in a similar vein to *Thunderbirds*. In fact, it would be very helpful to show the pupils some extracts from the film or the TV series (or other suitable science-fiction programmes) before you start the project, in order to help them visualise the story's settings, which make hefty demands on their young imaginations: the inside of a rocket; a planet where the colours of plants and trees are very different from those on Earth; and a barren wasteland. Although the locations are unfamiliar, the themes and issues of the drama are entirely pertinent to their young lives. For example, many of the situations faced by the PIR reflect a child's first few days in a new class, when so much is still unknown – the routines, the teacher, new classmates, the equipment and the curriculum. This particularly applies to the move from Foundation to KS1. The characters in the story are literally taking off to explore places they haven't seen before and to do things they haven't done before. In reality, at ages six and seven, brand-new experiences are being encountered all the time.

There are stories for KS1 pupils that contain space rockets, aliens and journeys to other worlds (such as Dav Pilkey's *Captain Underpants and the Invasion of the Incredibly Naughty Cafeteria Ladies from Outer Space; Q Pootle 5 in Space* by Nick Butterworth and *Fantastic Space Stories*, edited by Tony Bradman), but none of them have the real mettle of authentic science-fiction. The thrill of the genre does not lie in the entertainment value of futuristic settings and alien beings, but in its challenge to social, political and religious norms. Science-fiction creates a 'blank canvas' on which issues and dilemmas can be presented with great clarity. The journey into space, or to new dimensions, or through time, takes the characters away from the 'real' world and into settings where anything can happen. Consequently, 'universal' concerns (such as the right to interfere in other people's cultures) can be thrown into sharp relief and viewed with a fresh eye. In this regard, *Star Trek* is classic. Adult audiences are similarly gripped by *Babylon 5, Star Gate, Andromeda* and *Battlestar Galactica*. Science-fiction is serious stuff.

On a lighter note, episodes in the new series of *Doctor Who* tackle some major issues, such as the grip of the media, the unthinking nature of the mass population, the deception of politicians and the plight of single-parent families. *The Hitchhiker's Guide to the Galaxy* discusses the meaning of 'life, the universe and everything' (to which the answer is 42!) and even *Red Dwarf* has its mature moments.

Then we start on films. The central question in *Blade Runner* is, 'What does it mean to be human?'; *Alien* deals with the lengths to which governments will go to possess the ultimate weapon; *War of the Worlds* presents the inevitability of predation; and, of course, *Star Wars* deals with spiritual forces and the eternal battle of good versus evil. *The Remedy Rocket* is true to the science-fiction genre, but, of course, neither the plot nor the issues are anywhere near as complex as those of its grown-up counterparts. It is in the tradition of Gerry Anderson's famous creations, from *Supercar* onwards.

You will notice that a lot of attention is paid to health and safety in our story (for example, making sure that the spacesuits are fitted properly and that the air supply does not run out). This reinforces the message that adults are always giving to children to 'be careful'. These days, life is full of risks and we want children to be as safe as possible, so getting them into the habits of pausing, thinking ahead, weighing things up and being prepared can only do good. Related story books include *Rabbit's Golden Rule Book* by Pam Adams, which answers a number of personal safety questions, especially about going off with strangers; *Don't Talk To Strangers, Pooh* by Kathleen Weidner Zoehfeld, which deals with the same subject; and *Fire in the Fryer* and *Dangerous Pirate Treasure*, both by Hedley Griffin, which look at dangers around the house and garden.

Another aspect of growing up that concerns children is illness. Young children are interested in health problems, especially ones that affect them frequently, such as minor cuts and grazes. In the playground, a sticking plaster is as a badge of honour. This curiosity about people being poorly is all part of developing an understanding of how the body works and how it can be healed. Of course, the amount of sympathy received for a relatively minor bump and bruise also has its appeal! So, when the characters in the story are asked to help people who are sick, the pupils will easily empathise with them.

On a heavier note, the colony on the barren planet faces the prospect of death. Dealing with such a morbid, but inevitable, feature of life is hard for such young children. Nonetheless, many pupils will have experienced bereavement, or will soon do so (a pet or grandparent, perhaps), and so *The Remedy Rocket* might provide a way into sensitive discussion or counselling. Not surprisingly, there are few books for young children on the subject. However, *Ghostwings* by Barbara Joose (remembering a much-loved grandmother), *We Love Them* by Martin Waddle (the natural death of a pet dog) and *Michael Rosen's Sad Book* by Michael Rosen (dealing with the death of his son) are rare examples.

There are two further issues embedded in the story: how do you decide whether you can trust people you have never met before; and how far are you prepared to sacrifice what you want in order to help others? The story places the children in the mode of parents or carers. The pupils' characters have the skills and resources to help a sick colony on the barren planet, but there is a cost to themselves if they stay and provide the assistance. This situation confronts the class with questions about torn loyalties and competing responsibilities, as well as the tension between personal needs and the needs of others. These conflicts of interest raise the idea of deferring gratification, something that children of this age are beginning to explore. Perhaps you can help pupils to see a parallel with working parents or carers who have to earn an income, or who want to further their career, and at the same time need to care for a dependent child.

Notes for those interested in the history:

- Hippocrates was a Greek physician born in 460 BCE on the Greek island of Kos. He became known as the founder of medicine and was regarded as the greatest physician of his time
- Asklepios was the Greek god of healing

- The Asklepion is an ancient building on Kos that was founded by Hippocrates as a medical school and later used as a sanatorium.

Role-play area

The interior of a space rocket, plus an area for 'exploring' once the rocket has landed. A hospital with a laboratory.

The cast of characters

- The space rocket pilot: Anwen Llewellyn who is confident, competent, helpful and experienced in space travel (TIR)
- Astronauts: new to the job (PIR)
- Dr Hippocrates: a senior doctor who is friendly and helpful (TIR)
- Eirian: a representative of a community on a barren planet (TIR)

Summary of the plot

The story is divided up into scenes, which we suggest you photograph so that the pictures can be used for language activities at the end of the drama.

Scene 1   **The astronauts prepare for their journey into space**

The new astronauts meet their pilot and learn about the space rocket they will be travelling in. They practise putting on their spacesuits.

Scene 2   **The astronauts take off in their space rocket for a test flight**

The new astronauts are taken for a test flight by the pilot.

Scene 3   **The astronauts arrive at the planet Asklepios**

The astronauts are given their first mission, which is to collect some medicines from the planet Asklepios that are needed back on earth. This is their first opportunity to see a different planet and to use the space cars.

Scene 4   **The astronauts collect the medicine**

The medicine is loaded into the cars and taken back to the space rocket.

Scene 5   **Something goes wrong with the space rocket**

All seems to be going well, but then a loud bang is heard and the pilot announces that there is a problem with the space rocket. The pilot tells the astronauts she will have to land the space rocket on an unknown planet so that repairs can be carried out.

Scene 6   **The astronauts realise they are not alone on the planet**

The space rocket lands safely and the astronauts put on their spacesuits because they need air as well as warmth and protection. A radio message tells them that there are other people on the planet. The other people invite the astronauts to stay with them, but the astronauts are not sure what to do and don't know whether they should trust the strangers.

Scene 7   The other people send a message to say they are ill

Another message is received from the strangers to tell the astronauts not to come to their base after all because a number of them have fallen ill.

Scene 8   The people on the planet need further help

Arrangements are made to talk to Earth and get permission to give the medicines the astronauts collected from Asklepios to the strangers. The astronauts take the medicines to the strangers. The space rocket is ready to leave for home but the strangers ask for help to make sure their air-making machine is working properly. The astronauts go to help using an all terrain space vehicle.

Scene 9   The people on the planet want even more help

The strangers ask to borrow the space rocket to take some of their families home to Earth. The astronauts have to decide whether they are prepared to stay on the planet and wait for the rocket to return before they can go home themselves.

Scene 10   The end

The PIR decide how the story ends.

Getting going

Show the pupils pictures of rockets, space and planets (Spacepics.pdf in folder Remedy Rocket on the Resources CD). Discuss what space is and what planets are and explain that together you and the pupils are going to act out a story about a journey in a space rocket. Tell the pupils they will be playing astronauts.

Scene Drawing: the space rocket

With all the children gathered round, draw a large picture of a space rocket (a shape similar to the space shuttle would work well). Talk about the rocket as you draw it and incorporate as many of the pupils' suggestions as you can. Tell the children that they are going to be astronauts and that each of them has a cabin (a small bedroom) in the rocket. Give the rocket a name.

Building belief

Allocate an area of the classroom to be used as the flight deck of the space rocket throughout the drama. Get the pupils involved in designing and 'making' the flight deck, using the tables to represent instrument panels and other devices. Cardboard boxes can be used for computers and machines of various kinds. Use what you have readily available, such as lengths of fabric to 'dress' the imaginary setting. For example, a piece of fabric draped over a chair easily turns a piece of ordinary classroom furniture into a seat on a space rocket. Decide where the door is and where the where the spacesuits are stored.

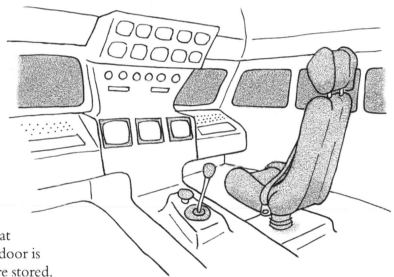

Optional Extra

Mathematics Ma 2 and 3

Pupils can be given tasks to do while they are in the role-play area. Set up some folders and explain to the pupils that they contain the astronauts' tasks. Put mathematical tasks and puzzles into the folders. These can be calculations, or activities to do with shapes, length or area. A classroom assistant can support pupils who are doing the tasks.

Tell the children that the astronauts are each allowed to take a small bag onto the space rocket with them. PIR as astronauts act out packing their own bag. As they do so, go round talking with them about what they are taking and why. Encourage the children to tell each other what they are packing.

Drawing in Role: items for the journey

Get the pupils into small groups of two or three and give each group a large sheet of paper and marker pens. Ask the pupils to draw what they are taking with them on the space journey. As you walk round, ask the pupils why they are taking this or that. Annotate some of their drawings with their reasons. We often get pupils to do this task because it indicates how their understanding of stories is developing. Over time, in different dramas, it is interesting to note how the choices pupils make become more reasoned and more appropriate to the situation they are about to act out.

It is worth preparing yourself for the next part of the drama in advance by thinking through the details of the spacesuit you are going to mime putting on. Being able to talk with confidence about details such as the fastenings and exactly how they are done up and undone really supports the pupils' imaginations. As you will see, we have provided a possible script to give you an idea of the level of detail.

Scene 1: The astronauts prepare for their journey into space

Tell the pupils that every person who goes out into space needs to wear a special spacesuit. The pilot of the space rocket is going to show them how to put the suit on and tell them why it is important to wear it when they are out in space. The suit and helmet are obviously required to provide warmth and an air supply. Also, the fabric of spacesuit is strong enough to stop small particles of rock travelling at very high speed from getting through.

Tell the pupils that you are going to play the pilot and explain how you will sign your role. You might do this with a pair of easy-to-slip-on boots, and a suitable jacket. Role function: benevolent authority figure. Tell the pupils that they are going to pretend to be new astronauts who have never been on a space rocket before.

Sign your role. Begin the drama by acting out (use tools if you have some, otherwise mime) fixing part of the radio communications system. You need to be engaged with your job and focused on the space rocket to make clear that your character is primarily interested in piloting the craft. Ask the PIR to gather round.

Possible script (the tone is confident and informal):

> 'Oh, hi! Sorry, just trying to fix this radio. It went on the blink last time I went out into space, but I think it's just a loose wire. I guess you must be the new crew come to work with me on the rocket. [Use the rocket's name if you have one]. I'm the pilot, Anwen Llewellyn. Gather yourselves round here, then. Right, what do you know about space rockets?'

Allow time for PIR to respond.

'Well, this rocket is the best of her kind: fast, easy to pilot and the crew's quarters are comfortable. Once we are in the rocket, I can turn on the air-making machine, which means we don't have to wear our suits all the time. But, as you know, there is no air out in space and some planets don't have an atmosphere, either, so these suits will be your lifeline! The rocket is also equipped with state of the art space cars and an all terrain vehicle big enough for all of us to ride in.'

'Now, I'm going to tell you how to put your suit on, so listen and watch carefully and follow my instructions.'

Get ready to take some digital photographs of the pupils as they act out getting dressed up in their spacesuits.

'Pick up the bottom part of the suit, hold it out in front of you. You can see that it's an all-in-one piece with boots and trousers fixed together. You need to step into the boots first.

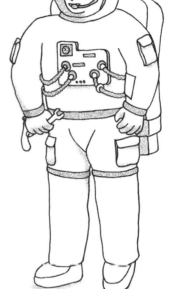

'Now put the top part of the suit on. The top part is very heavy and stiff and has no sleeves yet. Put your arms through the arm holes carefully. Pull the trousers up to your waist and make sure the trousers and the top are fastened together tightly with the metal ring fastener.

'Put the sleeves on and make sure the metal fasteners are fully closed. Now put this communications helmet on. It looks like a balaclava and it fits snugly on your head. It has the microphone built into it.

'Connect up your water tube.'

Give PIR time to respond.

'Make sure the straps are done up well. Have a walk around in them now. [TIR demonstrates walking in heavy boots]. Feels strange at first, doesn't it? You'll soon get used to it and, when you are out on a planet with less gravity than Earth, you'll be grateful you've got them.

'OK, air tanks next. These things are really heavy. They have two hours of air in them. Put your arm through the strap here and put it on your back like a backpack. See this tube? It connects to your helmet.

'Get your outer helmet next, put it on and secure the catches like this. Get the tube I showed you and connect it to your helmet like this.

'Put your gloves on. Make sure you have sealed them at the cuffs so the suit can stay pressurised. Press this button so that once the helmet screen is down we can still talk to each other. This button switches the radio on and is connected to the radio communication system, the one I was fixing just as you arrived.

'Can you all hear me? [If PIR say they can't hear you, do a little mimed fixing of communications systems].

'I hope you can all remember how to put on your suit because sometimes we have to "suit up" really quickly. You will need your suit to give you air and to keep you safe and comfortable.

'I'm going to take you for a ride in our rocket now so that you can see how she works. After the flight we'll all need a good night's sleep because tomorrow morning we have a mission. Our mission is to visit a planet called Asklepios a long way away and collect some medicine that has been made there. We'll be away from home for a few days so you'll need to bring your bags and I'll give you a cabin to sleep in. As the space rocket has an air-making machine, you won't need to wear your spacesuits when we are travelling.'

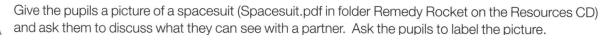

Optional Extra

Science Sc 1, Sc 2 and Sc 3

Pupils can be shown pictures and given information about spacesuits. Real spacesuits are known as *extravehicular mobility units* (EMUs).

Give the pupils a picture of a spacesuit (Spacesuit.pdf in folder Remedy Rocket on the Resources CD) and ask them to discuss what they can see with a partner. Ask the pupils to label the picture.

Scene 2: The astronauts take off in their space rocket for a test flight

Act out climbing into the space rocket and preparing to take off by making several checks on the systems by radio to people at launch control.

Possible script:

> 'Launch control, this is Pilot Llewellyn, on-line and requesting pre-launch checks.
> Communications? Check.
> Heat sensors? Check.
> Fuel? Check.
> Engines? Check.
> Navigation? Check.'

Count down to take off and then take off. Act out the flight. In role, talk to the pupils about your journey as an in-role narration. Explain that the rocket is travelling at 25,000 miles per hour and will soon be past the clouds and out of the Earth's atmosphere and into space. Tell the pupils that the rocket will head towards the Moon but will be turning back after a while. We can't go all the way to the Moon as it would take us three days to get there and three days to get back! Make the flight last long enough for it to feel as if the PIR have been on a journey, then bring the space rocket back to earth.

Stop the drama.

Out of role, show the children pictures of space and space rockets again. Explain again that in space there is no air, so the astronauts have to have an air-making machine in the rocket. Explain that people move about differently in space because there is no gravity. Demonstrate how people move in space. Show a video clip if possible.

Choice of pupil tasks

1. Ask the pupils to draw or paint a picture of the space rocket in the story. Encourage them to include lots of detail.
2. Make a junk model of the space rocket, again with plenty of detail.

Developing the story

Out of role, tell the pupils that, when the story starts again, it will be the next morning and the astronauts will set off on their mission to a planet far, far away. They have to collect some important medicines that are made on the planet and are needed on Earth. Tell the pupils that Anwen has been doing lots of jobs on the rocket all morning, making sure that everything is working properly and she will be there to meet them when they arrive for their first tour of duty.

Tell the pupils that they will have to pick up the bags that they packed earlier and, when everyone gathers back together, you will sign your role as Anwen and the story will start again. Show the pupils the pictures they drew earlier of the things they would take with them, to remind them of their imaginary bags. Ask the pupils to go into role as the astronauts and let them have some time to act out collecting their belongings, then gather them together as a group again.

In role as Pilot Llewellyn, greet the PIR by shaking hands with a few of them and congratulating them on being about to set off on their first mission. Get them to put their bags in the cabin rooms, unpack and report back to the flight deck. Any other areas of the classroom can be temporarily used as cabin rooms.

Take some more digital photographs during this scene.

Organise the PIR into small groups, all sitting on the flight deck with various jobs to do. It will help to allocate the jobs to different physical areas. The pupils will be pressing buttons on computer panels to:

- check the engines (Area 1)
- monitor the rocket's speed (Area 2)
- check the heat sensors (Area 3)
- keep the air machine working (Area 4)
- check the atmosphere and temperature inside the rocket (Area 5)
- measure the distance between home and the planet (Area 6)
- check the route to the planet (Area 7)
- seal the doors inside the rocket (Area 8)
- speak to launch control on the radio (Area 9)
- check fuel levels (Area 10).

NB: These jobs will mean very little to young pupils, but they sound 'right' and that makes it more 'real'.

Act out taking off.

Possible script (adopt a more formal, professional tone this time):

> *'Launch control, this is Pilot Llewellyn, on-line and requesting pre-launch checks.*
>
> *Communications? Check.*
>
> *Heat sensors? Check.*
>
> *Fuel? Check.*
>
> *Engines? Check.*
>
> *Navigation? Check.*
>
> *Cabin doors sealed. Check.*
>
> *Please fasten your seat belts. Forward rocket boosters ready. Crew, stand by for take-off. Take off in five, four, three, two, one. Here we go!'*

During the take-off, ask PIR if they can confirm that information. For example, 'Could Area 10 confirm that the fuel tanks are OK?' Ask the PIR to confirm by saying 'check'.

Act out a juddering climb into the sky. When the space rocket is out into space, TIR tells the crew they can undo their seat belts and relax for a while. Stop the drama.

Reflect on the drama

Out of role, ask the pupils to say what part of the story they've liked best so far and why.

Setting up a role-play area

You could set up a role-play area as the interior of a space rocket at this point in the project.

Developing the story further

Scene 3: The astronauts arrive at the planet Asklepios

Tell the pupils that the story has moved on in time and the space rocket has arrived at the planet Asklepios (the name of the Greek god of healing). The PIR must prepare to land the space rocket on the surface of the planet. TIR tells the PIR that this planet has air like our home planet Earth, so spacesuits will not be needed.

To land the rocket, act out the same checking routine you used for take-off.

Once the rocket has landed, lead the PIR out onto the planet. Tell the PIR you have never been to this planet before. Point out the very different colours.

Take photographs of the crew on this unusual planet.

Possible script:

'Careful how you come down the ladder. Hey, look! The trees and grass are all blue and red colours. Look at these flowers – they're green! The sky is green too. It's amazing! Look at that pond – the water's yellow. I've got to take some photographs. Come on, I'll take a photograph of you. Stand here by this blue tree.'

Tell the PIR that they will have to use the space cars to travel to the planet hospital to pick up the medicine they've come to collect. Tell them that the cars are in the cargo hold of the rocket. Act out pulling the big cargo hold door open and tell the PIR to select their car. Tell the PIR to follow you and act out driving the space cars. Make the journey exciting by going faster and more slowly, 'screeching' round bends, braking suddenly and so on!

Photograph the car journey.

Arrive at the hospital. Get out of the cars. Tell the PIR that you have just seen an old friend to whom you want to say hello and ask them if they will go and collect the medicine from Dr Hippocrates without you.

Stop the drama.

Optional Extra

Science Sc 2

Talk with the pupils about hospitals. Ask if any members of the class have been inside a hospital in real life; if it is appropriate, ask pupils to share their experiences. There may obviously be circumstances around hospital visits that could be distressing for individual pupils, so teachers and assistants will need to make their own professional judgements about the appropriateness of topics involving health and hospitals.

Make a list of people who work in hospitals. Provide the pupils with resources for research, such as books, video film of people who work in hospitals, posters, leaflets, websites on the computer and worksheets. Place the resources around the room at 'information stations'. Information should be accessible in a variety of ways so that different levels of reading ability are catered for.

Put the pupils into teams of three.

Ask the pupils to find:

- five facts about doctors
- five facts about nurses
- the names of three hospital departments and what they do.

Tell the pupils they can research the information in any way they choose but they have to be able to answer questions about doctors, nurses and hospital departments when it is 'test time'.

Tell the pupils how long they have to find information and at what time the 'test' will be.

Offer pupils either a sheet of plain paper or a worksheet to record their information.

'Test time' should be fun and be conducted in a quiz-show style, giving each team time to confer before answering. At 'test time' ask each team a question in turn and keep scores. Questions can be adjusted for each team so as to ensure success!

Debrief the process of researching. Questions might include:

- How did the teams organise themselves? (Did they split the team up or work together?)
- How were tasks allocated?
- How did pupils record what they found out from the resources?
- What helped the team to get the job done?
- What hindered the team from getting the job done?
- What would the teams do differently next time to improve the speed and accuracy of gathering information?

Tell the pupils that in the next part of the story they will be in the hospital. Discuss what a hospital is and what it looks like inside, and list some of the things that happen there.

The teacher changes role to become Dr Hippocrates. Tell the pupils who you are going to be and sign the role, ideally with a white coat. Role function: benevolent authority figure.

Scene 4: The astronauts collect the medicine

TIR as Dr Hippocrates greets the PIR and invites them to look around the hospital. Act out a 'tour' of the hospital, ending with the research laboratory, where new medicines are made and tested.

Possible script:

> *'As you can see, this is a very modern hospital and the staff are well trained. This is where we mend broken bones. Has anyone here ever had a broken arm or leg?'*

Give pupils time to respond. Then:

> *'I'll take you to where we look inside people's bodies with our special machines. These machines can show us pictures of bones and the parts of our body that are under our skin.'*

Show the PIR a biological picture of the human body (Body.pdf in folder Remedy Rocket on the Resources CD) or an X-ray, if you can get one.

> *'This is the department that tests blood. As you know, we can learn lots of things about a person's body from looking carefully at their blood. We have patients here from many different planets, so we have to teach our nurses about lots of different types of blood.*
>
> *'Here are some of the wards where patients who need to be looked after stay while we give them medicines or operations. [Move on]. And here is our medicine laboratory, where we make and store medicines. The medicine you are collecting is in here ready for you.'*

Show the PIR where the boxes of the medicine they have come to collect are stacked. Act out picking up the heavy boxes and loading them into the PIR's space cars.

Photograph the pupils loading the boxes of medicine.

As Dr Hippocrates, ask the PIR to tell Pilot Llewellyn that the hospital will not be able to supply any more medicine until next year, as they have used up all the ingredients. Wish the PIR a safe journey.

Stop the drama.

Reflect on the drama

Out of role, talk with the pupils about what has happened in this part of the story. Discuss their visit to the hospital. Ask them what parts of the hospital they visited with Dr Hippocrates and what jobs people were doing there.

Briefly discuss the character of Dr Hippocrates. Possible questions:

- Is she a good character? How might they judge?
- What words would describe Dr Hippocrates best?

Remind the pupils that Dr Hippocrates said the hospital had used up all the ingredients for the medicine they have just collected, so they won't be able to have any more for a whole year.

Optional Extra

Art

Make a collage picture of the planet Asklepios. This could be done as a small group activity, or individuals could make their own pictures.

Use different materials to show the different textures of the landscape. Remember that the colours of the planet Asklepios are not the same as they are in our world.

Pupils might find it interesting to see pictures by Fauvist artists, who used colours in unusual ways in their landscape paintings.

Scene 5: Something goes wrong with the space rocket

Tell the pupils that, when the story starts again, the pilot and the astronauts will be back in their space rocket and travelling towards home. Ask the pupils to get into their places on the flight deck.

Explain to the pupils that in the next part of the drama something goes wrong with the space rocket. Agree a sound that you will make that will indicate a loud explosion that is heard by all the astronauts. (The sound could be made by banging a drum or cymbal.) Teacher and pupils go into role.

Possible script:

> 'Oh, no! Did you hear that bang? That was the rocket booster engine blowing up. I'm going to have to land the rocket on the nearest planet for repairs. Everyone get into the emergency landing seats.'

Get the pupils to sit close together and remind them to fasten their seat belts. Seat yourself in front of the group, facing them.

> 'I'll just bring up the communications systems here. Yes, we're in luck: there's a planet nearby. It doesn't tell us whether anyone lives there or not. There's a very poor atmosphere, almost no air. OK, hold on tight – this will be a bumpy ride.'

Act out a bumpy landing. Once the space rocket has landed, increase the tension by noticing that the rocket's air-making machine has broken, too, which means that everyone must quickly get into their spacesuits.

> 'That was a rough landing and we've managed to break the air-making machine too, so quickly unclip your seat belts and get into your spacesuits. We only have about five minutes of air left in the rocket. Don't forget to connect your air tanks to your helmets. And switch your communicators on so we can talk to each other.'

Act out getting into the spacesuits. Take photographs.

TIR tells the PIR to pick up a toolbox each and leads them out onto the surface of the planet. Imagine for yourself a desert landscape with rocks and sand. The space rocket crashed into the sand and is part buried. Before you leave the space rocket, tell the pupils what you can see and impress upon them the need to be careful.

Possible script:

> 'This is a very different planet. There are no plants, trees or grass at all. All I can see is sand and a few large rocks. It looks pretty windy, as the sand is blowing about all over the place. We are going to have to fix our air-making machine as quickly as we can. There isn't much air out here, so we will have to keep our suits on outside and use our air tanks. Remember, they have only two hours of air in them, so we won't be able to stay out on the planet surface for long.'

Remind the PIR that it is harder to move around in the spacesuits. Demonstrate by moving slowly. Do not worry if some pupils are not able or willing to join in with the idea of the different way of moving, just continue to act out moving slowly yourself. Believe in your role and eventually the pupils will join in.

Explain that the space rocket is part buried in the sand and that it will have to be dug out. Give PIR jobs to do:

- digging (everyone)
- unscrewing metal panels
- taking the engines out and mending them
- building a screen to stop the winds blowing the sand onto the space rocket again
- mending the air-making machine
- checking that the landing legs of the space rocket are working
- checking that the doors can be sealed.

Young pupils are not expected to know exactly how to act out these jobs. Their actions are meant only to represent the kinds of things characters might do in a crisis of this kind. The intention of the jobs and the language used is to let the pupils know they are being taken seriously in 'adult' roles.

Photograph the pupils working on their tasks.

Move round each group and talk to them about what they are doing. Offer the children tools to help with their jobs and suggest that they borrow tools from other people.

Still working in role, stop the children and ask them to come back into the rocket to have some food. Act out having space meals (in reality, these liquidised meals in packs are 'eaten' via a 'straw' through the helmet). Comment on the fact that there isn't much food or water in the food store and tell the children you hope the rocket can be mended quickly.

Optional Extra

Science Sc 4, En 1

Make a dark den.

Identify an area of the classroom that can be used to make a dark den. Put the pupils into small groups. Give each group materials to make a dark den: blankets, boxes and so on.

When the pupils have made a den, let them play in it and tell them that they will have to explain what it is like inside the dark den.

Give pupils a torch and a box of different materials to take into the den. Some of the materials should have reflective surfaces.

Ask the pupils to look at the materials in the dark den and sort out:

1. which ones are easiest to see in the dark;
2. which ones reflect light back most effectively when a torch is shone on them.

Introducing a problem

Scene 6: The astronauts realise they are not alone on the planet

Tell the PIR that you have tried to get a radio message to Earth but the long-range radio transmitter is also broken, so it won't work over such a long distance. Notice a sound on the radio. Act surprised. Let the PIR know there is a message coming in, but it can't be from Earth. It must be short range. If you can have the message pre-recorded on tape, that will create a good effect!

The message is from a colony of people on the planet who saw the space rocket crash and are inviting the crew to take shelter with them.

Possible script:

'This is a message for the pilot and crew of the space rocket that recently crash-landed on our planet. We are a colony of people from Earth who are exploring this planet. We have a base station near to you and plenty of air and food to share. We have sent a message to Earth to let them know what has happened to you. Please come and stay with us until someone from Earth arrives to rescue you. We will send a radio beacon to guide you here, so just keep your communications tuned into this frequency.'

Discuss with the PIR whether or not they should go to the base station. The discussion will illuminate how well the pupils are following the story. If they have understood the circumstances the crew are in, they may be able to discuss the issues spontaneously:

- lack of food and water
- limited air
- the need to communicate with Earth
- can the people be trusted?

149

Prompt the pupils by asking questions such as:

* What do we know about these people?
* What questions should we ask them?
* Will it be OK to leave the space rocket?
* What if we don't like the other people when we get there?
* Could we ask them for food, water and air and not stay with them? How could we ask?
* Should we ignore them and hope that we can fix the space rocket before our air tanks run out?

Discuss the options with the PIR and make a decision. Stop the drama.

Model Making: the surface of the planet

Make a model of the setting using a large sand tray and sand, with stones to represent the rocks and toys to represent the space rocket, base station and people. Discuss human and physical features as the model is being made.

Photograph the model.

Let the pupils play with the model and talk with them about the story and what it might be like to be in a place that is sandy, windy and without plants. Ask the pupils if they think it is hot or cold on the planet.

Set up a sand tray on the floor that pupils can stand in with their socks and shoes off. Talk with them about what the sand feels like under their feet.

If possible, set up a deep sand pit outside so that pupils can have a go at digging in sand and moving sand around. Discuss what the difficulties of digging the space rocket out of the sand might be. Discuss the different ways in which dry sand and wet sand behave.

Optional Extras

Science Sc 2

Compare different landscapes. Discuss what the landscape of the planet is like. Refer to the sand and rock model. Show pupils pictures of fields and pasture land. Compare the two landscapes and then give the pupils time to think about the conditions needed for different sorts of plants and animals to live.

Ask the pupils to what kinds of plants and animals might be found in the area around the school. Make a record of ideas. Discuss how the pupils could check out the different sorts of plants and animals in the locality.

List the equipment needed and then take the pupils outside to investigate.

Record findings and compare them to the initial record.

If possible, do the same exercise for different locations, such as a wooded area, a beach, a park.

Geography

Sit the pupils in a circle. Place a large piece of paper on the floor (several pieces of flipchart-sized paper would work well). Draw a plan of the school's locality and discuss the human and physical features. Record where plants and animals have been seen on the plan. Compare this to a real map of the area and note the differences.

Art

Look at pictures that show scenes at night or in the dark. Discuss how the artists give the effect of light in the dark.

Use Georgia O'Keeffe's painting *Radiator Building*. Show pupils how to get the effect of light in windows.

Ask pupils to paint the base station at night with

Scene 7: The other people send a message to say they are ill

Another message is received from the colony. This can be done as before, with a tape recording posing as a radio message, or you can just tell the PIR what was said. The communication tells them not to come to stay with them after all because some of the people on the base station have an illness.

Possible script:

'Base Station to Space Rocket. So sorry. Please stay where you are. It may not be safe to stay here after all, as several people have become ill. We will bring air tanks, food and water halfway to you. Then you can collect them. We have radioed Earth to let them know what is happening. Base Station out.'

Ask PIR to get into their space cars and drive out to collect the air tanks food and water. Bring them back to the space rocket and act out making repairs as before.

Gather the PIR together to listen to a new message from the base station. Help from Earth will not be arriving soon, because there are no rockets available for a rescue mission.

Possible script:

'Base Station to Space Rocket. We have just had a message from Earth. No rockets available for rescue mission. We will do what we can to help you. People here are feeling very poorly. No medicine left. We will contact you later to see if you are OK. Base Station out.'

In role, remind the PIR that that there are medicines on board the space rocket that were collected from the hospital on Asklepios. Discuss with the PIR whether the space rocket crew should give the medicine to the people at the base station and if they have the right to do so.

Photograph the pupils making their decision.

Pros and cons to weigh up:

- the space rocket crew are collecting and delivering – they don't own the medicine themselves
- Dr Hippocrates told them that no more medicine could be made for a year, as all the ingredients had been used up
- it isn't known what the medicine is going to be used for on Earth – there could be an emergency there
- we don't know very much about the people at the base station
- we don't know if the people at the base station are telling the truth
- we don't know if it is the right medicine for the people on the base station.

Explain to the PIR that is it is difficult to make a decision without further information. Ask the PIR what questions we should ask the mission controllers back on Earth. Tell the PIR that you will radio the base station and ask if they will send our questions to Earth and then relay the answers back to us. Work with the PIR to formulate the key questions. Write the questions down (and draw attention to the use of the question mark).

Get the PIR acting out fixing the space rocket while TIR acts out speaking to the base station on the radio. When you have finished the radio message, inspect the work that the PIR have done and announce that the space rocket is, thankfully, fixed. Praise the PIR for their skilful and swift work. Get the PIR acting out tidying up the tools and packing their belongings back into the rocket.

Still in role, gather everyone together and tell them they are ready to leave and just waiting for the message from Earth about the medicine. Tell the PIR that if they are going to leave today, it must be before the sun rises or the space rocket will not be able to take off. The sunrise will mean that rocket and astronauts will have rotated too far away from Earth and there won't be enough fuel to get home.

Suggest that the PIR wait in the space rocket, turn on the repaired air-making machine, take their spacesuits off and make something to eat and drink while they are waiting. Stop the drama.

Out of role, gather the pupils together in a comfortable sitting space. Explain to the pupils that the crew of the space rocket have to wait for a few hours and then they get a message on their radio from the base station.

Possible script:

> 'Base station to space rocket. Here is the reply from Earth for you. Please use medicine to help colonists on the base station. Unable to get help to them for a long time. Hope you are able to fix your space rocket. Earth out.'

Explain to the pupils that, when the drama starts again, you are going to change your role and will play a person from the base station. Show the pupils how you intend to sign the role, perhaps with a long coat or shawl. This character's role function is: victim.

Explain to the PIR that the astronauts are going to use their all terrain space vehicle which has a large fuel tank and is therefore more suited to the longer journey they are about to make to the Base Station. Tell the pupils that the second half of the journey is also very rocky and the all terrain space vehicle will be safer to travel in than the space cars. Describe what the all terrain vehicle looks like on the outside and explain that everyone will be able to travel together as there are seats in the back.

Start the drama with PIR loading the medicines into their all terrain space vehicle and driving to the base station. Impress upon the PIR that they must be back as soon as they can so that the space rocket can take off before the sun rises.

Discuss with the pupils what the inside of the all terrain space vehicle would look like and how the astronauts would be seated. Use the chairs and tables in the classroom to make the layout of the vehicle. You might want to practise acting out driving over bumpy ground.

When the PIR have acted out the drive to the base station, gather them together and greet them in role as Eirian, one of the leaders from the base station. The character is worried and sad but dignified.

Adding tension

Scene 8: The people on the planet need further help

TIR first of all asks how the repairs are coming along and is very pleased to hear that the rocket is now fixed. She goes on to explain that many of the people at the base station are very poorly and are very grateful for the medicine. Eirian wonders if the space rocket crew might do one big favour before they leave the planet. She explains that, because so many people are poorly, it has been difficult to look after the machines that make the air in the base station. Some of the machines have started to break down and she hoped that the space rocket crew might help to fix them.

Act out walking the PIR to the air-machine room.

Possible script:

> '*Congratulations on mending your rocket. You must all be very skilful. It's so good of you to bring us the medicine. Please, can I beg one more favour of you? So many of our people have been poorly that we haven't been able to look after our air-making machines properly. Several of them have started to break down. Please would you stay a little while and help us to fix them? It shouldn't take long. Let me show you the air-machine room.*'

Photograph the pupils looking at the air machine.

Stop the drama.

Reflect on the drama

Using the illustrations of faces with different expressions (Expressions.pdf in folder Remedy Rocket on the Resources CD), talk to the children about which facial expressions the rocket crew might see on the faces of the people who live on the base station and why.

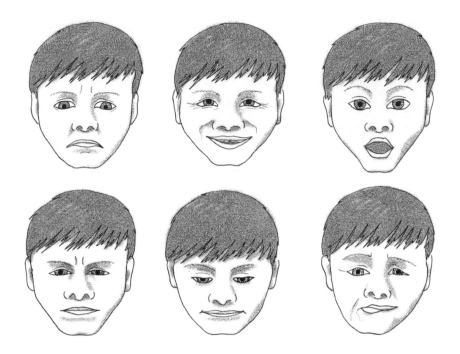

Reflection questions might include:

- What might happen if the space rocket crew decide not to stay and help?
- What might happen if the space rocket crew decide to stay and help?
- What do the space rocket crew know about the people on the base station?
- Are there any other ways of helping the base-station people?

Tell the pupils that, when the story starts again, the people from the base station have one further request.

Scene 9: The people on the planet want even more help

In role as Eirian, tell the PIR that a few people who are not sick would like to borrow the space rocket to take their families back home to Earth. It would mean that the crew would need to stay on the planet for a while longer, just until the rocket returns. Put a strong case for sharing the rocket.

Ask the PIR what they would like to do. Are they willing to share their space rocket?

Stop the drama.

- Ask the children to say how they felt when they were asked to share their space rocket.
- Ask them to think of times in school when we are asked to share things.
- Ask the children what makes people want to share.
- Ask them what makes people not want to share.

Photograph the pupils making their decision.

Finding an ending

Scene 10: The end

Help the PIR to make a decision. Here are two options for starters (ask the pupils what other possibilities they can think of):

1. The astronauts decide to stay and let some of the base-station people use their rocket to go back to Earth.
2. The crew decide not to stay, but promise to come and check to see how the base-station people are getting on when they are next passing the planet.

Whatever decision the PIR make, use Forum Theatre to improvise the moment when the crew and the base-station people have to say goodbye.

- Discuss what the people say to each other.
- Discuss what the people might be feeling.
- Act out a goodbye scene.

Photograph the ending of the drama.

Narrate the take-off of the space rocket. Leave the ending open for further adventures.

Possible script:

> 'The doors were sealed. The pilot made her checks to make sure everything was working well. The engines fired into action, sending the rocket zooming into the night sky. The people on the ground waved to their friends in the rocket. Soon, all that could be seen was a dot of a fire, a red glow in the dark, and then the rocket was gone.'

Final Reflection

Talk with the pupils about the story. Ask the pupils to tell each other what happened and in what order. Get the pupils into pairs and give them a set of the digital photographs you took during the drama to organise into a sequence of events. Jumble the photos first.

Put pairs of pupils into groups of four. Ask each pair to tell the story to the other pair using the photographs to help them explain the order of the scenes and to remind them what happened.

Using one of the photographs you have taken, discuss how to describe events, characters and settings. If appropriate, write a model descriptive piece about one part of the story with the class using the pupils' ideas.

Reflection questions might include:

- Are you happy with the decisions the astronauts made at the end of the story?
- Do you think they handled the situation with the colonists well?
- What do you think were the dangers the astronauts faced on the planet with the colonists?
- Do you think they could have done anything differently? What? Why?
- Are there any situations in real life like this?
- What advice would you give to other people about dealing with strangers?
- Was it difficult for the astronauts to decide whether or not to give the colonists the medicine? Why?
- Was it difficult for the astronauts to decide whether or not to share their rocket? Why?
- Did it feel the same when the astronauts were deciding whether to give the colonists the medicine as it did when they were deciding whether to share the space rocket? Why?
- How do you think the astronauts felt when they had to decide whether they would go home straight away or not?
- Have you ever been away from home by yourself? What was it like?
- What advice would you give to the people left on the planet who have to wait for the rocket to return?
- What have we learned about space while we have been playing this story? What would you like to know about space now? What kinds of skills do you think an astronaut needs? How could you find out more about astronauts?
- What have we learned about hospitals and medicine? What have we learned about landscapes, plants and animals? What have we learned about light and dark?
- Which people do you know in real life who have to care for other people? What do you think might be difficult about caring for other people? What do you think would be good about caring for other people?
- How well did we work together on this story? What helped us to work together? What stopped us working together well?
- Which activities did you like best and why? Are there any activities you would like to use again in another story?

Potential cross-curricular learning

Here are some of the areas of the curriculum that can be linked to the story and used as prompts for you to design activities of your own.

Cross-curricular links	
	Mathematics Ma 2 and Ma 3: Discussing shapes, sizes, measurements of length and area; carrying out calculations and number puzzles as part of the job of being an astronaut.
	Geography Discussing physical and human features; discussing space missions; learning about planets, stars, the solar system, day and night, the rotation of the Earth; learning key vocabulary such as equator, axis, poles; learning about scale drawing by making a plan of the Base Station; learning about different kinds of landscape, climatic conditions, and environmental features stimulated by the journeys to different planets.
	Science Sc 2: Learning about keeping the human body safe and healthy - understanding the need for air, water, shelter; discussing the use of drugs as medicines and the role of hospitals and other health services; learning about the skeletal structure of the human body and key vocabulary, such as names of bones; discussing plant life and the conditions needed to grow things in the context of the different types of planets visited in the story. Sc 3: Recognising a variety of materials and their uses; discussing ways of conducting and conserving heat. Sc 4: Using the various vehicles in the story as a stimulus, learning about forces and motion, for example making a bottle water rocket; electricity – using the space rocket crash as a stimulus for work on circuits and switches; using the story to learn about communications devices and how sound travels: identifying sources of light and how they can best be used in different circumstances and contexts.
	History Discussing famous people in space; the Apollo mission; Valentina Tereshkova as the first woman in space; the space shuttle missions; the history of rocket power; radio communications; telephone and television; satellites; how the world has changed during the development of space travel; reasons for the 'space race'.
	PSHE and citizenship In role, the teacher is helping to provide a model of leadership - speaking and listening, managing discussions fairly. This project asks the pupils to understand that humans sometimes have responsibility for the welfare of other people. The PIR as astronauts find themselves in a situation where they have to decide how much responsibility they are prepared to take for a group of sick strangers on a lonely and desolate planet. Their original mission was to collect important medicines and deliver them home to Earth, and in this way the pupils are learning about some of the issues around caring for others. Decisions are made collaboratively.
	Art Discussing light and dark; studying pictures of night skies and lights at night - candles in dark rooms, lights at windows – such as Georgia O'Keeffe's *Radiator Building*; working out how to represent light at night; studying the work of Fauvist artists who used colour in unusual ways; creating illustrations of planet landscapes; making a model of a space rocket, a hospital, the Base Station; drawing rooms and communal spaces inside buildings and vehicles

	featured in the story; designing costumes for characters. **Music** Composing music inspired by space rockets and space; listening to music composed for space films and programmes, such as the *Star Wars* and *Doctor Who* themes; listening to Holst's The Planets suite.
Literacy skills	Story construction; sequencing; character development; setting; including a problem; selecting a suitable ending; understanding the meaning of a story; familiarisation with a type of plot known as Voyage and Return; note making in pictorial and written form; asking and answering questions; speaking and listening in pairs and groups; critical viewing of film and TV programmes about space - such as clips from Star Wars (scenes such as Luke's successful attack on the Death Star) and the Thunderbirds puppet series; exposure to new vocabulary; learning points of grammar; learning about adjectives, verbs, nouns and question marks; writing descriptive passages.
Remember DfES thinking skills!	**Creating** Generating and extending ideas; applying imagination; looking for innovative outcomes. This story is set in a future when it is possible to travel to other planets and it requires a leap of imagination on the part of the pupils. Creative thinking is developed by making up imaginary locations and using imaginary equipment and technology. Pupils have to suspend disbelief and generate for themselves visions of a world that doesn't exist (as far as we know!). In role pupils are also asked to deal with the problem of crash-landing on a strange and relatively unknown planet. **Enquiring** Asking relevant questions; posing and defining problems; predicting outcomes and anticipating consequences. This type of thinking is developed through the PIR as they have to find out about the planets they land on. The planet the PIR crash-land on is a particular challenge, as they soon learn they are not alone. The PIR need to find out about the colonists and decide whether to make face to face contact with them. **Reasoning** Giving reasons for opinions and actions; drawing inferences and making deductions; explaining thoughts; making informed decisions and judgements. This type of thinking is developed through the discussions PIR have with TIR about whether or not to give the colonists the medicines that they are supposed to take back to Earth. The PIR must consider if they have the right to make a decision and if it would be right not to make a decision. **Information processing** Sorting and classifying; comparing and contrasting; sequencing. This type of thinking is developed by sequencing the story, taking photographs and organising them into a logical pattern that tells the story to others. Pupils can also develop this type of thinking through finding out about space travel, sorting and classifying materials, such as rocks, wood and metals, and comparing different locations, such as an area of fertile pasture land (first planet visited) with a dry rocky landscape (second planet). **Evaluating** Examining what the story means; judging the value of what you have read, heard or done. This type of thinking is developed through discussions about sharing the space rocket and the medicines. Pupils can be prompted through 'open' questions to think about the consequences of helping the colonists. This will help them to judge the value of what they have done in role as astronauts in the story. Reflection questions will also help the pupils to evaluate what they have learned and how well they have worked together.

Planning checklist

Subject matter	A quest to recover a precious item; rural life; a range of different landscape features such as fields, mountains, caves, a lake, a town and a village
Themes	Loyalty; trust; secrets; the threat of war; good versus evil; heroism
Key resources and equipment	Costume item to sign TIR as Keeper of the Rules, such as a cloak or draped cloth Costume items to sign TIR as Talgorn, such as a cloak and back pack Costume item to sign TIR as the Mayor, such as a hat, cloak, mayoral chain Costume item to sign TIR as The Lady of the Living Lake, such as a head-dress or flowing watery coloured cloak Costume items to sign TIR as Lord Grimlac, such as a gentleman's tie and handkerchief **Worksheet** (in folder The Quest on the Resources CD) Supplies worksheet (Supplies Worksheet.pdf) **Props include** Map of Good Land (Map.pdf) Silver and gold cardboard coins Pictures of fields, pastures, rivers, lakes, caves and farms (Landscapes.pdf) Picture of the mysterious house (House.pdf) Root and Top Supplies (Supplies.pdf) Letter (Letter.pdf) Castles Pack (Castles.pdf) Glass pebbles Junk to make model castles A Rules Scroll for TIR as Keeper of the Rules Equipment for TIR as Talgorn: rope; lantern; water bottle; purse with coins in
Organisation	**Time** Without Optional Extras: 8–10 hours With Optional Extras: 12–14 hours **Teaching space** Preferably a hall or large space Possible themes for the role-play area: • a market • a camp in a wood • a shop selling supplies for adventurers • a farm • a castle.
Main dramatic devices used	Teacher in Role Pupils in Role **Basic plot** Quest **Basic problem** Good Land is threatened with invasion because an enchanted sleep has been imposed upon the Queen (a friend needs rescuing; being tricked and trapped; threat of being invaded) **Basic tensions** Having great responsibility for the welfare of others (not knowing who to trust; lack of knowledge; running out of time; changes of plan; fear; threat of being outnumbered)

Teacher's overview

The Quest is an epic adventure, which means that it's long! In fact, it is the longest project in this collection. The story has many twists, turns, characters and settings that make it seem quite complex. Don't be put off. Actually, the dramatic activities are very simple, depending largely on TIR, PIR and Scene Drawing. The plot, however, contains all the ingredients needed to make a compelling story for young children. It resonates strongly with films they will have enjoyed, such as *Lord of the Rings* and perhaps *Star Wars* and *Troy*, all of which contain quests, along with stories that will probably have been read to them such as *The Lion, the Witch and the Wardrobe*, Hans Christian Andersen's *The Snow Queen* and Rupert Bear stories, which are not quests but set in a fantasy world. *The Quest* also draws on many elements of folk tales such as *Snow White, Little Red Riding Hood* and *Hansel and Gretel.* The pupils will readily identify with the idea of a castle, an object with special powers, with fantasy settings and rural life in olden days, with enchantment (sleeping without waking), with imprisonment, with 'goodies' versus 'baddies' and with last-minute rescues. In common with many children's adventures, nobody is really hurt in *The Quest* (despite overwhelming threats) and the heroes achieve their goal without a fight! Good overcomes evil and the world is saved. There's even an intervention of the gods, which connects the story to Greek myths (the *Iliad* and the *Odyssey*, for instance) and Biblical history (the Exodus is a classic case).

Other 'quests' in literature and film include *Pilgrim's Progress, Watership Down, Treasure Island, Tales of the Holy Grail, Around the World in Eighty Days, The Great Escape, The Guns of Navarone, Moby Dick* … The list goes on. This is an important and busy genre within the library of classic literature. Undertaking this project will help pupils, as they get older, to appreciate such works fully. There is also a strong connection with real historical quests such as black slaves travelling the 'Underground Railroad' from the Southern to the Northern American states aided by 'conductors' such as Harriet Tubman. You could also make a connection with the historical story portrayed in the Australian film, *The Rabbit-Proof Fence.*

For young children, there are the Sir Quinton Quest stories in the Jumbo Jets series, such as *Sir Quinton Quest Hunts the Jewels* and *Sir Quinton Quest Hunts the Yeti; Cyril's Woodland Quest* by Eugene McCabe; the Deltora Quest series and, for sheer fun, Captain Pugwash in *The Quest of the Golden Handshake*, which we suspect may be enjoyed more by some adults than by the target audience! A serious and also charming quest tale is *Mrs Frisby and the Rats of Nimh*, which is also a well-known children's film. There is also a children's version of *Around the World in Eighty Days* titled *Around the World with Phineas Frog.*

The themes in quest stories are heroism, trust, loyalty and good versus bad. The characters face situations that challenge their sense of right and wrong and require them to endure and be brave. Events determine who are the great leaders and who will be the loyal servants. So, for example, in *Mrs Frisby and the Rats of Nimh*, the meek and mild Mrs Frisby finds the courage to administer a sleeping powder to a fierce cat's dinner dish in order to rescue the rats. She has many difficulties to overcome as she works to do the right thing for her poorly son and for the rats, and as a result, little by little, she changes and becomes a stronger character.

Given the length of this project, it is recommended that you play it out in stages, perhaps over half a term. This is the kind of time you would take to read a book of this kind to the class. In fact, this makes an exciting alternative to that and would make an excellent introduction to the genre (ready for the study of Greek myths in KS2).

In order to prepare yourself for the adventure, here is all the information you need: the map; a list of the characters (many of whom you will play yourself) and a summary of the plot.

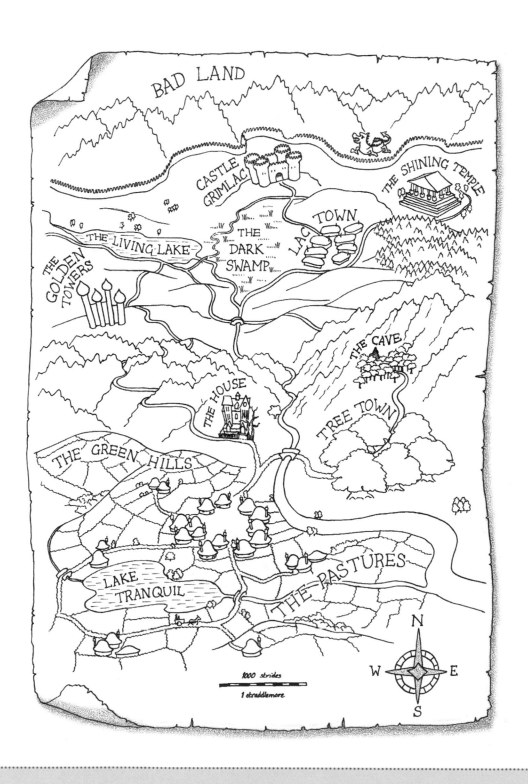

The Map (Map.pdf in folder The Quest on the Resources CD)

Role-play area

A castle, Tree Town shops, Green Town market, caves, a farm in The Pastures

The cast of characters

The Heroes	the People of The Pastures....	gentle, good people of Good Land (PIR)
The Keeper	Keeper of the Rules..............	a good, gentle Pasturite (TIR)
The Guide	Talgorn	mysterious but trustworthy ally of the Queen (TIR)
The Leader	the Queen...........................	powerful and good
The Baddie	Lord Grimlac........................	desires greater power and prepared to do very bad things to get it (TIR)
The Victim	the Mayor	a victim of Lord Grimlac's cruelty – loves his daughter (TIR)
The Protector	the Lady of the Living Lake ..	mysterious, elemental and very powerful (TIR)

Summary of the plot

Prologue

- There are two lands divided by a huge wall. One is Good Land and the other Bad Land.
- There are a number of different communities living in Good Land.
- The story begins in the area of Good Land called The Pastures.
- The people of The Pastures are peaceful and home-loving and govern themselves in a democratic manner by meeting once a year to review the Rules by which they live.

Part 1

The story opens at **Setting 1**, where the Pasturites are happily going about their daily lives – farming, fishing, buying and selling at the local market.

It is nearly Rules Day and preparations for this are being made. On Rules Day, the Pasturites have their own Rituals to mark the agreement of the Rules. After the celebrations for Rules Day, a group of Pasturites are asked to join a quest on behalf of the Queen of The Golden Towers.

In return for materials and help to construct some new buildings in The Pastures, the Queen wants some assistance with a problem that cannot be disclosed.

Part 2

At **Setting 2**, the Pasturites meet a guide called Talgorn, who has been sent by the Queen to explain the quest and be the leader of the group. Talgorn takes the Pasturites to Tree Town (**Setting 3**), a town built underground beneath giant trees. Here, Talgorn tells them that the Queen has been put into an enchanted sleep and she is the only person in Good Land who knows how to control the vicious serpent monster that is kept by the people of Bad Land.

The Queen's staff fear her enchantment is part of a Bad Land plot to attack Good Land. The Queen can wake only if she is touched by the Shining Crystal. The Shining Crystal has the power to do good, but its precious power can be used only once every hundred years and is therefore under the protection of the Lady of the Living Lake. The crystal is locked inside the Shining Temple and only the Lady of the Living Lake can give permission to use it.

The quest is to get permission to use the Shining Crystal, collect it from the Shining Temple and get it to The Golden Towers. The Pasturites have been chosen for the quest because it is known that the Lady of the Living Lake likes them more than any other people in Good Land.

Part 3

In Tree Town, **Setting 3**, the Pasturites buy equipment and supplies for their journey to the Living Lake. They meet the Mayor, who seems overly curious about what they are doing, buying so much equipment. The Mayor follows the Pasturites as they set off for a short cut to the Living Lake through the caves. When Talgorn is not around, the Mayor speaks to the Pasturites and tells them Talgorn is not to be trusted and is most likely leading them into a trap. The Pasturites have to decide whom to trust.

The Pasturites don't yet know it, but the Mayor is working for a character called Lord Grimlac. Lord Grimlac is holding the Mayor's daughter hostage in his dungeon. Manipulated by Grimlac, the Mayor is trying to delay the Pasturites from getting on with the quest. Grimlac is, of course, in league with the Bad Landers. Talgorn tells the Pasturites to ask the Lady of the Living Lake for answers to their questions about whom to trust, which they do.

At **Setting 4,** the Lady of the Lake tells them to trust Talgorn and gives them permission to use the Shining Crystal. The Pasturites are also warned about Lord Grimlac, whose lands they must cross to get to the Shining Temple.

Part 4

On their way to the temple, the Pasturites notice a lot of noise around Castle Grimlac. Lord Grimlac meets the Pasturites as they try to cross his land and, offering cordial hospitality, he tries to persuade them to stay with him in his castle on their way back from the temple.

Talgorn suggests that the party split up into smaller groups, each making its own way to the temple, while she stays to find out what is going on at Castle Grimlac. The party agree to meet back together the next day. Talgorn discovers that Lord Grimlac has not only imprisoned the Mayor's daughter, but also one family member from each household in nearby Lac Town. They are all being held as hostages while he forces the other family members to dismantle part of the wall and make a big hole through which the people of Bad Land can release their vicious monster. Lord Grimlac thinks he can control the Bad Land monster, but the people of Lac Town know that he cannot, and send a letter to Talgorn asking for help.

At **Setting 5**, the Pasturites successfully collect the Shining Crystal and make their way back to meet Talgorn.

Part 5

When the party have reassembled, Talgorn shows them a letter from the people who are being forced to dismantle the wall. The wall is almost destroyed enough for the Bad Land monster to get through and wreak havoc in Lac Town.

The Pasturites realise they need to decide how best to use the crystal, whose good power can be used only once in a hundred years. Do they use it to put Lord Grimlac to sleep so that the wall can be repaired before it's too late? Or, do they complete the quest as originally commissioned and take the crystal back to The Golden Towers to wake the sleeping Queen? The party must weigh the consequences of each option.

The decision presents the Pasturites with a true dilemma, as there is no way of solving the problem without unhappy consequences either way. On the one hand, Lord Grimlac is stopped immediately and no one is harmed, but the Queen is doomed to her enchanted sleep. On the other hand, the Queen is woken, but by the time the Pasturites reach her the wall will be broken down, the Bad Landers will have invaded with their monster and all the people of Lac Town will be in immediate danger.

Part 6

To provide a happy and intriguing ending, the Lady of the Living Lake arrives to save the day, declaring that she will herself protect Good Land and hold back the invasion because of the goodness of the Pastures people. Therefore, they can wake the Queen and everyone will be safe in the process. To let them know that all is well, she will place a bright star in the sky as her sign. She also tells the Pasturites that one day they will be called on again to help Good Land, but for now they can enjoy a time of peace and prosperity.

Epilogue

The Pasturites are magically returned to their home town – Green Town – where everything is peaceful and quiet. The adventurers go back to their normal lives of farming, fishing and selling produce at the market, but every night they check the sky to make sure the bright star is still shining down on Good Land.

Now you have the overview, the adventure may begin …

PART 1 – The Pasturites are happily going about their daily lives

Getting going

Explain to the pupils that the story they are going to act out involves characters who are going on a long journey. At the beginning of the story, the characters are living happily in their own land, which is called The Pastures. The people who live in The Pastures are mostly farmers and craftspeople.

Sit the pupils so that they can see a large piece of paper, either gathered in front of an easel or in a circle on the floor. Draw a basic plan of The Pastures (The Green Hills, Lake Tranquil, the village).

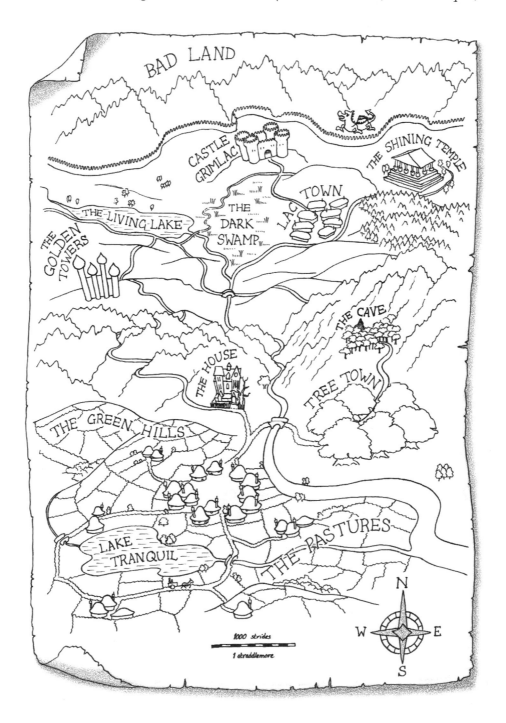

The purpose of the drawing is to give the pupils a visual cue that will help them to get into role and to act out life in The Pastures.

Building belief

If the pupils need information about rural life before they start working in role, give them pictures of fields, pastures, rivers, lakes, caves and farms to look at and discuss (Landscapes.pdf in folder The Quest on the Resources CD).

When the pupils are ready to start the drama, ask them what daily tasks they imagine the people who live in The Pastures do. The pupils can be prompted to consider a range of activities such as:

- mending hedges
- milking cows
- feeding animals
- looking after horses
- cooking food, baking bread
- taking things to the market to sell
- fishing
- planting
- chopping wood
- making furniture
- sewing
- making pots
- making a fire
- picking berries and other fruit.

Ask the pupils to pretend to be the Pasturites and let them practise acting out these tasks individually or in small groups. Encourage some of them to show to the rest of the class what they are doing. This could be done either by sitting the pupils in a circle and having volunteers perform in the centre, or by stopping the action several times and asking different groups to perform *in situ* while other members of the class stand and watch.

Optional Extra

English En 1

Tell the pupils that they are going to try to recreate a market day in Green Town. Help the pupils to think about an old-fashioned market by listing the kinds of things people are selling. If the items for sale are written on a large piece of paper, the class can read them together.

- vegetables
- fruit
- cloth
- pots and pans
- tools
- milk
- butter
- fish
- biscuits
- plants
- cheese
- bread
- honey.

Optional Extra continued

Items could include:

Divide the class into two groups. One group are going to be selling and the other group buying. Model what the pupils are to do by sitting the class in a circle and selecting two pupils to be sellers and two to be buyers. Help them to act out a short scene. At this stage pupils might need to have dialogue suggested to them by other pupils or by the teacher. The teacher or classroom assistant could model how to buy and sell by acting out too.

Next, sit the buyers where they can watch the sellers. Explain that the sellers arrive early in the morning to set up their stalls. The buyers are going to watch the sellers set up and get themselves ready for business.

Get the **sellers** into groups of two or three and give them one minute to decide what they are selling. Tell each group that they have a cart in which to bring their goods to the marketplace. Either the cart is pulled by a horse or they pull it themselves. If the concept of a cart is unfamiliar, the teacher will need to describe it briefly. On the cart are lots of boxes with the items they are going to sell. When the sellers get into the marketplace, they choose a stall and set out a display of their goods.

Ask the pupils to act out unloading their boxes and putting their goods out on display. The pupils may have some experience of markets either in real life or from the television and be able to use what they have seen to help them act out being market traders. If not, the teacher can help to give them a vision of the market by describing stalls and explaining what the seller does to display their goods. More detail in the acting out helps to build belief in the fictional setting, but it is important to keep the pace brisk, otherwise spontaneity will be lost. The teacher will need to judge how much rehearsal of the scene can be tolerated before the pupils lose interest.

Tell the **buyers** that market day is great fun because friends meet and chat and have a drink of juice together. People are excited by the shopping and the possibility of getting a bargain. You may need to discuss what a bargain is with some pupils!

Get the pupils into pairs. They are going to pretend to be old friends who haven't seen each other for a while and are going to meet at the market and go shopping together. Develop some dialogue by asking the pairs to decide what they say to each other when they first meet. To help, ask the class what people say to each other when they meet in real life. Practise a short scene where the pairs meet and greet each other.

Now that both the sellers and buyers are prepared, start the market scene in full. Tell the pupils that it's early morning and the sellers are just arriving and setting up their stalls. Ask PIR as sellers to start the acting out by setting out their goods on display.

You are in part narrating the scene by explaining what happens and in this way you are directing the action. Gradually send pairs of buyers into the scene and let them meet, greet and start to look around the stalls and buy.

After a while, stop the action.

Do a Scene Drawing exercise. Working in their pairs with large paper and marker pens, the sellers are asked to draw their stall in detail with all the things they are selling pictured on it. The buyers draw a picture of the whole market. Tell the pupils they have ten minutes to complete the task the best they can. The rule is that the teacher and classroom assistant can answer questions only with a 'yes' or 'no'. If pupils want help, they will have to work out which questions to ask the adults to get a useful answer.

Suggest the following openings to questions as examples:

- In the market is there …?
- Did the vegetable seller have …?
- Is the name for a person who sells fish a …?
- Do the stalls have …?
- Do people …?

Share the pictures and each other's perceptions of what the market is like.

Then sit the pupils (out of role) in a comfortable place to discuss what they know about markets. Talk about the sights, smells, sounds, tastes and what kinds of textures might be available to touch.

Devising the Rules Ritual

Tell the pupils that each year the people have a special ceremony to discuss and agree the Rules by which they will live. The ceremony involves a Ritual and the climax is when everyone solemnly says they agree to live by the Rules for the next year.

Out of role, the teacher and pupils devise a Ritual that has four parts to symbolise the four quarters of the year:

Part 1   a chant for spring

Part 2   a still, thoughtful time for summer

Part 3   a sequence of movements for autumn

Part 4   the agreeing of the Rules in a circle to represent the circle of the seasons

- A chant might be made from words that describe spring.
- A still, thoughtful time for summer might be started by leading the pupils through a guided visualisation of plants growing from seeds to maturity.
- A sequence of movements could be made up from tasks country people do in the autumn, such as harvesting, haymaking, storing foods.
- The rule-making needs to have a solemn atmosphere. For added effect, have a large scroll with a ribbon tied around it, on which the Rules will be written.

Out of role, the pupils can rehearse the Ritual. Music can be added—drumbeats, for example. Pupils might also practise processing into the marketplace at the start of the ceremony. When the Ritual has been sufficiently rehearsed, it can be played out, but only after the role of Keeper of the Rules has been introduced to the pupils ....

TIR as Keeper of the Rules

Role function: benevolent authority figure. Tell the pupils that there is one rule that has always been kept by the people of The Pastures from the beginning of their history. This is known as the Main Rule. It decrees that the people of The Pastures never fight, use weapons or harm anyone else in any way. Pasturites are peaceful, home-loving people. It is important to establish how important this rule is to the community at this point in the story so that the potential impact of a possible invasion from the warriors of Bad Land can be felt later. The Keeper of the Rules makes sure the Pasturites remember that this most important rule and helps them to make the new Rules by which they will live for the next year.

A costume such as a cloak or draped cloth would help to create the role of the Keeper. The Keeper needs a large piece of paper that will become the Rules Scroll, on which the agreed Rules will be written. At this point, only the Main Rule is written on the scroll, leaving space for four others to be added.

Tell the pupils that the Rules are discussed and agreed in the marketplace in Green Town each year on the day that they believe the sun is at its highest point in the sky. The Rules are made in the marketplace so that everyone can join in.

Acting out the Rules Ritual

Tell the pupils that they are going to play the role of Pasturites again. It is Rules Day and the Ritual is about to begin with the chant. Act out the first three parts of the Ritual leading up to Part 4, the Agreeing of the Rules. The Agreeing of the Rules is conducted as a formal meeting.

TIR as the Keeper welcomes the people of The Pastures to the marketplace and to Rules Day. She reminds people of the Main Rule that is always written onto the Rules Scroll before the Rules Day

meeting. The PIR are asked to suggest four other rules that might be discussed and agreed this year. Pupils often suggest rules such as:

- No being unkind
- No hitting
- No taking someone else's things.

TIR can deepen the PIR's thinking by asking them, for example, to explain what they regard as unkind behaviour. TIR may need to steer the pupils back into role if they forget, by asking how such-and-such a rule might apply to people in The Pastures. Young pupils usually take rule making seriously and often slip back into being themselves, discussing their own issues.

TIR can also help to reword ideas. If PIR suggest lots of rules about stopping antisocial behaviour, such as hitting, kicking, pinching, TIR can point out that Rule 1 deals with this. Likewise, if the pupils suggest 'stopping people from copying' or 'no talking to people when they are working', these could be reworded as, 'We all agree to leave people alone when they are busy.'

If pupils are unable to think of any rules, the teacher could, as a last resort, suggest some that have been 'agreed before'. For example:

- We will share with others who are less fortunate than we are
- We will listen to other people's views and ideas carefully before we speak
- We will make sure that everyone who wants to speak is given the time and space to do so
- We will have one rest day each week
- We will not take anything from anyone unless it is given to us
- We will be polite at all times

- We will care for our animals
- We will care for people who are in need through sickness or old age
- We will offer support to anyone who has a disability.

Pupils can then debate the order of importance and arrive at the 'top four'. Once the Rules have been discussed and written on the scroll, TIR leads the closing part of the Ritual, in which everyone repeats after the Keeper that they agree to keep the Rules.

If the pupils need a 'lighter' moment to conclude this part of the story, PIR can act out having a party to celebrate another successful Rules Day. Stop the drama.

Reflect on the drama

Out of role, ask the pupils to reflect on what they have understood about the people who live in The Pastures. For example:

- What kind of people are they?
- What makes them happy?
- What would make them sad?
- What is important to them?

Tell the pupils that a group of Pasturites have just agreed to do a job in return for help and materials to build some houses for the old people of Green Town. **This concludes Part 1 of the story**, during which time belief should have been well and truly built.

Part 2 – The Pasturites meet a guide called Talgorn

Developing the story

Still out of role, tell the pupils that two days ago a stranger came to Green Town offering the services of the Queen of The Golden Towers. The Queen would be happy to help with any project the Pasturites named in return for several skilled people who would be willing to undertake a secret mission. Tell the pupils they are going to be the Pasturites who volunteered to help.

The Pasturites were told to meet their guide at a house on the mountain road just outside Green Town. The guide would show them the seal of the Queen of The Golden Towers to identify herself.

The Pasturites have just arrived at the house. It is a strange-looking place. Show the pupils a picture of the house (House.pdf in folder The Quest on the Resources CD). Alternatively, any creepy-looking building will do!

Scene Drawing

Get the pupils into groups of four and give each group a piece of paper and one marker pen. Tell the pupils to draw what they think it is like just inside the front door of the house. Explain that they must share the drawing and the pen and that everyone's contribution must be included. They have ten minutes to complete their drawings.

Soundscape

Ask the pupils what kinds of sounds they might hear as they approach and then enter the mysterious house. Ask the pupils – working in a group of four or five – to use their voices to make a Soundscape for the house. Encourage groups to perform for each other.

Sit the pupils in a circle and ask for a few volunteer actors who are going to perform the arrival at the house. With help from pupils sitting in the circle (Forum Theatre style) devise and rehearse a short mimed scene. Next, discuss the use of musical instruments and what kinds of sounds would be needed to make a good Soundscape for the mimed scene. Give a selection of musical instruments to the pupils sitting in the circle and help them to create a Soundscape. Perform the mimed scene with the Soundscape.

Rehearse until the movements and Soundscape look and sound good. Allow pupils to have a go at playing the Soundscape and miming the scene.

Talgorn introduces herself

Role function: benevolent authority figure. Talgorn first appears as a mysterious person, so sign the role with some costume that looks like a cloak or cape, preferably with a hat or hood that can be used to cover the face. If you can find an interesting box to carry (containing the Queen's seal) this can be used as a prop. Talgorn is an experienced adventurer, although to begin with the role is played in a way that suggests a slightly more strange and mysterious character.

Before going into role, explain that the Pasturites nervously ring the doorbell. The door opens a little. Working in role, greet the PIR by opening the door. Shout at the PIR in a feigned manner, 'Go away!' and then quietly tell the pupils they must go round to the back door, as no one must see them entering the house. Act out letting them in through the back door, making a big fuss about being quiet and not being seen.

TIR introduces herself as Talgorn, who has been sent by her mistress the Queen of The Golden Towers to lead the Pasturites on their quest. TIR must make it clear that the quest will not be an easy one and will involve travelling far across the country. The PIR will also have to keep their identities secret and must never reveal who they are working for. TIR reinforces the good reputation that the people of The Pastures have all over the land and thanks them for agreeing to help with this quest.

TIR tells the pupils that they can take with them only what they can carry in a backpack. They must be prepared for many days and nights away from home and for sleeping outside at times. It won't be safe to leave until dark, so everyone is told to get some sleep. Stop the drama.

Scene Drawing: what the Pasturites need to take with them

Get the pupils, out of role, into groups of three or four and give each group a large sheet of sugar paper and marker pens. Ask them quickly to draw everything they think they will need to take with them on the adventure. Time the activity: ten minutes.

Acting out the Pasturites' departure

Back in role, TIR gathers the PIR together and everyone acts out getting ready to leave:

- packing bags
- putting on boots, cloak, hat
- making sure that no lights or torches are showing, because the group must leave without being seen.

Act out leaving the house and travelling silently and in a secretive way. TIR leads the way (around the classroom or hall) and describes the journey:

- *'We have to go through the woods here …'*
- *'We'll travel on the mountain road as far as the crossroads …'*
- *'We'll cut across this field to the bridge …'*

TIR gathers the PIR together to explain that she is taking the PIR to Tree Town, an underground town built by people who live in and under the Giant Trees. There, each member of the party will be able to buy food and any other items they might need for the quest. The details of their mission will also be explained to them.

There is a difficulty: the quickest way to get to Tree Town is to cross the bridge over the river, but, unfortunately, there are some people camped for the night by the bridge. TIR suggests the party walk along the side of the river and wade through the water so that they are not seen by anyone.

Act out sneaking along the river bank. At the crossing point, TIR tells the PIR to take boots and socks off and to hold their bags and possessions above their heads. TIR acts out taking a rope across the river for others to use to help them across. Act out securing the rope to a tree and then wading into the cold water and crossing to the other side of the river, holding the rope tight. A real rope can be used and a long cloth can represent the river, if these props are available. Encourage the PIR to wade across the river.

Freeze Frame and narration

When all the PIR are across the river, Freeze Frame the action. The teacher narrates the story to explain how cold, wet and uncomfortable the adventurers are. Thought Track the PIR to prompt them to think about the situation the characters find themselves in. Questions might include:

- How are you going to get dry?
- Are you worried about what is going to happen?
- What do you think about Talgorn?
- Is this what you expected?
- Why do you think Talgorn doesn't want you to be seen?
- How dangerous was crossing the river?

Talgorn explains the quest

TIR gathers PIR together and explains that the journey to Tree Town should be an easy one and soon they will be able to dry their clothes and sit by a fire with some good food. Act out the journey. Arrive at Tree Town. TIR takes the PIR into a house, gives them bedrooms, tells them it is safe to change their clothes and hang their wet clothes up to dry.

TIR tells the PIR she will make a fire to keep them warm and, when everyone is ready, she'll explain what the quest is and why there has to be so much secrecy.

Let pupils act out getting changed. TIR acts out making a fire and invites the PIR to sit around the fire. TIR explains the quest.

Talgorn says,

> 'A few days ago, the Queen of The Golden Towers fell into a deep sleep from which she cannot be woken. No one knows how it happened, but it is almost certainly because the Queen is the only person in the land who has the ability to control the serpent monster from Bad Land. There has been a rumour that the terrifying serpent has recently been seen near the wall that divides the two lands.'

Show the PIR the map of their land (Map.pdf in folder The Quest on the Resources CD).

Discuss the route that the group has travelled so far.

Tell the PIR that their quest is to get permission from the Lady of the Living Lake to take the Shining Crystal from the Shining Temple back to The Golden Towers. The Shining Crystal has the power to wake the Queen from her enchanted sleep. Actually, the Shining Crystal is very powerful and can be used for any good purpose, but only once in every hundred years.

The Lady of the Living Lake is very rarely seen by ordinary people, but she likes the people of The Pastures because of their good nature and Talgorn believes that she will speak to them and listen favourably to any request they make.

The quest must remain a secret because there are Bad Land spies in Good Land and they must not find out that the Pasturites are trying to wake the Queen from her enchanted sleep. If the spies find out about the quest, the Bad Landers will speed up their efforts to invade Good Land with their ferocious serpent.

TIR and PIR study the map. The quickest way to the Living Lake is to travel through the caves under the mountains. Also, they can travel through the caves without being seen. TIR explains that the caves are cold, dark and scary, but probably the safest route.

Ask the PIR what they have heard about other places on the map.

PIR then go off to buy the supplies and equipment they think they will need for the journey. **This concludes Part 2 of the story.**

Part 3 – Pasturites buy equipment and supplies for their journey to the Living Lake

Optional Extras

Mathematics Ma 2

Put the pupils, out of role, into pairs. Explain that the activity they are going to do next requires reading skills and some maths skills. Give each pair a 'Root and Tops Supplies' sheet and worksheet (Supplies.pdf and Supplies Worksheet.pdf in folder The Quest on the Resources CD).

Tell the pupils they have a chance to buy some items to take with them on the next part of their adventure. Talgorn has given each pair of them one gold piece and thirty silver pieces to spend.

They do not have to spend it all here – they can take some of it with them.

Give pupils some silver and gold (cardboard) coins to work with. Each pair has to look at the list:

1. Read the items.
2. Draw pictures of the items next to the words.
3. Decide which items you are going to buy.
4. Decide how many of each item you want to buy.
5. Add up the total number of silver and gold pieces you will need to spend.
6. Check that you have enough money.
7. Check how much you will have left.

If pairs don't have enough silver and gold pieces, they will have to rethink.

English En 1

When the PIR have finalised what they want to buy, tell them that the adventurers go shopping in Tree Town. Of course, Tree Town is an unusual place because it is all underground. Would the shops be any different from ones above ground? Sit the pupils in a circle and, using a forum-style technique, act out scenes where the adventurers buy their supplies and equipment. You can model the role of a shopkeeper for the first two or three PIR as customers. Once the routines of buying and selling have been established, hand over the role of shopkeeper to a volunteer pupil.

Put the pupils in small groups and ask them to make up their own shopping scenes. Give the class five minutes to 'play' at shopping.

Meeting the Mayor of Tree Town

Out of role, gather the pupils together and tell them that the Mayor of Tree Town wants to meet them. Play the role of the Mayor, signing it with a costume (a jacket, for example). The role function is: victim. TIR as the Mayor wants to know what the adventurers are doing in her town. The Mayor is clearly suspicious and asks lots of questions about what they are up to, where they have come from, where they are going, whom they are staying with, where they are staying, why they are buying so many things and so on.

TIR can choose to ignore diplomatically any comments that give the secret quest away, or can pick up the comments and question the PIR even harder! Stop the drama.

Reflect on the drama

Out of role, discuss with the pupils what has happened and encourage them to think about the questions the Mayor asked. What was the Mayor expecting to find out? What might she be thinking now? Why was she so curious? What if anything did the adventurers give away?

Optional Extras

English En 1

In order to build further belief, to deepen their commitment to the drama and perhaps provide some light relief, ask the pupils out of role to choose one of the following drawing tasks (fifteen minutes should be enough).

- Draw a picture of Tree Town. Put as much detail into it as possible.
- Draw a picture of yourself in the drama. Choose a scene that you think is exciting.
- Draw any part of the story that interests you.

English En 3

If you want to use the drama to provide a stimulus for writing, the pupils could be asked to write what they remember of the story so far. First, the events could be recalled by asking the children in small groups to draw a timeline, or to come out and stand on a 'line' at the front of the classroom with each pupil representing one event – they have to put themselves in the right order.

Discuss what is meant by a plot and any of the essential features of a good story that they have experienced so far. If you feel the pupils can manage it, discuss the importance of having tension in a story. Consider how the characters have been developed and how settings and scenes have changed.

Tell the pupils that the drama is about to start again and the adventurers have difficulty deciding who to trust.

Introducing a problem

TIR as Talgorn gathers the pupils together and tells them she is ready to leave for the caves as it's about to get dark. TIR asks the PIR whether they talked to anybody in the town, and, if they did, what was said.

If the pupils explain about the conversation with the Mayor, TIR must appear to be very worried. If the pupils do not mention their conversation with the Mayor, TIR must explain again how important it is to keep the quest a secret and tell the pupils that some people in the town cannot be trusted, especially the Mayor. TIR asks the PIR about their equipment and, under instruction from TIR, everyone acts out checking their possessions and sorting out their backpacks. TIR will point out where people do not have cloaks, torches or enough food, but say it is too late to worry now.

Act out part of the journey, trudging down a muddy road and occasionally hiding to avoid other people. At the end of an arduous day, act out making camp for the night, lighting fires, cooking food and settling down to sleep.

Narrate the next part of the story. Possible script:

> *'During the night, the adventurers were aware of noises, not far away from them. There it was again! The sharp crack of twigs being broken underfoot. Several of the adventurers sat up and looked around but even with torches it was too dark to see what might be moving around behind the trees and in and out of the shadows.'*

TIR wakes all the adventurers and gathers them together. Explain that you have found footprints near the camp and believe someone is following them.

Act out packing up the camp. TIR tells the PIR that she is going to travel ahead and check that everything is safe on the route to the caves; she'll be back soon and asks them to be ready to set off in a few minutes' time. Stop the drama.

Meeting the Mayor again

Out of role, gather the pupils together and tell them that the person who has been following the adventurers is the Mayor of Tree Town. The Mayor waits until Talgorn has gone, then spies her chance to talk to the adventurers. Tell the pupils that you are going to play the Mayor again and explain that you will sign the role as before.

TIR as the Mayor explains to the pupils that Talgorn is not to be trusted. Talgorn is leading them into a trap. The Mayor doesn't know what Talgorn has planned, but points out that the caves can be very dangerous. Give the pupils some time to ask questions and then, as a means of leaving the scene, TIR becomes worried that Talgorn will be back soon and suggests that the adventurers ask Talgorn a few questions to find out more about the quest they are on. TIR as the Mayor says she will stay in hiding, but will continue to follow the adventurers. She is willing to help them if they need her. Stop the drama.

Reflect on the drama

With yourself out of role, discuss with the pupils what has happened. Analyse the situation. Some of the reflection questions can be worded as if the pupils were still in role and some out of role. The pupils will be responding emotionally and critically simultaneously. The pupils are being asked to reflect on the effect that the conversation with the Mayor has had on their characters and they are also thinking critically about the story as if they were readers, not players.

Prompt questions might include:

- Did the Mayor surprise you in any way?
- Why do you think the Mayor is following the adventurers?
- What do we know about Talgorn?
- What do we know about the Mayor?
- Where did Talgorn go?
- What do we need to find out?
- How can we find out what we need to know?
- Whom could the adventurers talk to?
- How will they know if they are being told the truth?

List possible actions that the adventurers could take, the possible consequences of the actions and the risk levels.

For example:

Action	Possible consequence	Risk level
Question Talgorn	Talgorn will know the adventurers don't trust her.	High if Talgorn has companions nearby who could capture them.
Tell Talgorn about the Mayor	Talgorn might capture the Mayor – the Mayor might be telling the truth. The adventurers might then be in danger.	High – they might put the Mayor's life in jeopardy.

Discuss different possibilities with the pupils, but tell them that, before the adventurers have time to make any decisions together, Talgorn returns and wants them to set off for the caves as quickly as possible.

Developing the story further

PIR may argue for taking a different route or abandoning the quest altogether! Or, they may just follow TIR's orders. If necessary, TIR can look at the map again with the pupils and agree to a different route over the mountains, for example, or across the river and past The Golden Towers, but will point out that all other routes take longer. TIR can keep asking the PIR to give reasons for wanting to take an alternative route.

If the pupils press too hard, or want to capture Talgorn or question her, TIR can ask them to talk to the Lady of the Living Lake, who everyone knows is good, kind and truthful, and she will answer all their questions about the Mayor and about Talgorn. The quickest route to her would still be through the caves but the adventurers must decide.

Allow the PIR time to discuss what they want to do.

If the decision making at any point appears to be getting out of control, stop the drama and tell the pupils that the adventurers decided to take the quickest route through the caves and ask the Lady of the Living Lake for her advice. They agreed they would all keep a watchful eye on the Mayor and Talgorn and trust neither of them fully.

Acting out the journey to the lake

The route may have been renegotiated, but whichever way the PIR choose to go (or are told to go), the acting out can happen in the same way. The adventurers try not to use the roads and to take a route that keeps them out of sight as much as possible. The scene can be played out to music and in slow motion to add a more theatrical style to it if you wish. Either TIR can lead the acting out and pretend to be clambering over rocks and squeezing through gaps and over slippery surfaces, or the pupils can discuss the journey out of role and then act it out without the teacher. If the pupils act the journey out by themselves, the teacher can Freeze Frame the action from time to time and Thought Track pupils to say what the journey is like. Pupils could be encouraged to use past and future phrases one after the other, such as:

- I had to crawl on my hands and knees to get under that big rock
- I'm going to have to use my rope to climb up that steep pathway.

When the PIR arrive on the other side of the mountain, stop the drama and tell them that they can see the Living Lake and it is very beautiful.

Optional Extra

Geography

Talk to the pupils about lakes. Show pictures of real lakes and discuss features. How are lakes made? What are the different types? What do people use lakes for?

Preparing to meet the Lady of the Living Lake

Act out setting up camp by the shores of the lake, paddling in the water, swimming, cooking and eating and eventually sleeping. Then stop the drama.

Out of role, ask the pupils what they think the Lady of the Living Lake will look like. Discuss what kind of character she is. Prompt questions might include:

- How does she compare to an ordinary kind of person?
- Why is she called the Lady of the Living Lake?
- Where do you think she lives?
- How does she dress?
- Why does Talgorn think she will trust the adventurers?

Role on the Wall

Out of role, make a Role on the Wall of the Lady of the Living Lake.

Character Drawing: the Lady of the Living Lake

Give the pupils, still out of role, a large piece of paper and ask them to draw a large picture of the Lady of the Living Lake with as much detail as possible.

Optional Extras

Art

To help pupils think about a costume for the Lady, the teacher could provide samples of different fabrics and trimmings and discuss the properties of these materials. It is useful to include samples with a soft pile such as velvet, some with a shiny surface, some metallic trimmings and sequins, some flower shapes and other motifs that suggest creatures or features of a lake.

Discuss with the pupils:

- whether any particular colours should be used to suggest a connection with water

- what kind of material her clothes might be made from
- how the costume might be decorated
- what her hair is like and what she wears as a headdress
- her jewellery
- whether she carries anything in her arms – a book, a sword, a sceptre.

English En 3

Ask pupils to write about the Lady of the Living Lake using their pictures to help them describe what she looks like.

Tell the pupils that, when the drama starts again, you are going to play the Lady of the Living Lake. You can either prepare the pupils for the meeting with the Lady or work spontaneously.

Optional Extra

English En 1

Explain that the adventurers know that the Lady will answer only ten questions. Get the pupils into groups of three and give them a piece of scrap paper each and five minutes to write as many questions as they can.

The class then listen to each other's questions – a couple from each group of three. Discuss which questions the adventurers should ask the Lady and why. Remember, they can have only ten. The main question they have to ask is whether they have permission to take the Shining Crystal from the Shining Temple to wake the Queen from her enchanted sleep.

The pupils can also be prompted to ask questions about Talgorn and the Mayor.

Meeting the Lady of the Living Lake

Explain that the drama will begin again with the appearance of the Lady of the Living Lake. Get the PIR in position, standing on the shore of the lake. Describe how the water moves and changes and forms into the Lady. The Lady's role function is that of benevolent authority figure. Sign the role (a chiffon scarf, perhaps) greet the PIR and ask them what they want to know.

If the pupils are finding the questioning difficult, TIR can say she likes the people of The Pastures so much that she is going to break her custom of only answering questions and tell them the information they need to know.

One way or another, TIR needs to tell PIR the following:

- Talgorn is to be trusted
- The Mayor is not to be trusted
- They can take the crystal, but it can be used for one good deed only
- The crystal must be returned to the Temple once it has been used or its powers will stop working
- The people of Bad Land want to invade Good Land
- You will meet a man called Lord Grimlac – beware of him!

A nice detail to add to this scene would be to give each PIR a small glass pebble (the kind used in flower displays) as a 'key' to the Shining Temple. Stop the drama. **This concludes Part 3 of the story.**

Part 4 – The Pasturites meet Lord Grimlac

Approaching Castle Grimlac

Out of role, sit the pupils so they can see the map and tell them how the adventurers took a shortcut across the Dark Swamp. You may be able to use some ideas suggested earlier by the pupils about the Dark Swamp (if you remember, pupils were asked to say what they knew about different places on the map when they were in Tree Town), but if not, just give an impression of a dark, damp, muddy and miserable place.

Explain that to get to the Shining Temple the adventurers must pass through an area controlled by Lord Grimlac. As the adventurers get near to Castle Grimlac, they hear lots of noise that sounds like people chipping away at stone.

> ## Optional Extra
>
> ### History and Art
>
> Pupils work in pairs or threes. Each group is to make a model of Castle Grimlac, which should be as detailed as possible. They will need modelling dough and perhaps a supply of 'junk' items.
>
>
>
> Have lots of pictures of different kinds of castles around the room (Castles.pdf in folder The Quest
>
> on the Resources CD). Pupils can ask questions about the pictures: for example, they might want to know the names of various features and what they were for.
>
> Compare the models and discuss the features. You could go on to consider what purposes castles served in the past and how their architecture and technology developed over time.

Meeting Lord Grimlac

Tell the pupils that the adventurers continue on their journey, but just as they pass the castle they are stopped by a well-dressed gentleman. Explain to the pupils that you are going to play this role. Sign the role with some suitable costume (a gentleman's tie and handkerchief, for example).

This character is Lord Grimlac (role function: sinister authority figure) and needs to be played as a well-mannered, old-fashioned gentleman at this point in the story. Grimlac is charming in the hope that he will win their trust. He hopes that the adventurers will return across his lands on their way back from the Shining Temple with the crystal. Of course, he plans to steal the crystal from them so they cannot use it to wake the Queen. He doesn't know the adventurers have been warned about him by the Lady of the Living Lake.

Possible opening script:

> *'Goodness me! What a complete pleasure it is to meet you. If I am not mistaken, you are from The Pastures, aren't you? Welcome, welcome, everyone. Let me introduce myself: I am Lord Grimlac and the castle over there is my home. I'm just having some repairs done on it at present. All the stonework is being replaced on the far side. It is a rather noisy business, I'm afraid, but it will look lovely when it's finished.*
>
> *'I was just about to start my picnic and I'd be delighted if you would join me. I have plenty of food: look, jam sandwiches, sausage rolls, cheese, cake and fizzy pop. Come and sit down.'*

TIR develops a conversation with the PIR, asking them questions about where they are going and what they are doing so far from home. Whatever PIR say, TIR invites the PIR to stay with him to rest on their way home. TIR announces that he must go, wishes them well on their journey and says that he looks forward to seeing them in a few days' time.

Off to get the Shining Crystal

At this point, you change role and become Talgorn again, so remember to remove your Grimlac 'sign' and put on your Talgorn 'sign'. TIR suggests that the party splits up into small groups so that people can move faster and avoid being seen. TIR does not trust Grimlac and urges the PIR to get the crystal and meet back at this place as quickly as possible. While they are gone, Talgorn will see what she can find out about Castle Grimlac and look for other ways to travel across the Dark Swamp without getting too close to the castle. Divide the PIR into small groups and send them off to make their own way to the Shining Temple and bring back the crystal.

Let the PIR act out their own adventure for a few minutes, to the point where they return with the Shining Crystal. Then stop the drama.

Tell the pupils that they are going to have a chance to show each other what happened to their small group after they left Talgorn. Give each group ten minutes to practise a short play. If necessary, remind the pupils that they were given keys to the Shining Temple by the Lady of the Living Lake.

When the pupils have had time to practise their playlets, sit the class in a circle and remind them of the rules of watching performances.

Let groups show their plays to each other. Discuss the scenes to clarify what happened. Explain how the collection of the crystal is a very significant event in the story because inside the temple it was protected under lock and key, but, now it is outside, anyone could take it and use it. The adventurers have a big responsibility to look after it and make sure it reaches The Golden Towers safely. Remind the pupils that the crystal can be used only once every hundred years. **This concludes Part 4 of the story.**

Part 5 – Talgorn shows them a letter from the people who are being forced to dismantle the wall

The dilemma

> Dear People of The Pastures
>
> Forgive us for writing to you, but we desperately need your help. Lord Grimlac has imprisoned our families and is forcing us to take down the wall that separates Good Land from Bad Land. Soon the Bad Landers will be able to send their fierce monster through the broken-down wall, then Lac Town will be doomed. Lord Grimlac thinks he will be able to control the monster, but we know that he cannot. We also know that you have been to collect the crystal from the Shining Temple. Please use it to put Lord Grimlac to sleep so that we can repair the wall quickly and rescue our families from the dungeon.
>
> We beg you to do this. Time is very short.
>
> The people of Lac Town.

TIR as Talgorn meets and greets the returning adventurers and gets assurance that they have collected the crystal and that it is safe. TIR is worried. She asks the PIR to sit with her for a few minutes while she explains what she has found out about Castle Grimlac. TIR needs to tell the PIR the following:

- Lord Grimlac is not having repairs done to his castle: the noises they heard were the people of Lac Town destroying the wall that divides Good Land and Bad Land.

- Lord Grimlac has lots of people working on the destruction of the wall.

- The people are being forced to do this work because Lord Grimlac has imprisoned one member of each family in his castle dungeon.

- The wall is nearly destroyed; it is only a matter of hours before the first Bad Landers get into Good Land and let their monster through.

- The Mayor's daughter is being held prisoner by Lord Grimlac to ensure that the Mayor will do Lord Grimlac's bidding.

TIR shows the pupils a letter from the people of Lac Town begging for help (Letter.pdf in folder The Quest on the Resources CD). The letter must be large enough for everyone to see.

TIR leads PIR through a discussion about what they should do. Prompt questions could include the following:

- What could happen if the Queen is not woken?
- What could happen if Lord Grimlac is not put to sleep?
- If the Bad Landers invade Good Land, what will happen to The Pastures?
- What loyalty or duty do we have to the people of Lac Town?
- How could the people of Good Land defend themselves?
- Who would be the Good Land leader if the Queen is not woken?
- Do we have the right to make this choice?
- Is there a right choice?
- Are there any other solutions?

After discussion, the PIR have to make a decision about what they are going to do. A physical continuum line could be used to structure the debate. This would stretch from one extreme point of view (there is absolutely no doubt that we should use the crystal to put Grimlac to sleep) to the opposite point of view (without question, we should not use the crystal on Grimlac, but definitely must use it to wake the Queen).

TIR might need to help the PIR to decide how to decide!

- Does everybody need to agree on the same course of action?
- Will the group accept a majority vote?
- How will voting take place? Show of hands? Secret ballot?

One way or another, PIR make their decision. The decision is formally announced. Stop the drama. **This concludes Part 5 of the story.**

Part 6 – The Lady of the Living Lake arrives to save the day

The happy ending

Sit the pupils, out of role, in a comfortable place and tell them the last part of the story.

The adventurers did what they felt they had to do and … (explain the action they took). Suddenly a bright white light lit the sky and the adventurers could see the Lady of the Living Lake. They heard her soft voice saying:

'You are very brave, my dear Pastures people, and your goodness has saved Good Land for now. You have done the right thing. Because you have been faithful and true, I will do what you were not able to do. I will wake your Queen/put the evil Grimlac to sleep and ensure the wall is rebuilt [delete as appropriate]. *So, all will be well. I know that Good Land will need you again one day, but for now go home and enjoy your lives in The Pastures. While Good Land is safe, I will keep a bright star in the sky to remind you of my protection.'*

The adventurers suddenly found themselves back home in Green Town marketplace. It was quiet and peaceful. Everyone was going about their business as normal and, as soon as they saw the adventurers return, they were filled with joy, greeting them with tears and open arms. That night, a bright star filled the sky with light.

Final Reflection

- What happened at the end of the story?
- Is Good Land safe?
- Did you expect the Lady of the Living Lake to have such powers? Why?
- What do you think might happen to Good Land in the future?
- What do you think had happened to the Queen? Why?
- How do you think the adventurers felt when they realised they were home?
- Would the adventurers miss the thrill of the quest or would they settle back to their Pastures life easily?
- Where do you think Talgorn might be at the end of the story?
- What do you think Talgorn will do next?
- What do you imagine has happened to Lord Grimlac?
- Why did the Bad Landers want to invade Good Land?
- What do you imagine is happening in Bad Land now?
- Who were the bravest people in the story? Why do you think that?
- Would you say that Talgorn was a hero? Why?
- Was Talgorn a good leader? Why?
- What makes a good leader?
- Was the Mayor a good or a bad man?
- What would you have done if you had been the Mayor?
- If the Mayor loved his daughter was it acceptable that he lied and betrayed others to help her?
- Is it ever acceptable to tell a lie? When? Can you give an example?
- Do you think the adventurers should tell their friends and family what they saw and what they know about Bad Land? Why?
- The Lady of the Living Lake has stopped the invasion for now but is there any way of ensuring a lasting peace?
- What time is the story set in?
- Do you know any other stories that are like *The Quest*? Which ones? What are the similarities and differences?
- What was the main problem in the story?
- What made the story exciting?
- How would you describe the ending of the story?
- Did you like the ending? Why?
- What have you learned about people?
- What are the differences between the way people live in Good Land and the way we live?
- Would you like to live in Good Land?
- Would you like to know more about Bad Land?
- What would it be useful to find out about Bad Land?
- If you were to play the story again would you do anything differently? Why?

Potential cross-curricular learning

Here are some of the areas of the curriculum that can be linked to the story and used to design activities of your own.

Cross-curricular links	**Maths** Ma 2: Practising calculations – in particular buying and selling goods at the market in Green Town, adding up the cost of equipment items for the quest journey. Ma 3: Undertaking various measuring tasks as part of the role of being an adventurer - for example, working out distances travelled or the sizes of 'mystery' footprints that have been found near the adventurers' camp; weighing drinks containers and working out which one carries most liquid, is the least bulky and is easiest to carry.
	Geography Reading maps and plans; familiarisation with scales – especially if pupils have a go at working out distances travelled; using geographical language; describing what places are like; discussing human and physical features; learning about weather, the water cycle, rivers, river plants and animal life and also lakes and ponds, caves and mountains; learning about people who live in different locations, such as in mountainous regions or in cold lands; locating on real maps features such as rivers, flood plains, lakes, mountains.
	Science Sc 2: Using the imaginary landscape to discuss living, once-living and non-living things; working on the topics of plants and growth whilst acting out scenes of life in The Pastures; comparing different types of plants, such as trees and flowers; studying wild animals, animal habitats and what animals need to live; discussing day and night creatures; discussing human safety and welfare. Sc 4: Light and dark.
	PSHE and citizenship Developing confidence and responsibility; preparing to take an active role as a citizen; talking and listening in groups of different sizes; expressing opinions, hearing the opinions of others; taking responsibility for decisions and actions; coping with dilemmas.
	History Studying farming and costumes from the 'olden days'; looking at the history of farming from medieval times to the present day; castles and castle life, how castle walls developed over time to provide better defence from attack; strategically important walls and why they were built such as Hadrian's wall, the Great Wall of China and the Berlin Wall; famous people – landscape painters such as John Constable.
	Design technology Discussing walls – how they are constructed and the use of different building materials; comparing castle walls with modern house walls, garden walls with dry-stone walls on farmland.
	Art Learning about landscape painting, studying pictures such as Richard Wilson's *View in Windsor Great Park*, Theodore Rousseau's *The Forest of Fontainebleau, Morning*, Camille Pissarro's *Landscape at Chaponval*, Ferdinand Hodler's *Lake Thun*, John Robert Cozen's *Between Chamonix and Martigny* and Frederick Church's *Twilight in the Wilderness*; making landscapes in model form, collage and by drawing and painting.

Literacy skills	There are lots of opportunities to develop speaking and listening skills through drama and discussions. Pupils are centrally involved in decision making and are therefore involved in debating options and persuading others of a point of view. The pupils are also learning about how a quest story is constructed and about its key features. There are opportunities to develop story writing skills through discussions about settings, characters, the problems the characters face and, of course, the ending.
Remember DfES thinking skills!	**Creating** Generating and extending ideas; applying imagination; looking for innovative outcomes. This story demands a lot of imagination as pupils are asked to create a vision of a whole new world. In the drama pupils develop their creative thinking as they journey through a fantasy land - crossing rivers, clambering over rough ground, entering caves, sleeping under the stars near an enchanted lake and, finally, collecting the shining crystal that will save the Queen.

Enquiring Asking relevant questions; posing and defining problems; predicting outcomes and anticipating consequences. This type of thinking is developed through the many meetings pupils have in role with characters in the drama. Who can be trusted? What is the best route to travel? What equipment will be needed? Pupils in role try to understand what is happening to Good Land as they work out how to successfully complete their quest.

Reasoning Giving reasons for opinions and actions; drawing inferences and making deductions; explaining thoughts; making informed decisions and judgements. This type of thinking is developed through discussions in and out of role about the best course of action to take. As the pupils in role progress on their journey through Good Land they are given information and they have to decide what to believe, what to ignore, what is important and what should be acted upon immediately.

Information processing Sorting and classifying; comparing and contrasting; sequencing. This type of thinking is developed through sequencing the story. On their quest, the PIR visit five locations for different purposes, although each of these places is important in the story. Pupils also learn how stories can be broken into parts or scenes. Pupils also develop this type of thinking through using the map of Good Land and through reflective discussions about the nature of the landscape in which the story is set (for example, pupils might be asked to consider what they know about Good Land and how it is different from where they live in real life).

Evaluating Examining what the story means; judging the value of what you have read, heard or done. The quest plot is important, as it deals with people who are striving towards a distant but all-important goal. The journey the heroes of the story take will change their lives and this is an interesting and relevant message for young pupils who are just setting out on their own 'life journey'. This type of thinking is developed through reflecting on the experiences the characters in the story have and being prompted to imagine how the events might relate to real life. |

The Big Factory and River Trouble

Planning checklist

Subject matter	Factories, industrialisation and the effects of pollution on communities
Themes	Trust; secrets; loyalty; manipulation; the truth and lies; personal versus communal wellbeing; bribery
Key resources and equipment	Various costume items to sign TIR: cap and bunch of keys for the Gate Guard; clipboard; briefcase; white coat; large book with 'Chemical Formulas' written on the cover; spectacles; microphone. **Worksheets (in folder Big Factory on the Resources CD)** Character Chart (Character Chart.pdf) Chemical Protection Suit Details (CPS Details.pdf) House Prompt Sheet (House Prompt Sheet.pdf) Our Model (Our Model.pdf) Predicting Events (Predicting Events.pdf) The Ground Floor of My House (Ground Floor.pdf) Workers' Report (Workers Report.pdf) The Most Exciting Part of the Story (Most Exciting Part.pdf) Yes/No table (Yes-No.pdf) Car Request Form (Car Request.pdf) House Request Form (House Request.pdf) Instrument box worksheet (Box Worksheet.pdf) **Props include** Car brochures Magazines of house interiors Pictures of industrial landscapes (Industrial Landscapes.pdf) Pictures of houses from newspapers/estate agents Worker gate passes (Gate Passes.pdf) ID badges (ID Badges.pdf) Factory Rules (Rules.pdf) Worldwide Medicine Corporation secrecy agreement (Secrecy Agreement.pdf) Pictures of real chemical protection suits (CPS Pictures.pdf) Lab pictures for the broken pieces Optional Extra (Lab Pic Whole.pdf, Lab Pic1.pdf etc)
Organisation	**Time** Without Optional Extras: 8–10 hours With Optional Extras: 12–14 hours **Teaching space** Preferably the hall for the acting-out activities with the flexibility to return to tables for the writing and drawing tasks Possible role play area themes: • a factory – gate; office; shop floor; canteen; tools area • a laboratory – office; workshop; equipment room; staff room • a fishing boat • a television studio • a hotel.
Main dramatic devices used	Teacher in Role Pupils in Role **Basic plot** Tragedy, with elements of Rags to Riches **Basic problem** Pollution of the local river (a potential threat to life) **Basic tension** Secrecy and the possibility of industrial sabotage (lack of knowledge; being threatened with unwanted consequences)

Teacher's overview

This project is about pollution of the environment and the story deals with some genuine issues and dilemmas faced by communities around the world. Behind the story is the current widespread concern about the pernicious effects of water pollution. Young pupils may not be able to understand the global effect of water pollution yet, but the story will raise their awareness of the issue and prepare them for deeper understanding later on in their school lives.

In the project, pupils are in role as workers in a medicine factory. The workers have to face the prospect that the local river may have been polluted with chemicals that have leaked out of their factory. People in the nearby town are getting sick and the media are looking for someone or something to blame. To complicate matters, the workers have agreed to sign a secrecy agreement in exchange for a package of privileges from the factory managers. They also have to deal with conflicting information. It may not be chemicals from the medicine factory that have polluted the river, it might be industrial sabotage, it might be the farms up stream of the factory. If, however, their factory is responsible for the pollution and the workers 'blow the whistle', their jobs could be at stake. They might have to decide whether to keep quiet in order to retain their standard of living or sacrifice their jobs to save the local community.

In the fiction, the workers don't have an opportunity to seek a solution and are forced to react ever more quickly to events and information as the story comes to a climax. Towards the end of the project, the pupils change roles to become the Directors of the medicine factory, who have the option to close the factory knowing that this will mean an immediate loss of jobs for people in the local town. By experiencing the story from the point of view of two different roles, the pupils have a chance to build a broader understanding of the environmental and economic issues.

Serious stuff! But as you set up the drama, it may help you to base your thinking on *Charlie and the Chocolate Factory*. Some of the same devices are used in order to create a sense of excitement: secrecy; the threat of industrial espionage; making the PIR an elite group who enjoy special privileges; and the potential for the main characters to do good for others. The factory makes medicines, so it can be bright clean and reasonably cheerful.

So, this is not a simple goodies versus baddies story. Rather it is intended to give the pupils an insight into the complexities of pollution problems. Therefore the bosses are not 'the enemy' but stakeholders who find themselves in a difficult situation, facing the combined pressures of competition, potential sabotage and active protest. On the one hand, closing the factory will bring job losses and a decline of the local economy. On the other, keeping the factory on the same site may well cause damage to the local community and other businesses through bad publicity and it may be cheaper in the long run to move the factory elsewhere.

The workers are not 'heroes' but during the course of the drama become increasingly aware of what could be at stake for them: loss of jobs; of lifestyle; of privileges; of health. They face the moral question: is it right that people should have to sacrifice their way of life for the sake of others? They experience what it might be like to have to make tough life-changing decisions. In role the pupils taste the temptation to 'feather their own nests' and not to let the big picture, the community perspective, or worldwide issues affect them. As children get older, this may help them to understand the choices faced by people who are desperate to make a living, such as those who work for companies clearing the rainforest for timber or pasture. In a small way, the pupils are beginning to examine notions of community at local, national and international levels and the stresses of torn loyalties and competing responsibilities.

In the background, there are also issues around freedom of speech, the nature of protest and the power of the media, all of which can be explored further if it seems appropriate. Questions that could be discussed include:

* What right do people have to protest?
* How far should protests go?
* Is it ever right to break the rules or break the law?
* Should any information be censored or kept secret?
* Who has the right to know what?
* How far can we trust media reports?
* How far can we trust what manufacturers tell us about their products?

Going even further (perhaps too far for young children, but interesting for the teacher to bear in mind), the drama opens up a discussion about the dominance of commercialism in our society; the grip of multi-national companies; the ethics of research and experimentation (use of animals, for example); and the power of advertising (junk food for instance).

Pupils can also begin to understand that there are risks involved in an area becoming economically dependent on one major industry and associated businesses.

The tale of *The Big Factory and River Trouble* has been created from a composite of real cases from around the developed and developing world and especially from Sharon's experience of working in Bilston near Wolverhampton, an ex-steel town. In fact, the story connects with the recent history of most UK urban areas that have struggled to deal with the economic and social problems of post-industrialisation: the decline of the potteries in Stoke-on-Trent (where we live); the closure of the coal mines in the Welsh Valleys; the disappearance of shipbuilding from Teeside, Tyneside and the Clyde; the abandonment of the cotton mills of Lancashire and woollen mills of Yorkshire … the list goes on.

It is easy to see how this story can help to lay essential foundations for history (change and continuity, the relationship between economics and politics, Victorians …) and geography (people, places and environment) at KS2.

The drama is designed to give pupils 'food for thought' and although they have to make tough decisions, in role they are clearly not responsible for creating the situation, they are part of the solution to the problem even if it is not a completely satisfactory one.

There are moments in the project when the pupils have time to discuss the information they have been given about the pollution of the river. The picture plan of the area is an important resource for these discussions. We did not want the pupils to be able to easily dismiss the possibility that it is the medicine factory at fault, so the other factories are placed deliberately downstream of the Red Houses settlement. It is therefore highly unlikely that any substances they put into the river would affect the people who live in the town as the flow of the river would immediately take pollutants away (out to sea). This leaves the PIR with the options that it *is* their factory, or it is possibly chemical fertilizers and insecticides leaching from the farmer's fields, or it is another medicine company deliberately framing their factory in order to hamper the development of the new medicine. There is obviously some potentially good geography in this part of the project, but pupils will need help to understand the implications of the location of the potential culprits.

The other industries shown in the Red Houses locality (leather, paper, wine) have been chosen because globally they are known to contribute to water pollution and again it is a matter of simply raising awareness by mentioning them. It is not necessary at this stage for pupils to know how or where or why these particular industries contribute to water pollution, hopefully all that will come later on.

Defining this drama's plot-type is a little difficult for a couple of reasons. The pupils select the ending, which means that the story could end tragically or have a happy outcome. The plot could be developed as a Tragedy, which would make it a little gloomy for young children (actually, we can't find any examples of Tragedies in young children's literature). It is probably best to see it as a Rags to Riches story, but accept that it may well have a not-so-happy ending.

Famous Rags to Riches stories within the canon of English literature include Charles Dickens's *David Copperfield*, George Bernard Shaw's *Pygmalion* and Charlotte Brontë's *Jane Eyre*. Children's stories include *Cinderella*, *Dick Whittington*, *Aladdin* and the musical *Annie*.

The cast of characters

The teacher is asked to take on a number of roles in order to give the impression of a factory with lots of different people and departments – a big factory.

- **The Gate Guard**   A friendly and efficient person employed by the factory to look after security at the main gate (TIR)
- **Dr Codyne**   Senior researcher employed by the factory to train new workers in the most top-secret projects. A serious-minded person (TIR)
- **Human Resources Manager**   The 'go between' who brings messages from the factory bosses (TIR)
- **TV news reporter**   Breaking the news about health issues in Red Houses Town (TIR)
- **The Professor**   The most senior figure in the Top Secret Laboratory. Dedicated and honourable, but perhaps a little too pre-occupied with work (TIR)
- **The Mysterious Scientist**   A protestor who is prepared to break rules in order to protest and bring issues to the attention of the general public (TIR)
- **The Workers**   Honest and hard working (PIR)
- **The Directors**   The factory bosses who have a lot of responsibility and some tough decisions to make (PIR)

Summary of the plot

Scene 1 **The workers arrive at the factory gate**

It should be just another typical day at work, but someone has been searching through belongings left in the locker room. Something strange is going on, but what?

Scene 2 **Joining 'the Top Team'**

The workers are offered a glamorous new job.

Scene 3 **Recruited to work on a secret project**

The new job will pay well and have many benefits, but the workers will have to agree to keep what they do secret.

Scene 4 **Learning the new job**

It is becoming clear that there are some potential dangers involved in the new work.

Scene 5 **The TV interview**

The news reporter wants to know why so many people in the town nearest to the factory become ill. The workers are asked to reveal secrets.

Scene 6 **Working with the Professor**

The workers meet the most senior person in the top-secret laboratory.

Scene 7 **The break-in**

Someone has smashed up the laboratory and stolen the recipe for the newest and most top secret medicine.

Scene 8 **The challenge**

A mysterious scientist challenges the workers to go public with the truth about what they do in the top-secret laboratory.

Scene 9 **The Directors arrive for their meeting**

A decision has to be made about the future of the project, the factory and, therefore, the workers.

Scene 10 **The ending**

The PIR as the Directors decide what to do.

Getting going

Show the children pictures of industrial landscapes from different cities and countries (Industrial Landscapes.pdf in folder Big Factory on the Resources CD). Ask them to work in threes for three minutes, brainstorming orally (there's no need for them to write anything down at this stage) everything they know about factories. It might be useful to mount the pictures onto separate cards so that the pupils can pass them round and use them to prompt their brainstorm.

Use tokens to structure a whole class discussion about factories. Every pupil is given a token (perhaps a button or a plastic counter) and must spend it by contributing an idea or opinion to the discussion.

Use questions such as:

- What did you see in your pictures?
- What do factories look like?
- What happens inside factories?
- Why do people build factories?
- What jobs do people do in factories?
- Do you know anybody who works in a factory?
- Are there any factories near to school?
- Are there any factories near to where you live?
- What is a factory?
- What work is going on in the other places such as the building site?
- What docs a power station do?
- What kinds of things do people mine for?
- What does a wind farm do?
- What do you think happens to the logs after they are taken out of the water?
- What are the differences between these other 'industries' and factories?
- What are the similarities between these other 'industries' and factories?
- What questions do you have about factories?

Summarise what the pupils have said about factories and make a note of important points to remember on a flip chart or whiteboard so that it can be kept and referred to later if necessary. Also record any questions the pupils have about factories at this point.

Map and Plan Making: the area around the factory

Tell the pupils that the drama will be set in a factory that makes medicines and that they will play the part of factory workers. Using the illustration on Page 196 as a guide, draw a map to show them where the factory is situated. Sit the children so that they can see a large sheet of paper and draw a river running across it. Near to the river draw the factory building (the medicine factory). Add an outline of the hills, add the vineyard, the bridge and the other factories. Indicate the positions of Red Houses town and the Old Port. Label the drawing.

Once you have drawn this base map, ask the children to add details to the new town of Red Houses, which has swallowed up the original fishing village. Explain that as a result of the building of the medicine factory, followed by other factories along the river, the settlement expanded rapidly. Lots of houses and associated facilities had to be built to accommodate the workers. The pupils can do this activity in one of two ways.

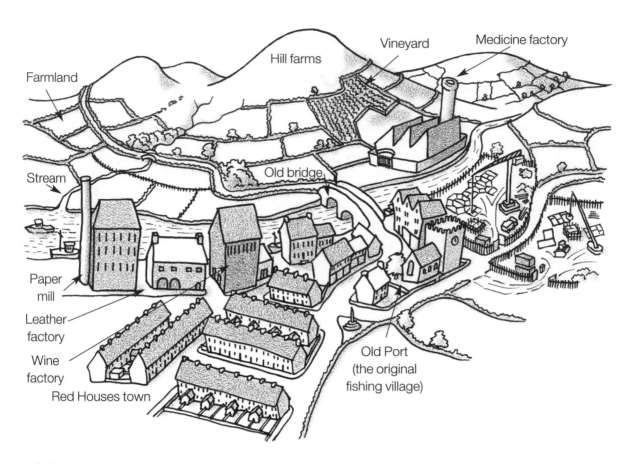

1. Ask them to get into groups of three; give each group a large piece of paper and a few marker pens. Ask them to draw, as a group, an expanded detailed plan of Red Houses town (including the Old Port). After ten minutes, call the groups together to compare their plans. Ask the children to spot similarities and differences.
2. Continue working as a whole-class group. Ask pupils to contribute ideas orally, which you draw directly onto the communal map for them.

Finally, check that the pupils have included all the facilities that the factory workers and their families will need, such as parks, a leisure centre, dentists' and doctors' surgeries, different types of shops, a recycling centre and so on. If necessary, add these in.

Building belief

The pupils need to have a feeling for the secrecy of the project that they are about to be recruited to work on. To help build belief in the situation, the start of the drama must quickly suggest the highly secretive nature of the work that the factory undertakes. You need to help the pupils to visualise a secure building with many locked and guarded gates and doors. Some areas of the factory are for specially authorised personnel only. Staff are always checked when entering and leaving the building. All chemicals and other ingredients have to be signed for. The factory does not have to be grim, but you must convey the impression of an insular, behind-closed-doors organisation. *Charlie and the Chocolate Factory* might provide a good model to work from. You will need to have made worker gate passes and ID badges (Gate Passes.pdf and ID Badges.pdf in folder Big Factory folder on the Resources CD) for all the pupils before the start of the lesson.

As teacher, you will need to play a number of different roles. Explain to the pupils that you will be playing different characters at different times and, each time you introduce a new character, you will sign your role differently (with a fresh piece of costume or a property such as a clipboard or a bunch of keys). For most of the drama, the pupils will be in role as factory workers who live in nearby Red Houses.

Give each pupil a worker gate pass (write a unique letter and number on each, e.g. A1, B1, C1). Tell the pupils that they must remember their special code letter and number. Explain that the factory gates will open at 7.30 a.m., at which time the gate guard (TIR signs with a cap and a bunch of keys perhaps) will be ready to collect their worker gate passes. Once they're inside, the gate guard will line everyone up for morning inspection and briefing.

Scene 1: The workers arrive at the factory gates

At the start of the acting out (out of role), lead the action by getting the PIR to line up outside the factory gates. Let the PIR line up and wait for a short while (this creates a little tension and anticipation).

Now Freeze Frame the action to give pupils time to think about their situation. Question the pupils to expand their thinking and build belief in the fiction:

- What are the gates of the factory like? Describe them.
- Would you like to do the gate guard's job? Why?
- What is the weather like this morning?
- What sounds can you hear?
- Have you had breakfast before you came to work? What did you have?
- What are you wearing for work? Do you have to have any special clothes to do your job?
- What are you looking forward to doing today?
- When you get home tonight, what will you most enjoy doing?

It doesn't matter if the pupils can't fully answer these questions, since they are only serving as prompts for their imagination. Suggest answers in a conversational tone, such as, 'I see, so you don't have to wear any special clothes for *your* job, but if you were to work in the chemical room, I bet you'd need an overall.'

At the sound of a bell or other suitable noise, TIR as the gate guard (role function: authority figure) unlocks the gates and lets the PIR as workers through. TIR collects their worker gate passes as they enter and reads the factory rules to the PIR (Rules.pdf in folder Big Factory on the Resources CD).

The rules can then be pinned up:

FACTORY RULES

✓ Workers must not tell other people about the jobs they do in the factory.
✓ Workers must not tell other people about any products made in the factory.
✓ Workers must not tell other people about any of the ingredients used in products made in the factory.
✓ Workers are not allowed to bring any equipment, tools, food or drink into the factory.
✓ Workers are not allowed to take any equipment, tools, ingredients, products, food or drink out of the factory.
✓ Workers must give their Gate Pass to the Gate Guard when entering the factory.
✓ Workers must wear their ID badges at all times once inside the factory.

Signed *M. Latif*

On behalf of the Directors of the Worldwide Medicine Corporation

---

TIR issues the PIR with their personal ID badges and insists that they make an orderly line by the door to the workers' locker room. TIR explains that all the lockers in which the workers store their personal belongings and special factory clothes have been opened and searched as part of a routine security check. All the workers are therefore allowed an extra ten minutes today to tidy up their lockers and get dressed in any special clothes before they are taken to the places where they work.

Act out letting the PIR into the workers' locker room through a door that is obviously heavy and has several locks. TIR apologises for the mess and, by chatting with PIR, suggests the kinds of things the workers have stored in their lockers.

Possible script:

'Oh, I'm really sorry about this. I hadn't realised the security guards had made such a mess of your things. Is this someone's photograph? Are these your socks? Someone's wristwatch is on the floor over there. I've just trodden on a hairbrush! Is this your notebook? Who owns this red towel? I think this must be your overall.'

Let the PIR act out the tidying up for a couple of minutes. Stop the drama.

Drawing in Role: items in the lockers

Give the pupils a timed task. The intention is to add detail to their visualisation of this scene and build further understanding of the situation the workers find themselves in. Use 'must, should, could' to prompt pupils to manage their time well. The task should take about twenty minutes, but the time needs to be set to suit the capabilities of the class. Each pupil:

Must draw the things that her character kept in her locker.

Should then use the drawing to write a list of items that her character kept in her locker, or label the drawing.

Could complete a worksheet showing what workers can and cannot bring into the factory (Yes-No.pdf in Big Factory folder on the CD).

Explain to the pupils that, when the drama starts again, the workers will get a surprise. They had expected to go off to do their usual jobs, but they will be taken off to a secret meeting room instead.

Scene 2: Joining 'the Top Team'

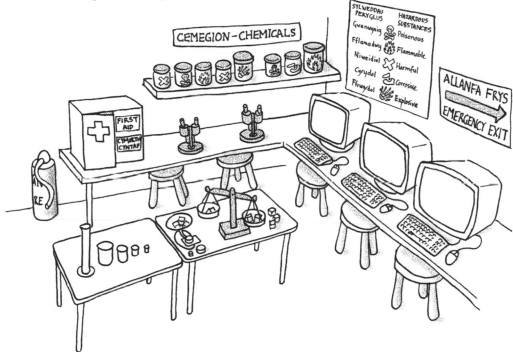

Now change your role to Dr Codyne, best signed with a white coat if possible. Role function: authority figure. Dr Codyne gathers the PIR together and tells them that the Board of Directors are very sorry that the security checks in the workers' locker room made such a mess of their possessions. The checks were necessary, as the PIR are now needed to work on the factory's most secret medicine ever. All of the workers present at this meeting have passed the security checks with flying colours and are invited to join the Top Team in the top-secret laboratory. Here, they will learn new skills and work on a most wonderful new product. TIR tells the workers that they will be paid more and will each be given a free house and a free car for doing their new job. PIR are asked to follow Dr Codyne on a tour of the factory's top-secret laboratory. TIR leads the PIR on an imaginary tour of the lab. (It may help to have drawn yourself a rough plan to show how the laboratory is laid out in the teaching space you are using.)

Stop the drama.

Optional Extra

English speaking and listening En1

Broken pieces exercise

Organise the class, out of role, into groups of four. In each group, the pupils need to sit so that they can hear each other well, but with enough space between them for each to hold an A4 picture without other members of the group being able to see it. You will need to print the picture of the whole laboratory plus its four fragments (Lab Pic Whole.pdf, Lab Pic1.pdf, Lab Pic2.pdf, Lab Pic3.pdf and Lab Pic4.pdf in folder Big Factory on the Resources CD).

Explain that each group has a picture of a laboratory, but the picture has been cut up into four sections. Each pupil has just one section. They have to describe their bit of the picture to everyone in the group. The task is to see if they can draw the whole lab just by listening to the other descriptions. They are not allowed to look at the fragments held by other group members.

Each pupil takes a turn to describe what they can see in their fragment of the picture. Time the 'rounds' to ensure that everyone gets a chance to describe their section in detail.

When all four children have had a chance to describe, split each group into two pairs. Give each pair a large sheet of paper and ask them to draw the whole picture the best they can, by putting together the descriptions they have heard. Time this drawing activity – ten minutes should be ample.

Put the pairs back into fours. Now ask them to put all four pieces of the laboratory picture together on their table top so they can see the whole thing. The pupils then compare their drawings to the original picture to see how accurate they were.

Debrief the exercise by looking at some of the drawings and discussing what was easy and what was challenging about the exercise.

Introducing a problem

Little do they know it, but the factory workers are about to take a job that will change their lives.

Move the story on in time by half an hour. Explain to the pupils that the factory workers have completed their tour of the lab and have just been called to a meeting in a room on the managers' corridor. Normally, workers are not allowed in this area, so they realise that it must be something very important.

Scene 3: Recruited to work on a secret project

TIR changes role again and becomes the factory's Human Resources Manager, perhaps signed with a smart jacket and clipboard. Role function: benevolent authority figure. TIR as the Human Resources Manager welcomes all the workers to the meeting. The workers are told that the factory has just invented a new product, which this group of workers has been chosen to manufacture. However, the workers will need to be trained and will have to sign a strict agreement to say that they will keep their work a total secret. TIR tells the PIR that they are trusted workers. The fact that they have already seen inside the top-secret laboratory is a sign of the faith that the managers have in them.

PIR are told that the factory already has a very high reputation for making quality medicines. But the new product will be the best ever. It will prevent illnesses for thousands of people and save many lives. The new medicine actually stops people becoming ill in the first place! It is a major breakthrough. Consequently, the PIR can be very proud of the work they will be doing.

TIR hands each pupil the secrecy agreement and asks them all to sign it (Secrecy Agreement.pdf in folder Big Factory on the Resources CD).

Acting out trying on chemical protection suits

TIR explains that each worker is going to need special equipment for their work and that the rest of the day will be spent gathering all this together. Tomorrow, the PIR will have their first day in the laboratory learning their new jobs.

First, each worker must have a chemical protection suit (CPS). TIR acts out leading the PIR through a number of locked doors to a room where they can try on CPSs for size. TIR introduces the room, which has no windows and only one door. Around the wall hang all-in-one suits and helmets. On a rack there are boots; on another rack there are gloves. There are oxygen tanks and breathing equipment stored in a box with a locked lid.

TIR leads acting out how to put on a CPS. Details make a real difference to whether or not the PIR enjoy the sense of danger that is building around their new jobs. TIR needs to instruct the PIR as if every detail were a matter of life and death! Here is a possible sequence:

1. Carefully take the suit from its peg.
2. Explain that the suit is made from a special fabric that is waterproof and also strong enough not to burn for five minutes should there be a fire.
3. At the ankles and wrists there are tight-fitting cuffs (demonstrated as difficult to pull over) that seal the suit.
4. The front has two fastenings, first a zip and then a fold-over flap that has Velcro to seal it into place.
5. Each worker needs a pair of boots.
6. Each worker needs a pair of gloves.
7. With keys, open the box where the breathing equipment is stored. Connect the oxygen tanks. These will be needed because some of the jobs will need to be done in special airless rooms so that nothing will become contaminated. Demonstrate putting on the breathing equipment, like a backpack. Switch it on.
8. There is an intercom system that has to be switched on when you want to speak to someone else who is wearing a suit.
9. Finally, switch on the air, switch on the intercom and walk around in the obviously heavy and cumbersome suit.

TIR must urge all workers to check their suits frequently, since any damage might allow a chemical to enter the suit and cause illness. Tell the PIR not to damage their suits by sitting down in them or by catching them against sharp equipment and tearing the fabric.

Let the pupils act out moving around carefully in the suits. Freeze Frame the action from time to time to ask pupils what it feels like to wear the suits and why they think they will need to wear them. Ask pupils what they think it will be like working in the suits.

TIR leads taking off the suits and storing them carefully, putting the air equipment back in the box and so on.

Optional Extra

Literacy

Pupils use the worksheet to draw themselves wearing their CPSs (CPS details.pdf in folder Big Factory on the Resources CD). They must be able to say what they think it looks like and what all the features are for.

Give the pupils a picture of a real CPS (any protective suits would work well, including those for nuclear, biological and chemical incidents – CPS Pictures.pdf in folder Big Factory on the Resources CD) and ask them to compare their drawings with the pictures. Ask the pupils to find things that are the same and things that are different about their drawings when compared with the pictures.

TIR takes the PIR for a refreshment break in the White Room. The White Room is a place that only workers from the top-secret laboratory can go to eat and drink. While handing out sandwiches and drinks, TIR explains that workers must never eat or drink in the laboratory. The PIR will be encouraged to have their midday break in the canteen with the other workers as usual, but they must of course not talk about the work they are doing. TIR needs to introduce the idea that some of the managers are nervous about the possibility that the chemicals that are used in the top-secret laboratory would pollute the river if ever there was a leak or an accident.

Possible script:

'These are just precautions and nothing to worry about. We are trying to keep what we do a secret so that other people don't steal our ideas. Some other medicine companies would not like the idea of a medicine that is a wonderful cure for all kinds of illnesses you know. It would mean their medicines would no longer be needed! And please don't worry about the chemicals we ask you to work with. We are very careful to make sure everything and everyone is very safe. I know there has been talk of the river being polluted but I am absolutely sure that nothing, not even one drop of anything poisonous, has leaked out of this factory into the river. So, you have absolutely nothing to worry about, just enjoy your new job and all of the benefits. Speaking of which ...'

TIR gives the PIR pictures of houses to choose from. A good resource for this would be newspapers or estate agents house detail sheets. These are houses that are available on the new estate being built in the town. TIR asks the pupils to choose one and put their name on it or gets them to fill out a house request form (House Request.pdf in folder Big Factory on the Resources CD). TIR also give out pictures of cars. A good resource for this would be brochures from car showrooms. TIR can either ask the PIR to draw the car they want, select a car from the pictures, or fill out the car request form (Car Request.pdf in folder Big Factory on the Resources CD).

'The new houses look so nice. We want to look after all our workers and those of you doing "special" work are particularly important to us. Please choose a house for you and your family; you can have whichever one you like. Put your name on the picture of the house you want. Here are some pictures of cars that the Worldwide Medicine Corporation is willing to buy for you. Please take some time to have a look and choose which one you would like.'

Stop the drama.

Optional Extras

Geography

Pupils choose to do one of the following two tasks out of role.

Task 1

Pupils *must* draw or write items that they would like to buy for their house onto the worksheet provided (House Prompt Sheet.pdf in folder Big Factory on the Resources CD). Get them to:

1. Look at the plan of the ground floor of their house (Ground Floor.pdf in folder Big Factory on the Resources CD). There are four rooms. Decide what the rooms are, such as kitchen, lounge, study, playroom. If they are unsure of what to do give them a list of rooms to choose from.
2. Write the names of the rooms into the separate boxes.
3. Either draw pictures of, or write a list of, the furniture and ornaments that they would have in each room.

Should draw a detailed picture or plan of one room.

Could compare the picture of the room they have designed with pictures of rooms in magazines and say what the similarities and differences are, what they might change in their design and why.

Task 2

Pupils *must* make a model of one of their rooms. Get them to:

1. Look at the picture of their house. Inside the house there are have five rooms downstairs: kitchen; living room; conservatory; dining room and playroom. Choose one room.
2. Make the furniture and ornaments for their chosen room using the shoebox provided and some modelling dough
3. Decorate the sides of the shoebox as if they were the walls of the room.
4. Place the furniture and ornaments into the shoebox.

Should draw a one-to-one scale plan of the model room so that it shows exactly where everything in the room is. They need to look down on the model room from above.

Could make the plan bigger, to the scale of two to one, using maths equipment to help you.

Scene 4: Learning the new job

Restart the story with TIR as the Human Resources Manager (don't forget to sign your role) taking the PIR to collect their tools from the equipment department. Act out travelling down several corridors, having to unlock and relock doors. Along the way, TIR (acting as if she had just heard a loud explosion) points out that explosions are all part of the work and nothing to worry about. In the equipment department, explain to the PIR that every worker will be issued with a toolbox. Ask the pupils to go and find the toolbox with their name on (this is entirely done in imaginary acting out with no props necessary) and bring it over to the meeting area. TIR acts out opening her toolbox and asks the PIR to do the same. Act out taking (imaginary) tools out of the box and handling them carefully. Suggested tools:

- tongs for gripping hot items
- special measuring jugs
- scales
- thermometers
- pestle and mortar
- electronic machine for testing salts
- litmus paper for testing acids
- mixing machine.

TIR demonstrates in mimed action how each of these tools works and asks the pupils to perform the actions with her as if they are 'having a go' too. It doesn't matter if the pupils themselves don't know or understand what these pieces of equipment are, as the PIR have been told they will soon be learning the necessary skills. The seriousness of the process is the most important factor in this scene.

TIR tells the PIR to bring their toolboxes with them, being sure to carry them carefully, and leads the PIR back out of the equipment department and into the room where the chemical protection suits are stored. PIR are asked to put their toolboxes next to their suits ready for tomorrow. Tell the PIR that they will be leaving work early today. Make sure house request forms and car request forms (if used) have been handed in.

TIR takes them to the workers' locker room, where they are allowed to collect their coats and bags, and then they are taken to the gate. ID badges are exchanged for worker gate passes and the PIR wait for the gates to open. Just before the gates open, TIR takes a call on the telephone. TIR calls PIR together and warns them that spies have been seen in the local area today. PIR are warned to be careful whom they talk to and what they say. She reminds them of the secrecy agreement. TIR wishes them good afternoon and tells them she will meet them in the workers' locker room tomorrow morning. Stop the drama.

Out of role, sit the children in a comfortable place and spend some time reflecting on the story so far. Remind the pupils what was said about factories at the beginning of the project.

Reflect on the drama

- What has happened in the story so far?
- What are all the different places that the story has been set in so far? (List them – for example, outside the factory gates, the locker room, a laboratory.)
- Which of the places has been most exciting? Why?
- What do you imagine the factory looks like? Inside? Outside?
- Do you think the medicine factory is different to other factories? How?
- Which characters have we met?
- Which character do you like most and why?
- Do you know what the main problem of the story is yet?
- Is there any advice you would like to give the workers?
- What do you think will happen next?

Optional Extras

Science Sc 2, Sc 3 and Sc 4

This is a good place to stop the story for a while and work out of role on some science tasks.

Pupils have built a belief in a factory that makes medicines and conducts experiments. Pupils could tackle aspects of Sc 2 about health and medicines. Pupils could interview the school nurse, visit a chemist shop, interview a pharmacist, set up the role-play area as a chemist shop, find out information about the doctor's surgery.

For Sc 3, pupils could do experiments with materials that change, such as ice melting or bread dough stretching and growing. Pupils could also talk about hazards in the home and how to protect themselves and others from danger. Pupils could also discuss school rules and which ones are particularly for the protection of people.

For Sc 4, pupils could experiment with making a simple alarm or buzzer system and this could be related to the idea of security systems for the factory. Or relate any activities to do with electricity to the building of the new houses for the workers in the story or to making the factory light enough for the workers to be able to do their work well.

History

Pupils could find out about famous scientists, such as Marie Curie, Alexander Fleming, Elizabeth Blackwell and Louis Pasteur and in particular about their contributions to modern-day medicine.

Geography

Pupils could study the types of housing in the school locality, use simple maps and identify key features of the area, discussing the human and physical features. Pupils could also list the characteristics of a community. They could also look at real-life communities that are similar to Red Houses town in the story, such as Liverpool, Bristol, Newcastle-upon-Tyne. These cities are much bigger than Red Houses, of course, but it is possible to see how they grew over time from much smaller rural or fishing communities into industrialised areas.

Adding tension

Scene 5: The TV interview

Out of role, tell the pupils that when the workers get into town there are lots of people in the streets. A TV news crew is broadcasting live from the shopping centre. People are being interviewed by reporters. A group of workers are stopped by a reporter for a live TV interview. The workers decide to answer questions, since it might seem odd not to, but are determined not to give any secrets away.

Sit the pupils in a semicircle with four chairs in the acting area. Ask for four volunteers to be the workers who are interviewed. Tell them that they can ask the other pupils for help if they need it. This is a type of Forum Theatre. (It would be very effective if the interview could be video-recorded, but it is not essential.)

Start the acting out by setting the scene with TIR as the reporter (speak in the style of a TV news reporter and sign your role with a microphone), explaining where the story is coming from. Role function: messenger.

Possible script:

> *'Yes, here we are in Red Houses town centre, talking to local residents about the number of people who report illnesses to their doctor every week. Red Houses has the highest number of reported illnesses per week in the whole country. Are the people of Red Houses really so ill or are they making it up? I'm talking to four people who work for the Worldwide Medicine Corporation just up the road from here ...'*

Out of role, ask the pupils in the semicircle what they think is going on, what the reporter is trying to find out about and why the TV people are suddenly interested in Red Houses. The class work in pairs and think of two questions that the reporters might ask the workers. They have two minutes. Record their ideas on a flipchart or whiteboard.

It is important for the questions to heighten the tension of knowing something that others don't. Use the pupils' questions, plus any of the following:

- Why do you think so many people are ill in Red Houses town each week?
- Are people happy to work for the Worldwide Medicine Corporation?
- Why is there so much secrecy about what the factory makes?
- Is it true that you have to have a gate pass to be allowed into the factory?
- Some people say that the workers who do the most difficult jobs are given free houses to live in and free cars – is that true?
- What exactly are you making in there?

Allow the volunteer pupils time to talk to each other about their answers and to consult with pupils in the semicircle (Forum Theatre style) if they wish to. Finally, gather the whole group together (ask them all to go back into role as the workers) and, with TIR as the reporter, ask the PIR to respond to two final questions.

Possible script:

> *'And our final questions tonight go to a group of workers who are on their way home from working at the Worldwide Medicine Corporation. Thank you, everyone, for agreeing to being in our report. I have two questions.*
>
> *'Is it true that workers are forced to sign a secrecy agreement?*
>
> *'And finally, are dangerous chemicals used in the factory?'*

Stop the story. If the interview was recorded, play the video back and ask the pupils if their answers were good or bad and why they think they were good or bad. Ask the pupils if anyone lied during the interview? If so, what lies were told and why? Discuss with the pupils whether they actually had a choice to lie or tell the truth. Did signing the secrecy agreement mean it was OK to lie?

Prompt pupils' thinking by asking some questions such as:

- Is it necessary to lie about what goes on in the factory?
- Why do the managers want to keep the workers' jobs so secret?

Ask the pupils:

- Do the workers really know what goes on in the factory?
- Should the workers find out more about what goes on in the factory?

Ask all the pupils to act out going home, making something to eat and watching themselves on TV. Pupils can work in small groups or by themselves. Allow five minutes for practising and then see some short scenes. You will need to keep the pace brisk by moving on quickly from group to group.

Freeze Frame the action with the workers in their homes. Teacher narrates the closing scene of this part of the story.

Possible script:

'The workers felt a strange mixture of emotions. They were so happy that their new jobs would bring each of them more money, a new house and a new car, but they also began to feel worried that things were not as they should be at the factory, and something was about to go very, very wrong.'

Developing the story

Scene 6: Working with the Professor

Tell the pupils that the story starts again two days later. The workers will be in the top-secret laboratory all dressed in their CPSs. They will be doing jobs using their toolbox equipment, mixing chemicals and testing mixtures that are being brought into the lab.

Ask the pupils to act out working in the laboratory. Remind them that they have their CPSs on so they can't sit down or move too quickly. Allow pupils to make up whatever actions feel right to them.

After a few minutes stop the story and, out of role, introduce a new character called the Professor, played, of course, by yourself. The Professor is in charge of everyone who works in the laboratory and is about to teach the new workers a specific job. Role function: authority figure. TIR as the Professor (signed with an ID badge and by carrying a large book with 'Chemical Formulas' written on the front) gathers all the PIR together. She demonstrates a step-by-step process for four people to carry out:

Person 1 measures the dry ingredients into the mixing dish.

Person 2 measures the liquids from bottles into the mixing dish.

Person 3 weighs the mixing dish with all the ingredients in and tests the mixture with the machine that checks the salts.

Person 4 takes a temperature reading, then heats the mixture up, then takes another temperature reading.

The Professor wants the workers to keep careful notes of what happens and warns the PIR to be careful and to ensure they use all the safety equipment. PIR are put into groups of four by the Professor and told to get their equipment and get on with their work.

Allow the pupils to get settled and start acting out. TIR encourages PIR to act out the whole task exactly as instructed by giving advice and praising those who are concentrating and getting the task right.

Stop the drama. Ask the pupils, out of role, to come and sit in a comfortable place where they can also all see the plan of the area that was drawn at the start of the story. Tell them that tonight, when the workers leave the factory, they will be stopped by people who fish for their living and are protesting about the chemical waste in the river. The fishing workers believe that the Worldwide Medicine Corporation is dumping chemicals into the river and that the chemicals are killing the fish.

Optional Extras

Science/Maths task

Now that the pupils, in role, have had experience of laboratory work, this would be a good place to stop the drama and give them tasks to improve accurate measuring.

Pupils might start with a 'measure hunt'! Place a variety of items in boxes around the classroom. In the boxes there should be various items that are used for measuring, for example:

Time – sand timer; clock; watch; calendar
Length – ruler; tape measure; metre stick; string with knots in; trundle wheel
Weight – scales; measuring scoops
Capacity – jug; bottle; can; pipette; measuring spoons

And perhaps other kinds of measuring devices, such as:

Air pressure – barometer
Blood pressure – blood-pressure machine
Level – spirit level
Angles – protractor, set square

Put the pupils in teams of three and set up a circus activity so that each group of three visits the boxes in order (probably two groups of three to a box). Pupils have to decide how many things in each box measure the four main categories of time, length, weight and capacity. Pupils will need a worksheet to help them to record their findings (Box Worksheet.pdf in folder Big Factory on the Resources CD). They don't have to write the names of the items, just record the numbers.

BOX	Time	Length	Weight	Capacity

Once the pupils have looked in all of the boxes, and filled in their worksheets, talk to the class about the different measuring devices by holding each up in turn, explaining what it measures and describing how it is used. Pay particular attention to items that the children may not have seen before.

Announce that everyone is going to practise measuring time. There is a circus of tasks to be carried out in the same groups of three:

Task 1 One pupil has to see how many beads she can thread in one minute. The other two pupils have a minute sand-timer and have to call out, as precisely as they can, exactly when the minute is up.

Task 2 Two pupils have to sort shapes into sorting circles and see if they can do it within a minute. The third pupil times them with buzzer-type kitchen timer.

Task 3 The classroom assistant teaches the group how to tell the time using a real large clock, paying particular attention to minutes.

Task 4 One pupil has a stopwatch. The other two have to guess, independently, when a minute is up and shout out. They have several goes to see how accurate they can become.

Given the size of most classes, each of these tasks will be undertaken by two groups simultaneously. When the first round of tasks is completed, groups move round.

Once the circus is complete, discuss with the pupils what they have discovered about their sense of time and about accuracy.

Similar tasks can be devised for measuring length, weight and capacity.

Ask the pupils what they think the workers should do.

Steer the discussion so that the pupils can see some options. For example:

- find out more about what the factory makes and whether chemicals are in fact being dumped into the river
- refuse to discuss anything with the fishing workers
- agree to listen to what the fishing workers have to say without telling them anything about the factory
- tell the fishing people that you have to wear special suits to protect you from the chemicals you use
- look for work in one of the other factories so that you can leave the medicine factory
- keep going to work and keep out of any arguments or debates with anyone.

Questions to prompt discussion:

- Do you think the workers ought to tell them that they work with chemicals in the factory?
- Why have the workers had to sign a secrecy agreement? Have the managers got something to hide?
- Could the chemicals have anything to do with the fact that so many people are becoming ill in Red Houses?
- What will happen to the workers and their families if they break the secrecy agreement?
- What if the problems of the dying fish have nothing to do with the medicines factory?
- Who else might be polluting the river? Look at the map. The farmers, the other factories, domestic waste?

If necessary, act out the meeting between the fishing workers and the factory workers. TIR should play a fishing worker who meets all the workers as they walk home. TIR must be very angry and accuse the factory workers of ruining her business and making her family poor. TIR represents the attitude that there is no doubt that the medicines factory is to blame. Allow the PIR to respond as they want. It may not be necessary to act this scene, it may have been enough just to talk about it.

Adding tension

Scene 7: The break-in

Move the story on in time to the next day. It is early morning and the workers are lining up at the gates with their worker gate passes. TIR as the gate guard lets them in one by one, taking their passes and giving out the ID badges as they enter, and asks them to sit down and wait. The Professor is coming to speak to them. Keep the PIR waiting.

The waiting time and not knowing what is going on are intended to build tension. The tension can be heightened by using the following devices:

- TIR takes a phone call and can be heard telling the person on the other end how many workers are present
- TIR phones someone to ask if she should let the workers into the workers' rest room yet. The answer is clearly no
- TIR phones to ask if the Professor is on her way yet. As a result of the conversation, TIR announces to the PIR that the Professor has been delayed and will be with them as soon as possible

- TIR asks the PIR if they are aware of what happened yesterday. TIR tells the PIR that last night some ingredients for a new medicine went missing from the top-secret laboratory
- TIR takes a phone call in which she is clearly told off for talking to the workers about the missing ingredients.

Stop the drama. Tell the pupils that the workers have to wait for a long time and then the door to the workers' rest room is opened and the Professor asks them to come with her. The Professor tells the PIR that they must put on their CPSs, but today they will be cleaning up in the laboratory because last night someone broke into the factory and smashed up all the equipment. There is broken glass and mess everywhere. PIR are asked to take cleaning equipment with them such as dustpans, brushes and vacuum cleaners. TIR unlocks the laboratory door and lets the PIR in. TIR and PIR act out cleaning up.

TIR stops the PIR and tells them they need a rest break in the White Room. During the break, as TIR and PIR act out taking off their CPSs and making drinks, the Professor tells the PIR that a rival company is spreading rumours that the Worldwide Medicine Corporation factory is polluting the river. The medicine that the workers have all been involved in developing through their experiments in the laboratory will be the most important medicine ever made. It will prevent thousands of people becoming ill every year. Other medicine companies don't like the idea of this new medicine. They make only medicines that help people to feel better when they are already sick. If people don't get ill in the first place, they won't need the other companies' medicines.

But last night something even worse happened. Someone stole the formula for the new medicine. The workers will have to start all over again and will have to work longer hours every day to make the medicine before anyone else does. TIR explains that new equipment was ordered first thing this morning and it has just arrived. PIR are asked to unpack it and set up the laboratory again ready for work.

Act out putting the CPSs back on and setting up the laboratory. Then stop the drama.

Out of role, sit the pupils in a comfortable place and spend some time reflecting on what has happened in the story. Help the pupils understand that it is possible that somebody wants to stop the Worldwide Medicine Corporation from making the new medicine. The theft of the formula suggests this and perhaps the pollution in the river is a way of 'framing' the Worldwide Medicine Corporation in order to close it down.

Reflect on the drama

- What do you think is going on?
- What evidence do you have?
- Do you think the workers can trust the Professor? How do you know?
- Who might want to steal the formula for the new medicine? Why?
- What will happen to the factory if someone else makes the new medicine first?
- What do you think the workers should do?
- Could workers from another medicine company have put chemicals into the river so that the medicine factory is blamed? How would that help them?

Bringing the story to a climax

Scene 8: The challenge

Explain that the Professor leaves the laboratory to sign for some more equipment that has just arrived. While she is gone, a stranger comes into the laboratory and asks them to gather round. Explain that this new character has some information for the workers. Sign the role, perhaps with a pair of spectacles.

TIR explains that she is a scientist who specialises in looking after rivers and water. She has been working in this factory for several months and she is sure that the pollution in the river is coming from here. It is true, she says: the chemicals are killing the fish. The birds that eat the fish are also dying. The crops in the fields are also affected, because the farmers water them with polluted water. People are becoming sick because the chemicals have got into their food and into the air. She wants the PIR to help her expose what is happening to the world by telling the newspapers and TV what's really going on. She believes the reporters would pay a lot of money for this information.

Discuss the proposal with the pupils. TIR presses the pupils with a persuasive argument. Areas of debate:

- No product is worth wrecking a community for.
- It isn't fair to trade the lives of local people (who have no choice in the matter) for the lives of others who will buy the new medicine.
- It is crazy that a product that is supposed to stop people becoming ill is doing so much damage.
- If the local fishing industry is wrecked, there will be nothing to fall back on if the Worldwide Medicine Corporation decides to pull out and move to a different location.
- The workers are being bribed with houses and cars; that's not right.
- It is selfish to look after yourself and your own family and ignore the needs of others around you.
- There are other types of work that people can do other than working in the medicine factory.
- What if it's not the factory doing the polluting?
- What if it's sabotage?

Give the PIR until the end of the day to consider what they are willing to do.

Stop the drama.

It would be easy for the pupils to get carried away with the idea that the scientist is right and the medicine factory is to blame as she has put a persuasive argument to them. It is unlikely that as young children they will understand the need to challenge what they have heard, so it is crucial that there is a reflection session out of role to help the children to think this situation through.

Reflect on the drama

- Who is this character the workers have just met?
- What do the workers know about her?
- Do you think the workers can trust her? Why?
- Is it possible she stole the formula?
- Could she be a spy from another medicine company?
- What evidence did she have that the factory was causing the river pollution?

- Could any of the other factories in the town be polluting the river?
- Do you think it would be wise for the workers to make a decision based only on what she told them?
- What advice would you give to the workers?

Replay the scene with the scientist again.

This time TIR will accept challenges to her argument and confess, if pushed by the right questions, that it is her 'best guess' that the medicine factory is to blame but she has no actual proof. She can conclude her argument by suggesting it wouldn't do any harm to tell people about the chemicals that are used and, if the factory isn't to blame, the reporters will find out and she will apologise to the managers.

Stop the drama.

Ask the pupils what they think the workers should do.

Optional Extras

Pupils can choose between writing in role and writing about the drama out of role.

Writing in Role

Give each pupil a worksheet with the title 'Workers' Report' (Workers Report.pdf in folder Big Factory on the Resources CD). Ask them to write and draw what has happened to the workers today.

Writing about the drama out of role

Give each pupil a worksheet with the title 'The most exciting part of the drama' (Most Exciting Part.pdf in Big Factory folder on the CD) and ask them to record in drawing and writing what part of the drama they have enjoyed most so far.

Finding an ending

Tell the pupils that there is one possibility that no one has discussed yet and the Professor will mention it at a special meeting that has been called to decide what is going to happen at the factory. Explain it is probably true that the other factories are too far downstream to be the cause of the pollution. However, the farms on the hillside and further upstream might be responsible. The farmers spray their crops with pesticides (explain what these are) and it is possible that some of these chemicals have got into the river and flowed down toward the town. Chemical sprays might have been carried in the air too and that is why so many people have been feeling poorly.

Scene 9: The Directors arrive for their meeting

Explain to the pupils that they are going to be different people in the drama for the last part of the story. When the story starts again, the pupils are going to be in role as the Directors of the medicine factory. Explain what Directors are and that they are the absolute bosses who know everything about the factory and can make all the decisions. The Directors do not live in Red Houses, so they have to travel and will stay in a luxury hotel in the hills beyond the vineyard. They will have to stay overnight. There are cars and a helicopter to bring the Directors to the hotel.

Ask the pupils to act out packing their bags for their overnight stay. Set up some chairs for the helicopter. Set up some chairs for the cars and allow the pupils to decide how they will travel to the meeting.

Act out travelling to the meeting. Freeze Frame the action to ask PIR what they can see from their cars and helicopter. Ask them what they think about the town of Red Houses.

Set up tables and chairs for the 'board meeting'.

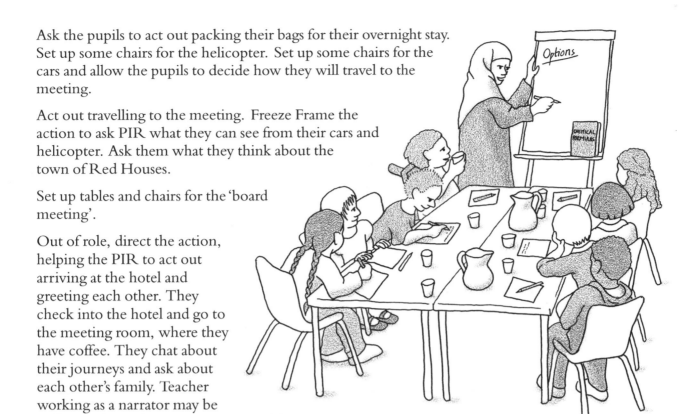

Out of role, direct the action, helping the PIR to act out arriving at the hotel and greeting each other. They check into the hotel and go to the meeting room, where they have coffee. They chat about their journeys and ask about each other's family. Teacher working as a narrator may be sufficient, but a few improvisations of the scene may help the pupils to get a feel for their new 'high-status' roles.

TIR as the Professor meets and greets the PIR and asks them to sit down ready for the meeting.

TIR as the Professor explains what has happened (as if the pupils had not been involved).

Possible script:

'I am very sad to report that things are not going well at the factory and this is why this meeting has been called. I am going to tell you what has happened and explain what I understand to be the facts.

1. A breakthrough was made on the new medicine last month.

2. New workers have been recruited to work in the top-secret laboratory.

3. Last week TV reporters covered the story about lots of people getting sick in Red Houses and some of the new recruits were interviewed (add any detail from that scene that enhance the story).

4. Three days ago the fishing people protested in the town centre and accused the medicine factory of polluting the river.

5. Two days ago there was a break in and the formula for the new medicine was stolen along with ingredients.

6. New equipment has been bought and installed in the laboratory.

7. Yesterday a person was caught in the factory without proper authorisation and it is believed she has tried to get the new recruits to sell information about what the factory makes and the chemicals it uses to the newspapers and TV. So far, nothing has happened and the workers seem to be considering what to do.

'I am not certain what is actually going on; whether a spy has stolen the formula; whether a rival company has put chemicals into the river make it look like it is us; whether the pollution is simply from somewhere else such as the farms up stream. But, if we can't prove our innocence, we'll be closed down by the government. Rumours are growing that we are responsible for the river pollution. It is getting more and more difficult to work in the factory without disruption from something or somebody.

'I understand that as the Directors of this company you need straightforward facts in order to make a decision about the future of the factory. There is a little more information that I think you would find helpful.'

In role, explain again that there are a number of potential causes of river pollution, including chemicals that have drained into the water from farming practices, leaks from a sewage works or a household dump, domestic waste being dumped in the river. Then there's the other factories, even though they are downstream. Explain that one of the consequences of the factory being blamed for the pollution is it will get a 'bad name' and this might make it difficult to sell medicines to people.

TIR offers options for the Directors to vote on. If the PIR wish to discuss each option, then TIR will need to ensure the discussions are brisk and the talking and thinking moves on quickly. In order to promote a feeling of tension, TIR could insist that PIR have to make decisions 'against the clock' as time is short. There's no telling what the workers might do.

Option 1

Move the factory to a different place. Recruit new workers and complete the making of the new medicine as quickly as possible.

Option 2

Move the factory to a different place. Offer to give the workers a job at the new site. The workers will have to find their own housing. Make the new medicine as quickly as possible and reward the workers if they make the medicine before a rival company does.

Option 3

Keep the factory where it is. Tell the workers they will have to take a cut in their pay, there will be no houses or cars given by the company. Spend the money saved from cutting the workers wages and privileges to prove that the factory is innocent of polluting the river. Make the new medicine as quickly as possible.

Option 4

Keep the factory where it is but stop trying to make the new medicine. Make medicines that people know about and want so that the public is not suspicious of what they are doing. Make the top-secret laboratory workers redundant.

Give the PIR as Directors in pairs three minutes to discuss which option is best. Then vote for the option they want. Tell the PIR that the agreed action will be taken immediately and close the meeting.

Pupil task

Give the pupils the 'Predicting Events' worksheet (Predicting Events.pdf in folder Big Factory on the Resources CD). Ask them to work in pairs and decide what three events happen as a result of the decision the Directors made. Ask the pupils to draw pictures and write captions (adults can write for those pupils who find writing difficult) to show these consequences.

Using the pupils' ideas from the 'Predicting Events' worksheet, discuss with the pupils the possible endings for the story.

Scene 10: The ending

Act out an event that signifies the way the story ends.

An example of an *unresolved ending*: the day the workers have to leave Red Houses because the factory has re-located or they take a cut in their pay. For example, PIR might act out packing up the last of their belongings, saying goodbye to friends and leaving on buses or trains or in cars, or groups of pupils in role as the workers decide how life will change with less money to spend.

An example of a *happy ending* that could work with Option 4: to insure a positive image of the factory, the workers have become involved in a Cleaner River Campaign. All the factories and farms have agreed to find a cleaner way of working and to ensure chemicals don't get into the water. PIR as the factory workers and as the people who live in Red Houses act out having a celebration day for the Cleaner River Campaign.

Final Reflection

- What did we learn from the story?
- Why is it so difficult to stop pollution?
- What have you found out about pollution?
- What settings were used in the story?
- What did you imagine Red Houses town was like?
- What did you imagine the medicine factory was like?
- If you could visit the town of Red Houses, what would you most like to see and why?
- What have you learned about secrecy?
- Do you think it is ever right to break an agreement?
- Do you think it is good that newspaper and television reporters try to find out what is going on – even if it is a secret?
- Do you know any other stories where the characters have to keep secrets?
- Who were the main characters in the story and what were they like?
- How did the characters in the story make decisions?
- Would you have done anything differently to the characters? Why? Explain.
- What was the most important event in the story? Why?
- What was the main problem the characters were trying to deal with?
- What made the problem more complicated?
- Do you think what happened at the end of the story was the best possible outcome? Why?
- How would you feel if you had to move away from your home?
- How do you think the workers in Red Houses felt when it seemed they might have to move house and live in a different place?
- Do you know of any people in real life who have had to move house because of their work?
- What do you think life in Red Houses will be like in a few years time? Will it be the same or different? Why?
- How did you feel about the ending of the story?
- Would you change the ending if you played the story again? Why?

It might also be interesting to look at some real case studies of pollution issues. In almost every local environment there will be areas that are affected by pollution – streams, ponds, land. Pupils could simply look at the effects of pollution and learn to recognise the signs.

Optional Extras

Use this story to consolidate pupils' understanding of the way in which all good stories are constructed. Discuss with them the component parts: characters; setting; plot; events; problems; tensions; ending. Explain that two of these elements are now going to be worked on in more detail.

Setting

Pupils must …

Using large, durable bases, such as Tough Trays (concrete-mixing trays from builders' yards), pupils work in groups to build a model of the Red Houses area including all the features on the plan. Ask them to find a way of making a model of the town and surrounding area from the plan we drew at the start of the story. Then …

Pupils should …

Complete the worksheet that categorises the features (Our Model.pdf in folder Big Factory on the Resources CD). Ask them to:

- draw or write all the physical features of the landscape represented on the model into the correct box on the worksheet;
- draw or write all the human features that are represented on the model onto the correct box on the worksheet.

Pupils could …

Design some symbols to represent these features on a two-dimensional map. Ask the pupils to design some small pictures that could be used as symbols on a paper plan to represent the features they made in their model.

Concluding task

Write a description of the area where the story was set. Ask the pupils to write about the people, the buildings and the countryside as well as the old and new parts of the town. Encourage the pupils to describe details of the setting, such as the banks of the river or the streets of the old fishing port. Encourage them to describe the factory buildings.

Characters: part 1

As a whole-class, identify all the characters the pupils can remember meeting in the story. List them on a large piece of paper. Pupils write them on their Character Chart worksheets (Character Chart.pdf in folder Big Factory on the Resources CD):

- workers
- gate guard
- Dr Codyne
- Human Resources Manager
- reporter
- the Professor
- the fishing workers' representative
- the mysterious scientist
- Directors.

Around the room, place different bags. Each bag has items in it relating to one of the characters on the list. The pupils are asked to work out from the evidence which bag belongs to which character.

Pupils work in teams of three. Give them clipboards for their worksheets. They have four minutes at each table to look at the contents of the bag and make a decision about whom it belongs to and to give reasons why. They fill in their worksheets as they go.

As a whole class, discuss the pupils' decisions and reasons.

Characters: part 2

Pupils must …

- work in their threes and choose one character they want to work on
- sit at the desk with the bag for that character
- draw pictures of their character; they can discuss the character together, but pupils must draw individual pictures
- write a brief description of the character; again, everyone must produce their own.

Pupils should …

- draw the character's family
- draw the character's house
- draw the character's most treasured possession.

Pupils could …

- write a story about a special day out the character had.

Sequencing the story

Help the pupils sequence the story.

Discuss with the pupils where the story was most interesting for them and what made it interesting.

Identify problems and tensions.

Some pupils may be able to write the story in their own words, or a class book can be made.

Potential cross-curricular learning

Here are some of the areas of the curriculum that can be linked to the story and used to design activities of your own.

Cross-curricular links	**Maths** Ma 2: Practising calculations – adding up lists of equipment items for the laboratory; working out money costings – lunch in the canteen and costs of equipment; solving number problems as part of the scientists' tasks in the story. Ma 3: Undertaking various measuring tasks as part of the scientists' roles, measuring length and capacity accurately; discussing the presentation of data in graphs and charts - for example by making a graph to show how much medicine was made on each day of the week.

Geography Map and plan making; using scales; using geographical language; describing what places are like; tracing the development of a settlement over time (the old fishing port has developed into the town of Red Houses); discussing human and physical features; recognising the impact of changes in the environment; discussing industry in the school's locality; learning about the water cycle, rivers, river plant and animal life; finding countries on a world map; locating on a map features such as river, flood plain, estuary. Case studies of communities who relied on one main industry such as mining, steel, pottery production.

Science Sc 1: Grasping the importance of evidence when making decisions. Sc 2: Using simple scientific language to communicate ideas and to name and describe living things, materials, phenomena and processes; discussing human health, drugs as medicines, care of the environment, learning about animals and creatures who might be affected by river pollution. Sc 3: Use of materials – using the laboratory as a stimulus, various tasks can be conducted to test different materials ; Sc 4: Using the factory and new housing development in the story as a stimulus for electricity, circuits, buzzers and switches.

PSHE and citizenship Developing confidence and responsibility; preparing to take an active role as a citizen; talking and listening in groups of different sizes; expressing opinions; hearing the opinions of others; understanding that there can be reasonable arguments on both sides; discussing the morals of secrecy – when it is important to keep secrets; recognising the dilemma of looking after close family versus wider community.

History Studying famous scientists such as Marie Curie, Alexander Fleming, Elizabeth Blackwell, Louis Pasteur; discussing the concept of chronological order through the development of the fishing village into a new town; using the story to stimulate questions about how historians know which historical period of time buildings were built in, when artifacts were made, when coins were minted, how people lived in the past; discussing factories in the past - for example the story of Cadbury's Chocolate Factory and the housing estate built for the workers in Bournville.

Design Technology Discussing bridge designs such as beam, arch, suspension and cable-stay using the story as a stimulus; planning and building |

	a model bridge; considering which bridge design would be most suitable for the job of linking one side of the river to the other if a new bridge were to be built. **Art** Investigating glass and reflective surfaces; drawing objects that could be found in a laboratory – glass containers holding liquids, metallic dishes, instruments; photographing and filming flowing water; making a multimedia display of a river or stream; looking at pictures of water, such as Turner's *Norham Castle on the Tweed*, Signac's *The Papal Palace, Avignon*, Monet's *Water Lilies*, Ruisdael's *A Mountainous Wooded Landscape with a Torrent* or Homer's *Breezing Up*.
Literacy skills	Story construction and composition; sequencing; character development; setting; including a problem; selecting a suitable ending; understanding the meaning of a story; note-making in pictorial and written form; asking and answering questions; speaking and listening in pairs and groups; understanding points of punctuation and spelling; learning to identify and explain component parts of stories and recognise them in literature; understanding how a debate is conducted; persuasive speaking; speaking to different audiences; learning the concept of interview – what it is and how it is carried out.
Remember DfES thinking skills!	**Creating** Generating and extending ideas; applying imagination; looking for innovative outcomes. This type of thinking is developed as pupils learn to work with different drama techniques and with storytelling devices such as the TV interview. In the interview, PIR are asked to apply imagination as they work out for themselves the most appropriate answers to the interviewer's questions. Another creative-thinking challenge is when pupils are asked to role-reverse at the end of the drama and become the factory bosses, who have to make decisions that will affect the characters they have played up to that point. In their roles as both workers and bosses, the pupils are required to find innovative solutions to problems that happen in the drama. **Enquiring** Asking relevant questions; posing and defining problems; predicting outcomes and anticipating consequences. This type of thinking is developed as the pupils experience situations that do not have simple solutions, such as the meeting with the protester who believes the factory is responsible for polluting the river. The workers do not know if the protester is telling them the truth or not and they need to seek information to help them decide what to do. Also, when in role as the bosses, the pupils have to anticipate the consequences of the decisions they make. **Reasoning** Giving reasons for opinions and actions; drawing inferences and making deductions; explaining thoughts; making informed decisions and judgements. This type of thinking is developed through meetings and discussions, both in and out of role, that prompt pupils to consider what might be the best solutions to the problems faced by the workers, the community and the factory bosses. **Information Processing** Sorting and classifying; comparing and contrasting; sequencing. This type of thinking could be developed through cross-curricular activities linked to the story, such as making graphs and charts, sorting materials, writing lists of equipment and so on. The drama can be sequenced

and presented as a complete written story or as a story-board with illustrations.

Evaluating Examining what the story means; judging the value of what you have read, heard or done. This type of thinking is developed through reflection on what happens in the story. For example, pupils can be prompted to consider the effect that the closure of the factory would have on the local population – would it be a good or bad thing, and why? There are no right and wrong answers to this dilemma, so pupils can safely have opinions and support them with their own ideas. This will help to prepare them for the concept of presenting evidence to support their arguments as they become more experienced at evaluating.

Appendix A
Professor Howard Gardner's Multiple Intelligence Theory

This explanation of Professor Howard Gardner's theory has been adapted, with permission, from *The Teacher's Toolkit*[1] by Paul Ginnis. For further information about Howard Gardner and his work, visit www.howardgardner.com.

We have come a long way since the days of intelligence tests that supposedly measured a person's 'intelligence quotient' (IQ). Nowadays, intelligence is not regarded as fixed at birth: it can be improved by every person during their life. What's more, intelligence is no longer thought of as a single thing; it comes in different shapes and sizes. Over recent years, various thinkers have come up with various types of intelligence, but the best known is Professor Howard Gardner of Harvard. As early as 1983, in *Frames of Mind*[2], he proposed what was then a radical break with tradition.

> *There is persuasive evidence for the existence of several relatively autonomous human intellectual competencies or 'frames of mind'. The exact nature of each intellectual frame has not so far been satisfactorily established, nor has the precise number been fixed. But the conviction is that there exist at least some intelligences, and that these are relatively independent of one another.*

He went on to define seven distinct types of intelligence (or 'frames of mind'), each, he claimed, traceable to separate areas of the human brain. Previously, many of these had been called gifts, talents, skills, capacities, abilities or human faculties, but never intelligences. In making this well-researched and deliberate linguistic switch, Gardner seriously expanded the world's thinking and broke the shackles imposed by the old school. Many years, twenty books and several hundred articles later, he now claims that all humans have eight types of intelligence:

- linguistic
- logical–mathematical
- spatial
- musical
- bodily–kinaesthetic
- interpersonal
- intrapersonal
- naturalistic

Gardner has strict criteria for defining intelligence. In 1983, he called it, 'the ability to solve problems or to create products that are valued within one or more cultural settings'. In *Intelligence Reframed*[3] (1999), he offers a more refined definition. 'I now conceptualise an intelligence as a biopsychological potential to process information that can be activated in a cultural setting to solve problems or create products that are of value in a culture'. He goes on,

> *... intelligences are not things that can be seen or counted. Instead they are potentials – presumably, neural ones – that will or will not be activated, depending upon the values of a particular culture, the opportunities available in that culture and the personal decisions made by individuals and/or their families, school teachers and others.*

---

[1] Ginnis, P (2002), The Teacher's Toolkit, Crown House Publishing, Carmarthen
[2] Gardner, H (1984), Frames of Mind, Harper Collins, New York
[3] Gardner, H (1999), Intelligence Reframed, Basic Books, New York

The debate is far from settled, though. For example, in the widely read *The Bell Curve*[4], Herrnstein and Murray re-presented the idea that intelligence is a singular, measurable commodity distributed among the population along a bell-shaped curve and passed on genetically from one generation to the next. With a dubious analysis of data, they drew the sinister conclusion that many social ills are due to the behaviours of people with relatively low intelligence. Professors Sandra Scarr and Robert Plomin argue that intelligence is genetically inherited, and Professor Alan Smithers of Liverpool argues for a core intelligence that underlies success across all fields, claiming that Gardner has misused the word *intelligence*.

Meanwhile, Professor John White of the London Institute has voiced serious misgivings about Gardner's definition and underpinning rationale, describing his theory as 'decidedly flaky'.

The questions of inherited intelligence, the definition of intelligence(s), the measurability of intelligence and the relationship between intelligence and social class will continue to be the subjects of fierce debate. In the meantime, in classrooms around the country, students' achievements and self-esteem are being raised by the optimistic and positive message that everyone is intelligent, but in different ways.

A friend and colleague, Tony Salmon, when he was a raising-achievement advisory teacher in Sandwell, put to Howard Gardner during a seminar, 'The strength we get from your work is that you do use the word "intelligence", because the kids have been told so often – not explicitly, but they have picked up the message – that they are not intelligent.' Tony was expressing just one of the benefits of Gardner's work, the flattening of the ancient hierarchy of educational values. The upgrading of ordinary household abilities to the status of 'intelligence' suddenly gives everyone a place in the world. Nobodies become somebodies overnight. Self-images and self-expectations are transformed.

What's more, the fact that this idea has a credible, internationally renowned, academic, weighty source makes it easier to persuade teachers to bring their habits into line with the new order, on three counts:

- teachers' thinking: they can't write anyone off any more; instead they can have high expectations of every child;

- teachers' language: they can now drop the limiting language of 'high ability' and 'low ability' and focus on pupils' 'developing abilities' instead; they can stop talking about a child's intelligence and start talking about his or her 'intelligence profile';

- teachers' classroom techniques: they can push the boat out and develop a range of learning and assessment strategies that suit the range of intelligences, so that every child has the best chance of success.

Strictly speaking, multiple intelligence (MI) theory is not a learning-styles model, although many teachers use it as such. This is because it describes a child's natural talents and aptitudes; it provides a framework for understanding why some pupils are drawn to particular activities and are very good at them, while other children struggle, only to find the situation reversed when activities are changed. This creates both an opportunity and a challenge. The opportunity: teachers can use MI theory to guide their lesson planning. It can prompt them to design learning activities to suit different intelligence profiles and thereby help them meet the needs of more children. The challenge: to find ways for children who are not naturally inclined towards logic and language to make progress in those areas by creating access routes that make use of other intelligences. Drama, for example, which primarily uses bodily-kinaesthetic, intrapersonal and interpersonal intelligences can be used as routes to reading and writing.

---

[4] Herrnstein, R.J. and Murray, C (1996), The Bell Curve, Simon- Schuster, New York

The chart below could be used as a rough-and-ready guide to the eight intelligences that might help with your understanding of individual children's needs. Remember, every child has all eight, but to varying degrees. Think of a child in your class – how would you rank their intelligences? Think of several children. How do their profiles differ?

Type of intelligence	Indicators of the intelligence
Linguistic intelligence	• thinks in words • likes to read and write • likes stories • likes to play word games • has a good memory for names, places, dates, poetry, lyrics and trivia • finds spelling easy • has a rapidly developing vocabulary
Logical and mathematical intelligence	• sees patterns easily • likes abstract ideas • likes strategy games and logical puzzles • works out sums easily in his/her head • asks big questions, e.g. 'Where does the universe end?' • uses computers • devises experiments to test out things he/she doesn't understand • thinks in categories and sees relationships between ideas
Spatial intelligence	• thinks in images and pictures • easily remembers where things have been put • likes drawing, designing, building, daydreaming • reads maps and diagrams easily • notices colour and shape • does jigsaw puzzles easily • is fascinated by machines • reproduces images accurately
Musical intelligence	• often sings, hums or whistles to him/herself • remembers melodies easily • has a good sense of rhythm • plays an instrument • enjoys listening to music • is sensitive to sounds in the environment • music helps him/her to concentrate

Continued

Continued

Type of intelligence	Indicators of the intelligence
Bodily-kinaesthetic intelligence	• remembers through bodily sensations • finds it difficult to sit still for long • has 'gut feelings' about things • is good at sports or dance or acting or mime • has excellent coordination • communicates well through gestures • learns best through physical activity, simulation and role play • mimics people easily
Interpersonal intelligence	• understands people well • learns best by interacting and cooperating with others • is good at leading and organising • picks up on other people's feelings • mediates between people • enjoys playing social games • listens well to other people
Intrapersonal intelligence	• likes to work alone • is self-motivating and self-directing • is intuitive • has a sense of independence • is strong-willed and has strong personal opinions • sets his/her own goals • is self-confident • is reflective • is aware of his/her personal strengths and weaknesses
Naturalistic intelligence	• is observant about the natural world • recognises flora and fauna easily • can easily group similar animals, plants or natural phenomena • uses criteria consistently • is drawn to keeping pets and is very responsible and skillful • is concerned about conservation and the environment

Appendix B
Dr Anthony Gregorc's Mind Styles™ Analysis

This explanation of Dr Anthony Gregorc's model has been adapted, with permission, from *The Teacher's Toolkit*[1] by Paul Ginnis. Gregorc's own website, www.gregorc.com, is very interesting; you can read his ideas first-hand (the 'FAQs on Style' section is especially useful) and buy some of his material. We particularly recommend getting a copy of the Style Delineator (and having a go at it yourself), along with a set of the Extenda Charts which describe the features of each Mind Style in some detail.

For Professor Anthony Gregorc, previously of the University of Connecticut, learning involves the dual processes of perceiving and ordering information.

Basing his theories on almost three decades of phenomenological research, Gregorc confidently proposes that there are differences in the way people both *perceive* (let in, grasp) and *order* (organise, store and reference) data. These differences in mental operation are the result of possessing common mental qualities to different degrees. Take perception first: the differences can be plotted on a continuum from concrete to abstract.

Concrete ————————————————————————— *Abstract*

PERCEPTION

Extremely *concrete* people are focused on physical reality. They are sensate. They concentrate on what they can see, feel, hear, smell and touch. They have little patience with arty-farty ideas and waffle. They are down to earth and live in the here and now. They have a strong tendency to be objective. When it comes to learning, the experience has to be physical. If the learning can't be seen, touched and 'done', little goes in.

Extremely *abstract* students, on the other hand, quickly and naturally turn experience into abstract thought. They live in their heads: they think; they feel; they look for patterns; make connections; seek generalities; want ideas; love theories and big principles. They 'see' the invisible. They tend to be subjective. Remember, this is a continuum with most people occupying positions somewhere between the two ends.

Ordering refers to the way in which people organise and store data in their heads. Again, there are big natural differences, from sequential to random.

Sequential ————————————————————————— *Random*

ORDERING

Strongly *sequential* people store ideas and facts systematically. They seem to have filing cabinets in their heads, they are logical and precise. To get from A to E mentally, they first go from A to B, then B to C, then C to D and finally arrive at E – and can describe all the steps clearly. They are linear, structured, step-by-step thinkers who will pursue only one idea or line of thought at a time. They are telescopic rather than kaleidoscopic.

---

[1]Ginnis, P (2002), The Teacher's Toolkit, Crown House Publishing, Carmarthen

By contrast, strongly *random* people seem mentally chaotic. They appear to store things all over the place, without rhyme or reason, yet can make intuitive connections and creative leaps that sequential people never do. They can go from A to E in one go, but have no idea how they got there! They store information in categories that make sense to them but to no one else! They tend to deal in big chunks, make connections this time that aren't the same as last time, see the whole rather than the parts and tend to weave many strands together simultaneously. They are kaleidoscopic rather than telescopic. Again, these are extreme positions and most people are somewhere in between.

Gregorc combines these mental qualities to form four distinctive styles and designates them: *Concrete Sequential* (CS); *Abstract Sequential* (AS); *Concrete Random* (CR) and *Abstract Random* (AR).

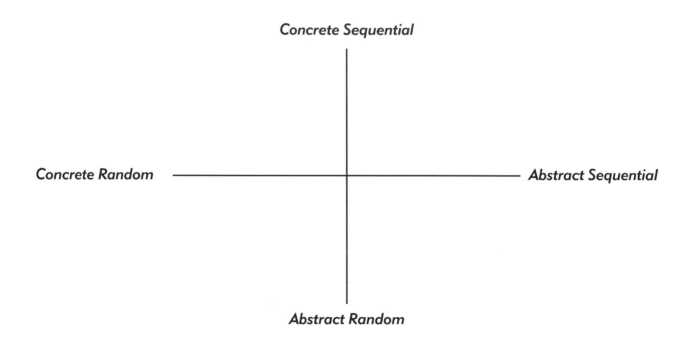

He is keen to stress that everyone has all four of these styles, but usually in different proportions. Some people might be fairly well rounded and have more or less equal facility in all four modes, but most have a natural inclination to one or two. Some people favour one style very strongly. If you imagine plotting your personal position on each of the four 'points of the compass' and then joining the dots with straight lines to form a kite or diamond shape, the area enclosed by the lines is your Mind Field. This territory is deeply rooted in your psyche, it is to be honoured and nurtured, it is not changeable, it is you. It could be said to be your comfort zone.

Although Gregorc does not have a precise percentage for each category, his extensive research across the two genders, across all age ranges, abilities, socioeconomic backgrounds and ethnicities, suggests that any class you teach will comprise students of all kinds. Some will have a strong propensity, others a mild propensity and a few (Gregorc's initial studies indicated about 5 per cent) will have no significant propensity at all.

This model and the consistency of findings over the years provide us with an excellent way of planning for diversity.

Students with a dominant Concrete Sequential Mind Style learn best through structured practical activities. They relish hands-on learning with step-by-step instructions, such as following a computer program, playing a game with clear rules, making a model from a set of instructions, completing a list of short tasks, following a prescribed route, painting by numbers, ticking off a checklist, observing and imitating an expert, working through a manual. Dominant Concrete Sequential learners like routine, take things literally, are usually neat and tidy, like to have concrete examples, are attentive to detail, keep to time and don't like to make mistakes (so it is very important to them that they know exactly what to do). It is very important that their learning activities be tactile or kinaesthetic and clear-cut, preferably with concrete examples and regular feedback from the teacher.

Students with a dominant Abstract Sequential Mind Style learn best through structured academic research and rational argument. They like to be guided to see the connection between ideas, the reason such-and-such is the case, the theory behind a concept. Usually preferring to work alone, they welcome structured worksheets, books and exercises in logic and detail, such as finding the missing link, extracting the core concepts, presenting the key words, comparing x with y. They take pride in carrying out instructions thoroughly. They like to think things through, use reason, analyse and evaluate information, find the causes, work out the 'big picture', compare and contrast and identify the pattern.

Students with a dominant Abstract Random Mind Style learn best through creative, open-ended, group-based tasks, preferably with an emotional or aesthetic aspect. They love to talk, to brainstorm, to reflect, to imagine, to explore ideas, to be spontaneous, to go off at tangents, to be intuitive, to make personal connections and to be allowed to make mistakes. The freedom to use images, symbols, sounds and movement, to be dramatic, to use a range of resources are all important to Abstract Random learners. Cooperative tasks that value feelings, impressions and holistic ideas are particularly suitable. Peer teaching is a powerful learning method and a touch of humour goes a long way.

Students with a dominant Concrete Random Mind Style thrive on open-ended practical work, especially if it involves a challenge, or a problem, or an investigation. They tend to resist prescription, deadlines and guidelines. Typically, they want to work out their own method and timescale and not be forced to follow routines or work with others if they don't want to. They usually want to explore alternatives, experiment, follow their intuition and use trial and error. 'See if you can work out a way of …', 'Come up with the best design for …', 'Can you find the answer to such and such …?', 'Prepare some teaching resources to help me with …', these are the best kinds of task. Dominant Concrete Random learners are naturally curious and want to be allowed to be unconventional, independent and inventive, and to have plenty of resources to get their hands on.

There are two levels at which teachers can respond to these differences. The first level is to incorporate these Mind Styles into their lesson plans. The simplest way of doing this is to check that, over a series of, say, four lessons, all four styles have been accommodated. Alternatively, different learning tasks can be designed and then offered to pupils as a menu of options for them to choose from. Or the teacher can negotiate learning strategies with students so that their natural preferences are built directly into a democratically created plan.

To help you to get your head round each style, here's an attempt at a summary in the kind of language that children might understand.

Abstract Sequential

- You like reading
- You are happy to work alone
- You like to find things out from books, from talks and from other sources
- You like reasons and theories
- You weigh up different ideas
- You are keen to do written work
- You organise your studies carefully

Concrete Sequential

- You like to do practical work
- You don't like thinking and talking too much – you want to get on
- You like to be told exactly what to do
- You like to tackle things one step at a time
- You like to be organised
- You pay attention to detail
- You like to get things right

Concrete Random

- You like to be given open-ended problems to solve
- You like to work out answers for yourself
- You have lots of ideas
- You like to try your ideas out even if other people think they are odd
- You like to find out how things work
- You like to be allowed to make mistakes and learn from them
- You like to have something to show for your efforts

Abstract Random

- You like group work so you can talk things through with other people
- You want to use your imagination
- You want the freedom to create your own ideas
- You understand how people feel
- You like to use drama, art and music
- You like your work to be fun
- You like your work to be about people

The second level of response is for teachers to take account of Mind Style differences in their *interventions with individual students*. Consider, for example, a child who is off task. If the child is dominantly Abstract Sequential, she will probably respond to knowing why the work needs to be finished, what it's leading to, how it connects conceptually with what's been done already and what will be done later. A strongly Concrete Sequential child is likely to benefit from having the task broken into small, crystal-clear steps, each with a clear deadline, while a dominantly Abstract Random learner might be best teaming up with one or two other like-minded pupils for a few minutes and letting off some steam about how boring it all is and then be asked to tackle it together. Try asking the strongly Concrete Random child to find his/her own way of getting the learning finished by dinnertime; they can change the task as long as they do the same learning.

Index

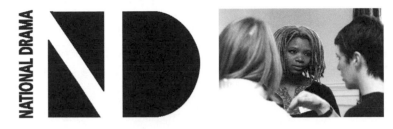

NATIONAL DRAMA

ND

Join National Drama - the leading UK subject association for drama and theatre educators

Membership benefits include access to other drama teachers and theatre educators, free copies of *Drama Magazine* (published twice a year), the newsletter *Reflections*, reduced prices for regional, national and international conferences, publications and courses, networking opportunities and access to specialist advice and support, as well as a voice in the future of drama at national and international levels and access to current drama research.

Name	
Job title	
Address	
Town	
Postcode	
Telephone	
Fax	
Email	

Membership rates
Individual £40   Student £15   Retired/non-working £20   NQT £30   Overseas £50   Affiliated groups £65

**Please join online at
www.nationaldrama.co.uk**

**or photocopy the form above and send with a cheque
(made payable to 'National Drama') to:**

**Christine Cutting, ND administrator,
9 Eastern Close, NORWICH, NR7 OUG
admin@nationaldrama.co.uk**

Also available:

Covering the Curriculum with Stories
Supplementary Projects for Foundation and KS1

This supplementary CD contains two further projects complete with all the worksheets, photographs and illustrations required:

- *Little Bo Peep (for 3-5 year olds)* Why can't Bo behave? Bo's mum is at her wits' end and is about to take action that will deeply affect her relationship with her daughter. This is a new take on an old tale which is set on Bo Peep's farm with some additional characters, all of whom get caught up in the problem of Bo losing the family sheep.

- *The Giant Pet Escape (for 5-7 year olds)* Village celebrations are interrupted one evening when strange noises are heard coming from the cellar of the nearby giant's house. Tensions mount as the nervous villagers deal with an escaped creature and the injured giant. In the cold light of day, there are some 'home truths' to face.

ISBN 184590045-6 (978-184590045-8) *£9.99*

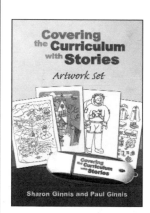

Covering the Curriculum with Stories
Artwork Set

This poster pack and memory stick set contains all Sue Hagerty's wonderful illustrations from the eight projects contained in *Covering the Curriculum with Stories* and the Supplementary Projects CD:

- A selection of the original artwork by Sue Hagerty on 24 A1-sized posters which can be used as visual aids for all the projects. These posters have been particularly selected to provide a perfect backdrop to the projects and include all the plans and maps.

- The entire collection of artwork is contained on an accompanying memory stick allowing you to customise, print, project and import the images to suit yourself.

ISBN 184590045-6 (978-184590045-8) *£35.00*

The whole *Covering the Curriculum with Stories* bundle to include:

- the book
- the Supplementary CD
- the Artwork Set.

ISBN 184590054-5 (978-184590054-0)
£59.99 (price if purchased separately £69.98)

For full details and to order your copies visit www.crownhouse.co.uk